PHIL HILL: Yankee Champion

Automotive Books By William F. Nolan

Omnibus of Speed (with Charles Beaumont) – 1958

Adventure on Wheels (with John Fitch) – 1959

Barney Oldfield – 1961

Phil Hill: Yankee Champion – 1962

Men of Thunder – 1964

When Engines Roar (with Charles Beaumont) – 1964

Steve McQueen: Star on Wheels – 1972

Carnival of Speed – 1973

PHIL HILL:
Yankee Champion

First American to Win the Driving Championship of the World

Revised, Expanded Edition by

William F. Nolan

Brown Fox

Books

CARPINTERIA
CALIFORNIA

First published in 1962 by G.P. Putnam's Sons, New York

Brown Fox Books
P.O.Box 5000
Carpinteria, California 93014
805-684-5951

Second Edition—revised

Library of Congress Cataloging-in-Publication Data
Nolan, William F., 1928–
Phil Hill : Yankee champion, first American to win the driving
championship of the world / by William F. Nolan. — Rev., expanded ed.

   p. cm.
Includes index.
ISBN 1-888978-10-4

1. Hill, Phil, 1927– .
2. Automobile racing drivers — United States — Biography.   I. Title
GV1032.H5N6 1996
796.7'2'092 — dc20
[B]   96-32029
         CIP

Body type is Sabon, titles set in Walbaum, and captions are Gill Sans.
Printed on acid free paper in the United States of America.

This one is for

Mark Godfrey

without whom...

Hill is Ferrari's No. 1 — an intense, taut, fluent and intelligent man, a theoretician who possesses a profound understanding of the behavior of race-cars at high speed.

–Ken W. Purdy,
  Kings of the Road (REVISED EDITION)

CONTENTS

Preface   9

Introduction   10

Chapter One
Nerve and Speed at Pebble Beach   13

Chapter Two
Of Conformity and Rebellion   16

Chapter Three
Midgets to Jaguars   28

Chapter Four
And Finally a Ferrari   36

Chapter Five
An International Effort   43

Chapter Six
Of Danger and Death   50

Chapter Seven
El Batallador   58

Chapter Eight
From Wisconsin to Argentina   67

Chapter Nine
A Brisk Introduction to Europe   73

Chapter Ten
Rain, Reims, and a Run on the Salt   84

Chapter Eleven
Many Crashes in Caracas   92

Chapter Twelve
Team Triumphs–and a Cuban Kidnapping   99

Chapter Thirteen
Masterful Driving at Le Mans   105

Chapter Fourteen
A Battle and a Beginning

111

Chapter Fifteen
A Fast Start in Formula 1

118

Chapter Sixteen
Victory and Frustration

128

Chapter Seventeen
Breakdowns, Behra–and a Bash at Lisbon

136

Chapter Eighteen
A Season Ends at Sebring

145

Chapter Nineteen
From Argentina to Monte Carlo

149

Chapter Twenty
Fighting the Odds

157

Chapter Twenty-One
After 39 Years: *Bravissimo!*

165

Chapter Twenty-Two
The Tables Are Turned

172

Chapter Twenty-Three
A Dutch Duel and Some Ring Records

180

Chapter Twenty-Four
Hill vs. Trips

188

Chapter Twenty-Five
A New World Champion

197

Chapter Twenty-Six
The Post-Championship Years

207

Table of Phil Hill's
International Successes

223

Index

226

PREFACE

TO THE SECOND EDITION

In the 46-year history of the international Formula 1 Grand Prix Championship, the highest prize in global racing, only two Americans have taken home the coveted GP Crown: Phil Hill in 1961 and Mario Andretti in 1978.

Phil Hill: Yankee Champion stands today as the only book-length biography of our first American World Champion — from his California boyhood in Santa Monica through his championship victory in Europe. However, when *Yankee Champion* was originally published in 1962, Hill was still an active driver, with many races ahead of him; his career had not ended.

With this revised edition, Hill's full story is finally told. Racing enthusiasts can be assured that the record is now complete within these pages. I wish to acknowledge the generous help of *Road & Track's* executive editor, Richard Homan, and the magazine's librarian, Otis Meyer. I also wish to acknowledge Alma Hill for her courteous response to my questions regarding her husband. Of course, Brown Fox Books' Mark Godfrey made this present edition happen, and carefully worked with me on the updating and revisions. Finally, a tip of the helmet to Jim Sitz, who reviewed the text for historical accuracy. My profound thanks to all of you.

Except for minor updating, the basic text of *Yankee Champion* (through 1961) has not been altered, but for this revised special edition I have replaced Chapter 26, "Of Speculation and Statistics," with an extensive new chapter, "The Post-Championship Years," which details Hill's last six seasons of racing and updates his life from retirement in 1967 through his present-day activities in the 1990s. Additionally, the photos gathered between covers are all newly-selected, providing dramatic visual testimony to Phil Hill's career as one of America's legendary racing champions.

William F. Nolan
West Hills, California
June, 1996

INTRODUCTION
FROM THE ORIGINAL EDITION

Phil Hill was the first American to win the classic 24-Hour race at Le Mans, the first American to win three times at Sebring, the first American to win a modern championship Grand Prix*—and had finally become the first American World Champion.

My initial view of Phil's spirited driving was at Pebble Beach, as a spectator in April of 1955, and we did not meet until the following year, when I talked to Hill in the pits at Palm Springs, California, during a sports car meet at the desert spa. He recalled that I'd already written a short profile on him for the West Coast magazine *Fortnight* earlier that year—and when I asked him if he'd consent to a tape-recorded interview he agreed. I wanted to know more about Hill and I was certain that many other sports fans did too. Our talk was quite successful. I found Phil to be a very articulate individual, strong-minded and quite introspective, possessing an ability for self-analysis which extended well beyond that of the average professional sportsman.

We've often met at races around the world since that initial interview, and I have seen Phil drive at Monte Carlo, Nassau, Sebring, Torrey Pines, Riverside and many other road circuits over the years. During this period, I continued to gather material relating to his life and career. We made additional tapes together at his home in Santa Monica. As a result, I sold some half-dozen major articles on Phil to various magazines. However, I was only able to use a fraction of my collected data in these published pieces, and a full-length racing biography seemed the logical solution. In May of 1961 I began work on this book—and its scope was naturally enhanced by Phil's championship at Monza.

---

*Only one other fellow countryman had ever scored a similar victory: Jimmy Murphy, in 1921, captured the French Grand Prix in a Duesenberg.

I wish to acknowledge Hill's generous help in the preparation of this story, and the reader will note that I have made extensive use throughout of our taped interviews, not only to allow Phil to speak for himself, but to show (through his own words) the kind of man he is. Strict biographical form would not have served as well. Therefore, much of what has happened in the colorful career of America's finest road driver is seen from a very personal perspective—just as the diaries of Stirling Moss were utilized by Robert Raymond when he wrote the first biography of that fleet Briton in 1953.

It seems appropriate to close with a quote by an anonymous young dueling student from the University of Heidelburg, relating to all who choose to enter any form of highly competitive endeavor, be it swordsmanship or auto racing:

> Sport has always possessed an element of honor, a test of endurance and courage in crisis. It gives each man a chance to find his own merit and to demand more of himself than anyone can demand of him. His duel is not a personal fight with another, but a test of the spirit and of the will to defy his own nature. From such tests, champions emerge.

Phil Hill passed such tests, and he truly earned his championship. America can be proud of him.

William F. Nolan
Burbank, California
June, 1962

CHAPTER ONE

Nerve and Speed at Pebble Beach

WHEN THE HANDSOME, night-black Jaguar Special, with its white number 2 in sharp contrast against the dark body, was rolled into a fifth-row position for the Pebble Beach Cup Race, the afternoon's 25-lap main event was about to begin. The date was November 5, 1950, and California's Monterey Peninsula was hosting its first annual sports car meet over the wicked, tree-lined 1.8-mile Pebble Beach circuit.

The site was ruggedly picturesque, set in a lush, 20,000-acre private playground near fashionable Del Monte Lodge overlooking the blue-glitter sweep of Carmel Bay. Sponsored by the San Francisco region of the Sports Car Club of America and the MG Car Club, three other contests had already been run that afternoon. In the last of these, the Monterey Unlimited Class Race, for the large, fast cars, the black No. 2 Jaguar, driven by brash, aggressive Santa Monican Phil Hill, had finished in second position, despite a severe handicap. While Hill was attempting to speed-shift into fourth gear in an effort to close the distance between his machine and the leading Allard, the lining had pulled loose from the clutch plate, dropping the pedal to the floor. Repairs of such a major nature were out of the question.

Therefore, in this 45-mile main event, Hill would be forced to practice the hazardous and difficult art of shifting without disengaging the clutch. Tendrils of fog moved ghostlike between the tall pine and cypress trees ringing the circuit, and Phil knew that the surface would be damp, slick from the rubber deposited by other cars. Mistakes could be costly here. He sat nervously in the cockpit, hand poised over the starter button as Al Torres prepared to wave the green flag. Hill's XK-120 Jaguar was in gear; theoretically, when the engine fired, the car would move away — but this was not the case.

As the flag dropped, and the other machines exploded into action, the Jag's engine refused to fire. Frantically Hill punched the button, then waved his arm for a push start. His pit crew, led by Richie Ginther, put their muscles to work, and the modified 3.8-liter powerplant abruptly burst into Jaguar thunder. Hill's car was last off the grid by a full 300 feet, but he wasted no time in self-pity. By the end of the first lap he had gained two positions, and could already see the leader, Arnold Stubbs in a V-8 60 MG Special, approximately a quarter mile ahead on the front straight. On lap three, pushing hard, he had moved up behind the XK-120 driven by Bill Breeze, and the two Jags stormed around the turns, nose to tail.

Phil was having his troubles, as expected. Several times, in downshifting from fourth to third, he would misjudge his revs and drag the rear wheels, as the skidding machine headed for the hay bales. Yet he kept the car on the road, and continued to hound the other Jaguar.

By the ninth lap Stubbs had pitted with the MG Special, and Mike Graham's big Cadillac-powered J2 Allard was in command. But Breeze and Hill were pressing close behind, and Graham steamed into the hairpin, saw he couldn't make it, and shot up the escape road, giving the lead to Bill Breeze.

Hill increased the pressure, forcing the pace, and now he could see that Breeze was slowing down earlier for the sharp turns—meaning his brakes were failing. On lap 11 Hill blasted past the other Jag, and Breeze retired on the following lap, drums smoking.

With more than half of the race remaining, Phil Hill had taken over the number one position, but he was confused by a chalked pit signal from Ginther reading: LONG LEAD. Was some driver named Long up there ahead of him in another car? Having started last, Hill had no way of being sure that this fellow, Long, had not been ahead of Stubbs from the beginning.

As a result, Phil began pushing the Jag to its limit in his effort to overtake a mythical opponent. But now his own brakes were rapidly failing. He skidded into bales, dragged the rear wheels and roared up escape roads when his speed was too great to negotiate a turn. The crowd, totaling more than 7000, roared approval at his hair-raising performance as he brutalized the black Jaguar around the twisting circuit.

Now the fog was thickening, closing in, and as Hill passed the pits he read a scrawled ONE on the board held by Ginther. Again he misunderstood, assuming that he had only one lap to go, and that it was too late to worry about catching Long. Actually, seven laps remained in the contest. Behind him Don Parkinson had moved his XK Jag into second spot, and Graham was rapidly making up lost ground in the Allard after a time-consuming pit stop to replace a broken fan belt.

Hill finally accepted the fact that he was leading when the checkered flag did not appear, but with the fog rolling in, and with his brakes all but nonexistent, his position was far from ideal. If he slowed to a safe speed it might well mean defeat at the hands of Parkinson.

Hill maintained his furious pace, abruptly swerving to avoid a deep hole which had opened on the second turn, regaining control as the circuit straightened. His gearbox threatened to disintegrate under the forced shifts, and engine heat was climbing—but Al Torres was ready with the checker on the last lap as Hill slid the hairpin and aimed the nose of the Special at the final straight. Torres leaped high in the air, dipping the flag down with a matador's flourish as the black Jaguar howled past the finish line to claim the 45-mile victory.

At twenty-three, Phil Hill had won his first important road race in a wild, impressive display of nerve and speed. His brakes and clutch were gone; the fenders of his Jaguar were battle-scarred by contact with numerous hay bales—but he had won the Pebble Beach Cup.

Eleven years later he would win the Championship of the World.

———————

CHAPTER TWO

Of Conformity and Rebellion

PROFESSIONAL MOTOR RACING is a demanding sport. Far more than basic talent is involved in hurling a sports car or a Grand Prix machine over the twisting, treacherous road circuits of Europe at speeds ranging up to 180 miles per hour, weaving around other cars, downshifting at the precise instant required to properly negotiate a turn, struggling to hold a position or to gain a better one, avoiding curbs, trees and oil on the course, aiming, always, at the checkered flag waiting at the finish line. Courage and a fighting spirit are required certainly, so is a wizard's sense of timing and the instinctive ability to make split-second life-or-death decisions. Physical strength and stamina are also major requirements, although the novice spectator is generally unaware of this. It seems, to him, that the *car* does all the work; the driver merely sits behind the wheel. Not true. Exhaustion due to poor physical condition has often been the cause of defeat. At Sebring, two drivers alternate at top speed for 12 hours; at Le Mans, through daylight and darkness, for *double* this period; on the Nürburgring, battling this roller-coaster 14-mile circuit for over seven hours, physical letdown can easily spell disaster.

Grand Prix champions are strong men, and Phil Hill is a good example of this. He is not tall, standing just 5 feet 10 inches, but his 160 pounds are distributed over a tough, wiry frame. His shoulders and arms are incredibly muscular, similar to those of a professional prizefighter, and his legs are rock solid. During his career he worked out in a gym for an hour a day, three days a week. He lifted weights, rode a bicycle, swam. He hated smoking, gave it up on numerous occasions, yet his nerves often seemed to require tobacco.

Hill still retains a skilled mechanic's interest in machinery. He lived, during the European season, at the Reale Hotel in Modena, near the Ferrari test circuit, where he could check out the latest chassis or engine improvements. He made suggestions, noted any changes made, mentally filed data for use in a race. When his Ferrari began to fail Phil usually knew why. The technicians respected his judgment. He spoke excellent Italian and could pinpoint difficulties, leading to faster, stronger, safer racing cars. His life depended on them.

$$\cdot \qquad \cdot \qquad \cdot \qquad \cdot \qquad \cdot$$

When the international racing season ended in Europe Phil Hill went home — to a large, white, Spanish-Moorish house on a tree-shaded street in Santa Monica, California. He has lived in this same house since his college days, and after several frantic months on the continent following the Grand Prix circus each season he looked forward to this quiet refuge near the Pacific Ocean. Until her death in 1959 the house and grounds belonged to Phil's aunt, Helen Grasseli, who occupied the premises with her servants, Fred and Julia Grant (butler and maid to the Hill family since 1916). With the Grants' retirement, Phil took over the house, utilizing two rooms of the lower floor as his personal living quarters, having converted these to modern decor. The ceiling is acoustical tile, since the main room contained a complex floor-to-ceiling stereophonic unit built into one wall. Here, also, were hundreds of tapes and LP discs, a couch, bookcases (in which Tim Birkin's *Full Throttle* was stacked next to *The Encyclopedia of Great Composers and Their Music),* and a glittering array of silver trophies won in races around the world. At one time he owned 2000 boxed rolls of music which he had collected.

Caught up in the roaring maelstrom of a Grand Prix race there was no time to think of the past; only the present mattered, the onrushing turns, the 180-mph straights, the fast bends and twists of a continental road circuit. But here, in Santa Monica, Phil Hill could experience a rare sense of personal security. He could let his mind move back to his childhood years; he could trace the entire pattern of his life, the elements which shaped his personality and career, which led him to his ultimate success as an international champion. . . .

$$\cdot \qquad \cdot \qquad \cdot \qquad \cdot \qquad \cdot$$

Phil's mother, Lela Long Hill, was born in 1896 on an Ohio farm, and she grew up in Cleveland where she became a loyal fan of the

Cleveland Indians. Her family had originally settled in this country in 1812, from France.

Once described as "an old-fashioned fire-and-brimstone revivalist as well as a staunch Republican," Lela manifested her zeal in several hymns and religious tracts which she wrote and published. One of the hymns, "Jesus Is the Sweetest Name I Know," was widely distributed; and Lela also displayed a talent for popular music when she produced the ragtime ditty "Down at Miami's Beaches." She was living in Miami when she met Philip Toll Hill in the early twenties. He had been a Navy lieutenant in the First World War and had later served as city editor of the Schenectady *Gazette*. In Florida, he was sales manager for the Mack Truck Company. (Of Dutch origin, Hill's family had been in America since 1675.)

Philip T. Hill was seven years older than Lela Long, and his solid, no-nonsense character impressed the Cleveland girl. They were soon man and wife, having married in Miami where their first son, Philip T. Hill, Jr., was born on April 20, 1927. Just a few weeks after the baby arrived they moved hastily to New York in order to escape the threat of a hurricane, said to be moving toward the Florida Coast. Mrs. Hill had survived one of these destructive storms, and she wanted no more of them. Jerry Ellis Hill, Phil's brother, was born in New York on August 2, 1928. The following year the family moved again, to California, where a new baby, Helen Hill, joined the family on May 28, 1930.

After they had lived briefly in Hollywood and Pasadena, the heat drove the Hills to Santa Monica, along the cool Pacific, and the family settled at 218 20th Street. It was here that young Phil, who was then called "Sonny" by his parents, began to take piano lessons in 1931, when he was four.

Of this period, Hill recalls: "I was far more interested in my mother's shiny new Marmon Speedster than I was in learning to play the piano. It had been one of a pair of New York show cars. Barney Oldfield bought one, Mom bought the other, and even at four I knew it was a beautiful thing. At this very early age cars held a strong attraction for me, and I remember peering under the Marmon's hood whenever I got the chance. Of course my Aunt Helen had this marvelous Packard town car which she had bought new in 1918, the same car I have today, and I was always *fascinated* by it, with its huge wooden steering wheel and big electric side lamps. She had actually designed it herself. Sketched out the plans and had the Fleetwood Body people in Pennsylvania build it for her. She bought the Pierce-Arrow Le Baron new in '31 also, and that's the car I later restored with Jerry. It's still a great automobile."

In 1935, Phil's father gave up a government appointment as Foreman on the Los Angeles Grand Jury to take over the job of postmaster in Santa Monica (a position he held until his death in 1951), and the Hills became socially prominent in the area. Phil had been sent to kindergarten at a private school, later switching to the Franklin Grammar School, and he recalls the discomfort involved in being delivered to class in his aunt's chauffeur-driven Packard. "Jerry and I hated to let the other kids see us. This was during the depression period, and we felt just *awful* being taken to school like a couple of royal princes, complete with Buster Brown haircuts. We'd try to hide on the floor, but my aunt would pull us back up on the seat, and we'd squirm there miserably while all our schoolmates gawked at us. It was then that I first began to resent our social status."

Phil's mother and father were politically divided, since the elder Hill was a strong-minded Democrat, and they would often exchange angry views on the current political scene over the dinner table. These sessions were quite painful for the three children, and Phil came to dread the occasions when he would be asked to eat at "the big table" with his bitterly wrangling parents. (His marked dislike for loud social dinners can be traced back to these unhappy meals.)

Religion, too, became a sore point with Phil, since he was forced to spend many of his boyhood summers at revivalist camp meetings; and his mother's passionate soul-saving lectures only intensified young Phil's desire to form a personal philosophy of his own.

In 1935, after his father became postmaster, Phil was sent to the Hollywood Military Academy. He spent three years there, learning to play the alto horn and drums with the school band, and diligently obeying his superiors in an attempt to fit into his family's social structure. His father expected him to be "a good little soldier," and Phil stolidly accepted this responsibility.

"Actually," he says, "I didn't know much else in the way of a living pattern, since we always had a considerable amount of regimentation around the house. Our father believed in a strict upbringing, and we were carefully disciplined. My mother liked to sleep late, and we were trained to tiptoe until it was time for her to be up. A buzzer rang, which announced to the help that she was awake. Then we could play. I called my father 'sir' and we could never seem to establish any kind of really close relationship. He didn't approve of my lopsided automotive interest, for one thing, and so I could never talk cars with him."

Phil recalls a game he used to play in grade school with the neighborhood boys. "We'd stand on San Vicente Boulevard and try to see who could guess the name and year of a car at the farthest distance. I kept getting better and better at this, until I could recognize almost every car made since the Kaiser's war! Maybe three or four hundred of them. After a while the other kids quit playing the game, since it was no fun with me around. I was a fanatic at it, and you can't compete on level terms with a fanatic."

Model railroading was another consuming interest, and young Phil had toy trains running throughout the house. On weekends he was learning to steer the 1918 Packard while sitting on his Aunt Helen's lap. Unlike his father, she encouraged the boy's interest in automobiles, and would instruct her chauffeur to climb into the back while she took over the driving seat. Then she would handle the brake and clutch while Phil (perched on her knee) would grip the large, wood-rimmed wheel as they motored slowly along the street. Occasionally, she would allow him to shift gears as she worked the pedal.

In 1936, when Phil was nine, a family friend stopped by to pay the Hills a visit in his new Oldsmobile. Screwing up his courage, Phil asked if he could drive the car around the block, and the gentleman agreed to this, obviously amused by the request.

"He didn't figure any nine-year-old kid could handle that big Olds of his," says Phil, "and I wasn't sure I could either. But I'd long since memorized every detail of shifting, braking and so on, hoping for a chance like this one, and I wasn't *about* to admit any doubts. My parents didn't like the idea, but this fellow told them not to worry, that he'd be right next to me all the way. I had pillows behind me in the seat, and I had to hold myself close to the windshield in order to see over the hood, but at least my feet could reach the pedals. So off we went, with a kind of lurch as I shifted into second. At the first corner I almost nailed the curb, but got around okay. Then, to my great embarrassment, I stalled the engine twice at San Vicente and 19th Street, but got it started again and completed the trip, foolishly happy in the knowledge that I could now drive without assistance."

During this year of his life Phil was suffering a great deal due to a sinus condition, which grew severe enough to warrant an operation. The boy was taken to the hospital, where the frontal bone in his upper nose was removed to ease the pressure.

Hill explains: "Now they can relieve the pressure with drugs, but in my case the bone had to come out, and for a whole year I had a drain tube in my nose."

Phil's aunt, realizing that the boy needed extra attention, began to let Phil drive her car on Sunday afternoons along deserted back roads. She then lived in San Fernando Valley, and the children would often visit her there on weekends.

"My aunt was very fond of us kids, being a divorcée and rather lonely and withdrawn," says Hill. "I was her favorite. My brother and sister had no inclinations toward driving, but the minute we'd get to the house I'd begin pestering Aunt Helen to take me out in the car. She understood me better than my parents did, and we grew very close. I could tell her how I really felt about things and knew she'd listen. She'd always been intrigued by fine cars and so she never objected to this obsessive automotive interest of mine. I didn't let my father know about these Sunday drives, because I was sure he'd try to put a stop to them. None of us said a word."

Helen Grasseli was previously active in Cleveland society, and she liked to dwell on the "glorious years" of her past. Well educated, she had once been a sophisticated member of the social register, and her tastes and values were stamped with quality. As Hill put it: "She seemed to have an instinctive feeling for things which were solid and worthwhile, and she influenced me subtly along these lines. It has taken me a long time to fully appreciate the extent of that influence, and I'm grateful for it."

Following her divorce, Phil's aunt began to withdraw from outside contacts. When the Hill children were not with her she would "take to bed," unwilling to involve herself with strangers. She became a recluse who lavished her affection on the three children of her sister, and her sole joy in life came about through bringing happiness to these children.

"My aunt loved doing things for us," says Phil. "And we rarely took advantage of her in this sense, but when we wanted a certain thing badly enough, and Aunt Helen knew about this, she'd see that we got it. That old Model T was just one example."

The year was 1939, and Phil was strolling with his aunt on Figueroa Street in Los Angeles, passing the used car lots, sometimes peering inside the showrooms at the new models. Abruptly, the boy stopped. A car had caught his eye in a lot behind one of the showrooms. There, silent and gleaming under the California sun, its top up, side curtains neatly in place, was a black Model T Ford, looking as though it had just rolled off a Detroit assembly line.

"I *had* to have a close look," recalls Phil, "because right away I could see that this car was in absolutely *amazing* condition. The seats were perfect, the tires were not worn, the top was like new. I hopped up on the running board to see how many miles it had on it. The odometer read just over 8000."

The going price for a Model T in 1939 was $10, but the salesman quoted an astronomical figure for this particular jewel: $40. Phil sighed. It was obviously far beyond his grasp.

"When Aunt Helen saw the look on my face she opened her purse and paid the man in full. So, at twelve, I suddenly had a car of my own—and I can honestly say that this was one of the most memorable days of my life."

The Ford was delivered that evening, and when Phil heard it approaching his aunt's house he ran to the upstairs window.

"I peeled back the curtains and there it was, shuddering back and forth in the street below, with that familiar whine of the planetary box, an unmistakable sound in low and reverse. I rushed down into the yard with my aunt not far behind me, savoring my excitement. The salesman told me, 'Now, you get low by pushing the left-hand pedal down, high by letting it out. The middle pedal is for reverse and the throttle is on the right of the steering column. Have you got that, boy?' I nodded impatiently, and within five hundred feet of the house I was driving the thing myself. I remember I couldn't even sleep that night, and I didn't go to school the next day."

Philip T. Hill strongly disapproved of the purchase, and warned his son not to operate the Ford on public streets. Young Phil readily agreed to this, since he already had an ideal area picked out for his driving, involving private roads and a quarter-mile dirt horse track.

"By then I knew George Hearst, the grandson of publisher William Randolph Hearst, and he also owned a car," recounts Hill. "We'd met at the Military Academy, and when he told me about this dirt track they had on his family estate in Santa Monica Canyon I was all for trying it out."

The two boys spent many hours on the private roads of the estate, staging two-car races around the dirt oval, sliding, spinning, skidding the turns, learning to handle their machines. This was Phil's first taste of fast driving, and he reveled in it.

He also learned about the interior workings of a gasoline engine when a rod went out on the Ford. Phil overhauled the powerplant with the help of his aunt's butler, proving his natural talent as a mechanic. He began wearing ripped T-shirts and scuffed blue jeans around the house in what he now admits was "an unconscious effort to annoy my parents." On one hand, he was proud of his family background and social position, but he found that it hampered his personal adjustments, and he began to rebel against the role of "postmaster's son." This rebellion was intensified when he began attending Santa Monica High School.

"The rich and the poor were funneled into those classrooms," he recalls. "And, in my opinion, there just wasn't a free and natural relationship between students. We well-to-do kids were terribly envious of the others. The kids from poor families seemed to have a freedom denied us. They seemed more worldly, more knowledgeable when it came to sports and dating and everyday living. We'd been sheltered while they roamed free. So we began to ape them, to swagger and smoke and raise hell. My scruffy clothes were a part of this pattern."

Hill had been experiencing this dilemma since attending his first public school, and blames this "social difference" for much of his early unhappiness.

"Take sports, for instance," he says. "I was just awful at baseball and football and the rest. When the other boys were learning to handle a bat and hit a ball I was out of school, removed that year and privately tutored because my mother heard about a polio epidemic and didn't want me exposed to it. As a result, I came back to find that all the guys had a year of baseball behind them and I didn't even know which end of the bat to grab. So I pretended I didn't want to play ball; instead I'd wander through junkyards, looking at all the old rusted cars. Dancing was the same thing. I was down in Florida when my brother and sister took their lessons—so there I was, scared to death to begin because they already knew how. I was mixed up in these matters, and I somehow always blamed myself, feeling that for some odd reason I didn't know how to do things that other people could do."

Unable to deal with such personality problems, Phil withdrew, became defensive and introverted. In his high school years, when he was asked what profession he intended to follow he would shrug the question aside. Deeply afraid of failure, he refused to commit himself to any single goal.

"My father was determined to send us to Union College in Schenectady because *all* the male members of the family had attended that college since it was founded in the late 1700s," Hill says. "Jerry and I were equally determined *not* to go there, just to prove we could break the mold. I had no real idea of what I wanted to do with my life. From the time I was very small, people would ask me 'What are you going to be when you grow up?' and I honestly couldn't tell them. I didn't know. Even in high school I didn't tie in my automotive interest with any kind of livelihood. The future was something I didn't want to think about."

Phil had seen his first automobile race in the winter of 1940, a night event at Gilmore Stadium, and was fascinated by the racketing, gaudily painted midget cars, as the helmeted drivers hurled them around the banked oval in a daredevil exhibition of wheel-to-wheel driving.

"It never occurred to me I could ever do anything like this," Hill confesses. "It was simply an exciting spectacle—and I enjoyed it purely from this standpoint. I only attended a few more midget races before the war stopped them. I didn't become a real fan until the late forties, when the postwar midget craze took over."

In order to supplement his regular allowance, Phil worked part-time in local service stations after high school classes and on weekends. Using this extra money, he bought a variety of cars during this period, including a V-8 Model A Ford, a Plymouth, a Chevrolet and a Packard, all used and all painstakingly modified by Phil, who was rapidly becoming a highly skilled self-taught mechanic.

"One of my illegal pastimes was 'dragging' away from stop lights," Hill confesses. "This was in wartime, and the streets were nearly always unpatrolled. We all had chrome pipes on our cars, which we figured made beautiful music by amplifying certain harmonics in the exhaust, and a couple of us would meet at a light, rev our engines, and squeal away in a cloud of black tire smoke. Of course my father was furious when he found out about this, and I was subjected to long, stern lectures on the advisability of *never* breaking the law, I guess I deserved those lectures, but they'd go in one ear and out the other. My mother just ignored the whole business."

Phil began attending hot-rod meets on the dry lakes, and although he didn't choose to compete he helped prepare some of the cars, Don Parkinson, who later married Phil's sister, was a member of this group. Young Parkinson had inherited an interest in fast cars from his father, a wealthy enthusiast who collected Lincoln Zephyrs and exotic foreign machinery.

"Don's father usually owned three or four cars at once," says Hill, "and he'd always have at least one Zephyr. I remember seeing Bugattis, BMWs, and a big eight-cylinder Alfa Zagato roadster in his garage. He let me borrow a couple of books by a British writer, Barré Lyndon. The titles were *Combat* and *Grand Prix*. They formed my introduction to European racing, the first being a history of the MG, and through them I discovered a whole new world of speed!"

In 1944 Phil worked briefly as a nose-gun assembler for Douglas Aircraft, then entered the University of Southern California after he had been turned down for the armed services (due to his sinus condition). Although he chose to major in Business Administration he was actually still unable to focus on a career.

"I didn't *like* Business Administration," he declares, "but it seemed a logical choice because my aunt told me that someday I might have to handle her estate, and that I should pick up some knowledge in this field. Up to then my school grades had been barely satisfactory, due partially to the fact that I never received any family encouragement. For example, my mother would tell me about how my grandfather and my great-grandfather had both been lousy at arithmetic, so this fully justified my being lousy at arithmetic. I had no basic inspiration to be a good student, and Jerry reacted just as I did. Helen was the only one of us who was able to overcome this and sail along on her own. She got fine marks."

At the university, however, Hill had a special reason for buckling down to work during the first semester, and his grades improved immediately. It had to do with his pride.

"A rule at USC stated that unless your marks were up to snuff for the first semester you couldn't be pledged to a fraternity," he explains. "Now, I was by no means the typical frat member; it was simply a way of life for fellows of the better families, and so I went along with the tide. Once I agreed to join Kappa Sigma, though, I determined not to let poor grades keep me out. I'd been a frat member in high school, and we'd get flogged black and blue with huge wooden paddles, part of the ritual then. College was, in some ways, even worse. In the beginning of Hell Week at USC each pledge had to undergo a 'heart-to-heart' session before a senior member of the frat house. He'd come into this dead-quiet room, blindfolded, and sit down in front of a desk. Then this calm voice would begin to ask very direct questions which must be answered honestly if the pledge wished to become a full-fledged frat member. Questions about your personal life and your girlfriends and the whole bit — and there you'd be, stumbling along, trying to answer, getting all panicky, with this guy telling you it's better to level now, in private, than have them investigate publicly. And finally, when you'd reveal something really horrible, the whole room would burst into laughter. Because, sitting around in the dark listening to this, would be *all* the frat brothers! You just wouldn't believe some of the things a pledge had to go through."

Hill adapted himself to fraternity life as best he could, but he never felt wholly at ease with the other members, even when he moved into the frat house for two months. ("The rest of the time I lived at my aunt's place to escape the pressures at home.") This again related to his feelings of inadequacy in a "worldly" sense; he found the forced social life disturbing and strained, which indirectly affected his studies. Once again the pattern reasserted itself and his marks began to drop.

"But I continued to do well in one special subject," he says, "and this was a course in psychology called 'Problems of Human Behavior.' Up to then, I'd been unaware of just *how* I had become the person I was; I hadn't realized that it was largely an environmental process — and all this was absolutely fascinating to me. I began to see myself from an objective viewpoint for the first time in my life, and this opened several mental doors. But, for the most part, college proved to me that I would never be able to function as my father did, in the role of the Good Citizen and Solid Businessman. I didn't want to continue at USC, but for the moment I had nowhere else to go."

It was George Hearst who provided Hill with a new direction, by informing him that a mechanic named Rudy Sumpter was looking for a pit helper on an Offenhauser-powered midget owned by Marvin Edwards of Hollywood Spring and Axle. Phil's revived interest in midget racing prompted him to seek out Sumpter and ask for the job. He was immediately hired.

This was the excuse he needed to quit college, and at the end of the term, in June of 1947, he joined Sumpter on a full-time basis. Gib Lilly was Edwards' driver, competing in the car twice a week, at the Rose Bowl on Tuesday nights and on Thursday nights at San Bernardino.

"This was wonderful for me," says Hill, "and I loved the work. I was just a mechanic's helper, but I had an identity; I had a real label which I could hang onto at last."

Phil Hill had left school behind him, and set out on his own. Now he could forget the past and lose himself in the dust and roar of a banked track.

The mold had been broken.

CHAPTER THREE

Midgets to Jaguars

T HE EDWARDS-SUMPTER-HILL combination did exceptionally well that season, and their car won many events with Gib Lilly at the wheel. Phil readily admits that his part in these victories was negligible, but he nonetheless basked in the aura of a winning team.

"Gib was an idol of mine at the time," Phil says. "He was a very good driver, with great potential, and he won a lot of races for us. When he didn't win he was always near the top. It was a challenge to see how to keep on improving the car, and Rudy deserves all the credit for the smooth way that midget performed. I was strictly a fetch-and-carry member of the team, but I kept my eyes open and picked up a lot about race preparation."

Despite his absorption in the midgets, Hill maintained his interest in exotic European machines, and was intrigued by photos of the new MG-TC models produced in England. He got his first glimpse of a TC while cruising down Wilshire Boulevard in his modified '46 Ford. The MG was parked, and Hill stopped his car to have a close look at the buglike little roadster.

"Just a few days earlier George Hearst had told me that they were selling MGs over at International Motors, in Beverly Hills," says Phil, "and right then and there I determined to go over and test-drive one. Louis Van Dyke, who ran the place with Roger Barlow, took me out and slid a few corners, then I wheeled it around the block and was hooked."

Hill immediately sold his Ford, borrowed $200 from his aunt, scraped up the remainder from friends, and purchased the TC. In November of 1947 he was the proud owner of a brand-new MG sports roadster, and he compares his emotional state to the elation he experienced in acquiring the old Model T.

"I could see so much classic beauty in that car," he says. "Red leather, nice carpets under your feet, the dash with the big round tach. Everything was so neat and different—with the little cubbyholes where the side windows fitted in the back. What a puzzle it was to get them in there without scratching the isinglass!"

Soon after he had bought the TC, Phil quit his day job as mechanic with a local Packard agency to work for International Motors, beginning an association that lasted for seven years. He continued to work with Sumpter in the evenings, and on weekends he would tinker with the TC.

"I was always getting in Dutch with Barlow due to my enthusiasm," Hill relates. "I'd stop work to talk at great length about cars and certain drivers and about the advantage of one kind of suspension over another. With almost every customer who came in the place! Naturally, this annoyed Barlow, and Louis Van Dyke was always coming to my rescue to keep me from being sacked. Later; when I started to earn a racing identity, things were different. Then I became something of an asset for International. Those early days, though, were touch and go as far as my job was concerned."

Phil ordered a Nordec supercharger for the MG, and while this was pending delivery he entered the small British roadster in a rally at Palos Verdes in January of 1948, finishing just a few points behind Van Dyke, who won in another MG.

"This was my first competitive event," he says, "and I got a real kick out of the thing—so I sent in my entry for the Chatsworth Rally on February 1. This started at a drive-in on Laurel Canyon and Ventura Boulevard, went way the heck down Ventura, then twisted up into the hills, ending in Chatsworth. And when the results were tabulated I was declared the winner! Got a dash plaque and a bottle of Mumm's champagne."

Hill also competed in the Santa Barbara Time Trials, running solo against the clock; but he had to wait until the summer of 1949 to get a taste of real competitive racing. Meanwhile, Edwards and Sumpter had added a second midget to their team, piloted by Walt Faulkner, and the operation was on a seven-nights-a-week basis.

"I was going around then with a girl named Kay Wathan," states Phil, "and she also worked at International. We'd hop into my TC the minute work was over and head for the midgets. Carrell Speedway, in Gardena, was a popular track and we often ran there, with Kay munching hot dogs while we sweated over those two cars."

Hill had traded in his first MG for the latest model by year's end, and quickly converted this new TC into what he called "a real charger." The conversion included a Shorrock supercharger, special red-and-black paint job with white striping along the doors and louvers — and a modified powerplant.

"We lowered the compression ratio way down," says Phil, "and put in huge inlet valves, hollowed out the combustion chamber and so on, with the net result that here was an efficiently blown machine, with no pinging or roughness in the engine, and tremendous stamina. It had the performance of about a two-liter car by then."

     •   •   •   •   •

A group of California enthusiasts had banded to gether as the Foreign Car Racing Association, and their first meet was scheduled for July 24, 1949, at Gardena's Carrell Speedway. Several MGs were due to appear, with a mixed variety of other sports machines, and Hill hoped to have his new car in the lists. He'd never driven on the fast, half-mile oval at Gardena, and he was anxious to practice there with the TC.

"Arnold Stubbs and I took out our MGs one afternoon," he relates, "and Rudy went with us to see the fun. To my humiliation, Arnold turned a faster lap in his unblown car than I did in my hotted-up one, and Rudy slapped me on the shoulder and said, 'Well, kid, too bad you can't drive like Stubbs. Your *car* looks fast enough.' Boy, that did it! I got out there again, all arms and elbows, and whipped that thing around, sliding, kicking up chunks of asphalt — but I beat his time by just a shade. I think Rudy was impressed."

The meet at Carrell was a night race, attracting some 8000 curious spectators. They had no idea what to expect from this unfamiliar assortment of wire-wheeled sports machines, which included one other blown MG (driven by Jack Early), several stock TCs, a 1936 MG Magnette, a BMW, a Talbot, a Hotchkiss and a snarling SS-100 Jaguar, as well as a sprinkling of Morris Minors, Simcas, Renaults, Fiats and an Austin.

Phil was placed in Class B, and throttled his TC to an easy victory against the other MGs. He next entered the three-lap trophy dash, pitted against Don Parkinson's BMW, the SS Jaguar and Stubbs in another MG. Again he won, and wrapped up the evening by taking the all-MG main as well, despite being handicapped a third of a lap at the start. It was a clean sweep for the young Santa Monican in his initial track event: Class B, Trophy Dash and Main!

"I guess I should have been delirious with joy, but instead I was actually depressed," Phil says. "I felt my *car* had won, not me. And this feeling carried over to the next event at Carrell, in which I also took first in three more races."

Hill felt guilty about using his experience in car preparation, gained from his many months with Sumpter, in order to win these races, and although his guilt was unjustified (since each novice driver did all he could to guarantee a fast mount) it tarnished his early victories at Gardena.

"We used to take off the left front springs and have them re-arched by Marv Edwards in his shop," Phil relates. "Then we'd be able to keep the inside rear wheel down. This was an old midget trick, and it worked fine with the TC. We even kept the car jacked up between races to be certain the spring set was not affected. We also found that worn tires got a much better bite, blown way up to 55 pounds, and this kept us from going into the fence."

Edwards and Sumpter were amazed at Hill's performance with the MG, and when Doug Grove (who had replaced Gib Lilly) broke a leg in a Carpinteria crash they asked Phil to step in and qualify Grove's machine for the main event at San Bernardino that August.

Phil had never even warmed up a midget, and he was extremely apprehensive about qualifying in the fast 40-car field, paced by such luminaries as Vukovich, Hanks, Ruttman, Bryan and Faulkner. He spun the car wildly on his first try, then settled into a steadier groove, increasing speed, finding out that he could dive well into the turns, then catch the sliding car with the throttle and set it up for the straight. His time was fast enough to put him among the top twelve.

"In the race itself, since I was a novice, I was not allowed to pass anyone else," Hill says, "but the fact that I had managed to qualify our car for starting money convinced Rudy that I should take Grove's place on the team. My whole attitude suddenly reversed itself, and I began to think that perhaps I had extraordinary powers as a driver, that these powers were simply handed to me and that I was unique in having them. Of course, this was as stupid as my earlier feelings. Maturity was a long way off."

Phil drove the midgets twice after this, at Gilmore Stadium and again at San Bernardino. But each time he had trouble; the car had been repaired after a crash and handled erratically. Hill finished far back in the field at Gilmore, and ended up scraping the fence at San Bernardino.

"I said to hell with this," Phil recalls. "And Rudy seemed just as glad to lose me. He claimed the car was perfect, but *I knew* it wasn't right. So we both agreed to call it quits. After that I gradually lost interest in midget racing. In a sense, I was relieved at not having to play the midget game, because I felt sure I'd crash sooner or later. I am honestly afraid of those little bombs. I was glad to turn my full attention to sports cars."

Hill soon decided that the TC was too small for his needs and determined to replace it with a racing Jaguar. The new XK-120 was creating a sensation in England, having won handily at Silverstone — and it had been officially timed at 132.6 mph on a straight run along the Jabbeke highway in Belgium, establishing a new world's record for a stock production car.

Therefore, in the fall of 1949, with the financial assistance of International Motors, Phil went to England. There he planned to buy an XK-120 and attend special courses in various plants in order to increase his mechanical knowledge.

"I still couldn't imagine my ever making a living as a driver," he declares. "Oh, I'd made some money at it, up to $500 a night at Carrell, but my future now seemed to be as a mechanic, and here was a real chance to learn. First I went to SU, in Birmingham, then to the Jaguar factory in Coventry, then to Rolls, then to MG. I spent three to five weeks at each place and found it all very rewarding. That's when I bought the Jag, drove it for a nice break-in period, then shipped it home."

England made a great impression on Hill; he had been anxious to break away from California for a few months, to escape the pressures of his family and to "think things out." He found both peace and excitement in England.

"When I got off the boat I was astounded at the foreignness of it all," he confesses. "Everything was so different from the States. Riding a bus, for example. Here was the driver in a sort of little cubicle up on the right side, herding this slow-revving old diesel-engined bus through traffic with its Wilson pre-select gearbox.... Even the *buildings* were unusual."

Phil found the peace he'd been seeking on a farm south of London, near Sussex, in the rolling green English countryside. He had survived the cold winter in boardinghouses; now it was spring, the hills bright with color, the weather mild and bracing.

"I lived with a family called the Dunts, on their place at Billingshurst," he says. "During that final month down there, in May of '50, before I headed home, I swore that I would never let myself get tense or nervous again. The area had an old-world calm that settled into your bones. I'd roam the hills, walking the country which was really beautiful at that time of year—and nothing seemed important enough to worry over. But it ended, of course, and by June I was back, sweating out the road races at Santa Ana."

· · · · ·

The postwar road racing revival in the States had gained momentum during the time Hill spent in England. In the East, spurred by the success of the initial Watkins Glen race late in 1948, competition interest was rapidly developed. In September of '49, when the event was repeated at the Glen, crowd attendance increased by 400 percent—to 100,000! Emphasis then shifted to Florida where a 105-mile road race was held at Palm Beach Shores. In April of 1950, at Palm Springs, California, the West Coast took over with a spirited 40-lapper at the spa's airport circuit. Santa Ana was slated to host the next event, and it was here that Hill re-entered the stateside racing scene.

A new and potent British threat had risen to challenge the Jaguars. This was the J2 Allard, a big, brutish machine in which modified American engines were used with marked success. On the Pacific Coast, Roy Richter had installed a Ford powerplant in his new Allard, and even though Hill had carefully prepared his British machine the Jag was clearly outclassed.

The two-mile circuit was laid out in the shadow of the massive blimp hangars at the Santa Ana Lighter-Than-Air Station, and incorporated numerous hay-bale chicanes and a half-mile straightaway, allowing the power of the Allard to be advantageously utilized. Two other Allards and Jack McAfee's XK Jaguar were the only big-bore challengers, but Richter had no trouble with them.

Hill, however, proved himself the hero of the day. He began by spinning out in the first turn, gunned back into the battle in last position and finished second ahead of McAfee after 20 laps.

Richter stated: "Hill's very aggressive handling of the Jaguar made it necessary for me to use all of my advantage of superior acceleration and top speed. I was always aware of Phil in my rearview mirror."

· · · · ·

In the Pikes Peak Hill Climb, that September, Hill got a chance to try out an Allard, with disappointing results. Booming up the wind-swept 12.4-mile slope in Basil Panzer's J2, Phil was setting a hot pace when he entered Glen Cove turn, halfway to the summit, found a large rock in his path, dodged it, and left the road. He lost a minute and a half in the ditch, dropping him to 22nd in the final results.

· · · · ·

In mid-October, Phil returned to Carrell Speedway in his XK for a try on the dirt. The basic half-mile oval had been lengthened to a mile by running the course out the pit gate, up a hill, across a parking lot, then back to the original track. Hill won the three-lap unlimited heat race by outsprinting the other drivers in a Le Mans-type start. He was first into his car and was never headed. But trouble beset him in the Trophy Dash when he spun in front of McAfee's Jaguar and was soundly clouted. He borrowed a suspension unit from another Jag driver, entered the 20-lap main event, and finished fourth.

"I was disgusted with myself," says Hill. "A spin at Santa Ana, off the road at Pikes Peak and then another spin at Carrell. I was driving too hard and although the Jag was well prepared, mechanically, I was pushing it beyond its limits. And my mental attitude wasn't helped by the fact that International Motors had talked me into becoming a salesman over at their new showroom on Wilshire. I just hated the whole idea of selling cars, and I was a miserable salesman. I could never get over the feeling that it was all some kind of dark conspiracy—which, of course, was nonsense. But there I was, extolling the virtues of Talbots, Simcas, MGs and so forth with a hollow voice. Luckily, Richie Ginther was then at International and we both profited from a close friendship which has persisted over the years."

Ginther credits Hill with the fact that he is driving today: "My interest in racing stemmed from knowing Phil. In fact, he's always been instrumental in whatever I've done. If I hadn't known him I don't have any idea what I'd be doing now. Maybe working in a gas station or digging ditches, who can say? We originally met in '46, when my brother had a fraternity party at the house. Phil came along, and we talked casually together. About a year after this, since we lived within only four blocks of one another in Santa Monica, I wandered over to his garage, and next thing I knew I was helping him prepare his MG."

Ginther was working for Douglas in 1950, when Hill returned from England, and he took a leave of absence to accompany Phil on a "delivery" trip.

"We drove a Rolls Royce to Palm Beach, picked up an older Rolls there and drove 'em both on to New York," says Richie. "Then we flew to Houston, picked up a Simca and tooled it back to L.A. Phil knew I was tired of aircraft work, and we talked a lot on that trip. When we got back, in July, I quit Douglas and he got me a job as mechanic for International."

The last big event of the 1950 season was run at Pebble Beach in November, and when Hill won this race in the clutchless, brakeless Jaguar, Richie was his pit chief.

CHAPTER FOUR

And Finally a Ferrari

HILL'S PEBBLE BEACH VICTORY occasioned a rebirth of the "unique natural gifts" theory which Phil had previously adopted. He refused to realize that great drivers develop over a long period during which they study their craft, using each new lesson to advantage. At this period of his life, Phil shut his mind to this developmental process, continuing to operate at an almost instinctive level.

"I needed to satisfy my ego by believing that I was *born* a fine driver," Hill now admits. "Had I been capable of lowering myself to the point of really learning how to drive a racing car in the beginning I would have progressed much faster and more smoothly. My having done so poorly in other competitive areas warped my thinking; when this success in racing came along I began to give myself much more credit than I deserved in order to compensate for the early failures. I seemed to require this ego gratification, and I couldn't approach my driving with any kind of objectivity."

Phil drove his XK Jaguar for the last time in a California mountain rally early in 1951, then sold it in order to finance the purchase of a classic 2.9-liter 8-cylinder Alfa Romeo. This had been a European team car in the Mille Miglia in the late thirties, and was ancient by modern standards, but Hill was unable to resist the fierce, blazing-red machine with its long louvered hood and twin superchargers.

"I've seldom enjoyed a car the way I enjoyed that old Alfa," he says. "It was one of a number of cars in the Tommy Lee estate offered for sale after his death in '50, and had been driven at Pikes Peak and

Watkins Glen before I got it. Trouble was, they'd hopped it up too much. The compression ratio was wrong, and it overheated. Besides which, the scavenger pump kept packing up on me — and that engine just gulped oil. My first time out with it, at Carrell in February of '51, I had to keep pitting for oil. But I loved the way it handled."

In the meet at Carrell (Hill's last race on the famed speedway) he won the Trophy Dash with the Alfa, then switched to the cockpit of Bill Cramer's V-8 60 MG, to score a fourth in the main ahead of Panzer's J2 Allard. He next fielded the Alfa at Palm Springs, where he stormed up from 25th place to third in the first two and a half laps before being forced out of the contest.

"I was boiling through this left-hand turn when I saw a wheel going by," he explains. "I wondered whose it was, and a split second later, when I felt the axle dig into the pavement, I had the answer. It was mine."

Phil's mother died ten days before this Palm Springs event, following a long illness. And on Phil's 24th birthday, April 20, 1951, his father also succumbed, victim of a fatal heart attack.

"He was in the hospital at the time, undergoing a routine physical exam," Hill relates. "He was very active in the Naval Reserve, and was being checked out just prior to a cruise when this thing hit him. There was no previous record of heart trouble, so it was completely unexpected."

The two deaths in the family didn't affect Phil's competitive plans. A month after his father's funeral, in late May, he was back at Pebble Beach, scene of his most important victory, for the second annual running of the event.

The Alfa/Hill combination garnered top honors in the 10-lap Del Monte Handicap, but could not maintain that pace in the 48-lap main for the Pebble Beach Cup. Pollack's huge 6-liter Cadillac-powered Allard won, with another Allard and the Breeze XK Jaguar edging out the overheating Alfa. Several stops for oil kept the 2.9 out of serious contention.

Reluctantly, Hill got rid of the red Alfa, knowing that further competition with the erratic machine was impossible. He was still a year away from owning his first Ferrari, but he filled in the gap with a remarkably handsome Aston Martin DB-2.

"I had no idea of buying this new Aston when they rolled it into our showroom at International," states Phil. "But when the *Road & Track* people wanted to take some photos for use in their publication I was sent along to drive the car—and that drive convinced me. I had the Alfa money, plus my inheritance, so I signed the papers."

Hill never competed in the DB-2, using it solely for transportation while he lined up rides in several more races that season. His reputation was steadily growing, and his ardent Coast following made their voices heard wherever he drove in California. Charles Hornburg, Jaguar distributor for the western states, was sending a pair of special Silverstone machines to the big August race at Elkhart Lake, Wisconsin, and he had chosen George Malbrand, a Grand Prix driver from Buenos Aires, to handle one of them. The other he assigned to Hill.

"They were modified XKs," Phil says, "with light, aluminum bodies and Rudge-Whitworth wire wheels, and they were slightly faster than my old XK—but not quite fast enough to get the job done at Elkhart."

Eastern ace John Fitch was a solid winner on the long 6¾-mile circuit, thundering home in a massive blue-and-white Cunningham ahead of a briskly driven Cad-Allard. Hill was third overall in the Silverstone Jag, taking a first in class just ahead of teammate Malbrand, who had broadsided into a tall stack of bales in the early stage of the contest. Phil had driven one of his best races, and as one reporter observed: "There were no wild detours down escape roads."

Hill competed with the white Hornburg Special twice more that October. At Reno, on the 12-turn, 2.5-mile Nevada circuit, twisting around the shores of Virginia Lake, he engaged Bill Pollack's huge Cad-Allard in a potent duel, overcoming the 2-to-1 advantage in engine capacity by faster cornering. For 25 laps they were locked together; then the white Jaguar began dropping back, smoke pouring from its hood. The oil-pressure relief valve had blown, and Hill's bid was over.

Back in Palm Springs a week later, he gained third overall with the Hornburg Jag in this airport event; and wrapped up the '51 season in early December by taking second in class to Jack McAfee's blown MG in "2 Jr.," the snappy Cramer-owned V-8 60 MG.

Phil got an abortive crack at one of Briggs Cunningham's big cars when he returned to the desert resort area of Palm Springs in late March of '52, but his brief attempt ended on the first turn as a cardan shaft U-joint snapped, immediately putting the Cunningham out of action.

"Pebble Beach was coming up again in April," says Phil, "and I wanted to make a good showing there—so I contacted Luigi Chinetti, the Ferrari distributor in New York, and found out that he would sell me a 2.6 model for about $6000. Now, that was just half the price most Eastern drivers were paying for a Ferrari, and so I was able to swing the deal with the money left from my inheritance. The particular model I got had been restored by the factory after a crash at Le Mans, but it had won the Tour de France in '51."

This "bargain" price was no accident. Chinetti had recognized, in Hill, a future champion, and wished to encourage the young Californian. An excellent driver in his own right (having won many events), Chinetti was noted for his wizard's ability to assess first-class driving talent. Over the years this canny Italian had been instrumental in helping to develop champions (including Raymond Sommer, Guy Moll, Tom Cole, Castellotti, Portago and Harry Schell). "I look for the fighter," Chinetti once declared. "I am not interested in finding a driver like me, who goes too carefully. I look for the spark in a man who could be tomorrow's World Champion."

It was Chinetti who became Enzo Ferrari's stateside distributor after the war, selling Briggs Cunningham the first sports Ferrari to be raced in the United States in 1949. The moody, dark-haired Italian who established Chinetti Motors in New York City has always tended to underrate his own skill at the wheel. In 1949, competing at Le Mans with Lord Peter Seldon of England, Chinetti won his third victory in this fabulous contest (in a small 2-liter Ferrari) by driving for a staggering 23 hours and 47 minutes. Lord Seldon was only in the cockpit for 13 minutes of the grueling 24-hour race! This exhausting feat has never been matched in the long history of the French classic, and becomes all the more remarkable when it is noted that Chinetti was then forty-two years of age!

•   •   •   •   •

Unhappily, Hill was not able to drive the 2.6 at Pebble Beach that year, since he honored a promise he'd made Hornburg to handle the white Silverstone Jag. Arnold Stubbs was permitted to take over the revamped Ferrari. Hill was forced to pit twice for water in the Jaguar, and Stubbs tooled the Ferrari gingerly and safely around the tree-lined circuit, enjoying the ride. Neither of them gave winner Bill Pollack's Allard any trouble.

But it was an entirely different story at Golden Gate Park in San Francisco the following month. Aboard a Ferrari for the first time in his career, Phil was proudly determined to extract the last ounce of performance out of his new Italian mount.

The date was May 31, and it seemed that all of San Francisco had turned out to view this event. From 75,000 to 90,000 spectators excitedly crowded the winding 3.1-mile circuit, and Bay City police as well as jeep-mounted Army units were on hand in force to control the huge throng. Chief interest centered around the "invincible" 6-liter Carstens Allard with Pollack aboard, Parkinson's modified XK and Hill in the 2.6 12-cylinder Ferrari.

Graham jumped into a brief lead at the flag, but Pollack boomed past out of the first turn. Hill had started sixth, but within three tours of the course had edged into second, although Pollack was rapidly putting distance between his car and the field. Parkinson and Graham were having at it behind Hill, and as the minutes ticked away Phil began increasing his speed. On the fast, sweeping bend beyond the pits he was timed at 112 . . . 113 . . . 115, picking up three seconds a lap on Pollack. The vast crowd, sensing a close finish, roared encouragement.

Now the Allard's 25-second lead had been cut to just four seconds, and Hill was timed through the traps at 118 mph! Blocked by a smaller vehicle, Phil threw the Ferrari into a four-wheel drift and got by on the inside. Phil was winding the red car up to nearly 7000 rpm. But his gallant effort was to no avail; on the final lap he dropped the coil off the right bank of cylinders, sputtering across the finish line at half power for second overall and first in class.

Despite this near victory, Hill was not entirely satisfied with his new mount, although convinced of the car's potential.

"The handling characteristics bothered me a bit," Phil says. "The shock absorbers needed to be worked over, which we did. Then an anti-roll bar was added in the front. This cured the trouble, and I was able

A very young (age nine) but confident driver. Phil is behind the wheel of his aunt's 1918 Packard; his sister, Helen, and a friend share the back seat.

Three years later, at age twelve, Phil tinkers with the engine of his first car, a Model T Ford, as an awed schoolmate looks on.

Phil Hill drove his MG TC against the clock in 1949 in a time trials at the former Goleta Marine Air Force Base at Santa Barbara. (Jack Campbell)

In July of 1949 Phil drove his supercharged MG TC at Carrell Speedway in Gardena. The crowd of 8000 saw the young man from Santa Monica win all three events he was in that night—his first track outing. (Jack Campbell)

George Hearst (grandson of publisher William Randolph Hearst) told Phil Hill that
Marvin Edwards midget team needed a pit helper. Hill was hired in June 1947, and
filled in as driver on three occasions at Carrell Speedway and Gilmore Stadium.

Phil Hill's only attempt at Pikes Peak was in 1950. Driving the Allard J2 of Basil Panzer,
Hill avoided a large rock halfway up the 12.4-mile hill climb, left the road, and lost a
minute and a half in a ditch. (Courtesy Pikes Peak Library District / Stewarts Photography)

A wild ride in 1950 at the first Pebble Beach road race. In the main event, Phil Hill finished first in his clutchless, brakeless Jaguar XK-120 after driving to the limit in an attempt to overtake a nonexistent opponent. (Jack Campbell)

Al Torres drops the checkered flag as Richie Ginther jumps in celebration of his friend's first road racing victory. (Jack Campbell)

Phil Hill and Arnold Stubbs pictured with an Indy car Hill had bought from the estate of Tommy Lee. They never did complete the project. (Jack Campbell)

Phil sold his Jaguar, and bought a 1938 Alfa Romeo 2900B. He is pictured driving the twin supercharged Alfa against Don Parkinson's XK-120. In his first outing with the Alfa in 1951, Hill won the Trophy Dash at Carrell Speedway. He then switched rides, and drove "2Jr" to a fourth in the main event. (Jack Campbell)

At Pebble Beach in 1951, Phil drove the 13-year-old Alfa Romeo to win the 10-lap Del Monte Handicap. Stops for oil kept the Alfa/Hill combination from being a contender in the main event. The Alfa had been a team car at the '38 Mille Miglia. (Bob Canaan)

In October 1951, Phil Hill drove this lightweight Jaguar XK-120 at the Palm Springs airport circuit. Hill scored a third with the aluminum bodied "Silverstone" Jaguar, owned by Charles Hornburg, Jaguar's distributor for the western United States. *(Bob Canaan)*

Phil Hill pilots "2Jr," the MG TC of Bill Cramer, at the first road race at Torrey Pines in December 1951. Hill retired the overheating Ford V-8 60 powered special, but was credited with a second in class for the 50-lap San Diego Cup. *(Griffith Borgeson)*

At Torrey Pines in July of '52, Phil lapped the entire field in his Ferrari 212 Barchetta on his way to a win. Purchased from Luigi Chinetti, the Ferrari distributor in New York, this car had been restored by the factory after a crash at Le Mans. The Ferrari's history also included a win in the Tour de France. *(Ralph Poole)*

Phil Hill is handed a cool drink by Josie von Neumann after a winning run at Torrey Pines. Dave Sykes is beside the car, waiting to congratulate his friend. *(Ralph Poole)*

to keep the inside rear wheel from lifting. The 12-inch finned aluminum brakes were fantastically good, though, and showed no sign of fade, so I knew I could really punish them in the next race if I had to. No car I'd driven up to then had pleased me as much in this regard."

During this Korean War period Richie Ginther had been taken into the service, and now Phil was due for his Army Reserve training. His sinus condition was still severe enough to keep him out of the regular Army, but each year he reported for two weeks of Reserve training at Camp Liggett—and he was due there in late July when the Torrey Pines Road Races were scheduled.

"I got permission from the C.O. to compete at Torrey," he states. "I felt I had a good chance with the 2.6 and I didn't want to miss it."

．　　．　　．　　．　　．

Located directly on the shores of the Pacific 17 miles north of San Diego, laid out on grounds that sloped down to the ocean, the 2.8-mile circuit at Torrey Pines was ideal from a spectator's viewpoint. For a driver, it offered special hazards: lack of proper escape roads, a dangerously uneven asphalt surface and some abrupt turns involving ditches and reverse camber. One climbing turn ended at cliff edge; the sea waited below.

A record entry of 120 cars and drivers made it one of the Coast's major attractions, and the star of the show was Tony Parravano's big new 4.1-liter Ferrari "America." Bill Pollack had stepped out of the Carstens Allard into this Italian machine for Torrey, and most pre-race betting favored him in the large 30-car field lined up for the main event of the afternoon.

As the battle got under way Sterling Edwards stormed his Chrysler-engined Special into an early lead, but by the end of the initial half mile, Hill had snapped past him in the 2.6 Ferrari. Pollack was not hanging about. Having disposed of the other contenders, he took over second when Edwards pitted on the sixth tour. Hill was revving up to 7500 rpm to pull away, but his straightaway speed was only 111 to Pollack's 115. Then Pollack spun in traffic, bottomed the 4.1 and retired with his track rods rubbing the brake drums.

Despite frantic slowdown signals from his pit crew, Phil continued to stretch his lead. Actually, as he later revealed, he had dropped his top revs down from 7500 to 7000, then to 6500, finally to a maximum of 5500 — and he was still pulling steadily away from second-place runner Chuck Manning in the big Mercury Special. By the fall of the checker Phil had lapped the entire field, including the Mercury, and the crowd applauded happily when he took his final cool-off lap.

Hill's Ferrari victory that sunny afternoon at Torrey Pines was the beginning of an association with the marque of the Prancing Horse which would lead to the continental circuits of Europe and to the official factory team of Enzo Ferrari himself.

———————

CHAPTER FIVE

An International Effort

WELL AWARE that the Jaguar XK-120 had become outdated, the factory in Coventry had released a new and
more potent model, dubbed the C-Type, or XK-120 C. This
was an all-out racing machine, in the best Jaguar tradition, and when
properly geared its 3.4-liter 210-hp engine could push it to 150 mph
on a long straight. When a team of Cs debuted at the 1951 Le Mans
24-Hours they vanquished all other marques, and by 1952 they were
definitely the car to beat in Europe. Charles Hornburg replaced his
XK Silverstone Specials with a pair of new Cs that season, and Phil
Hill agreed to try one out at Elkhart Lake in early September.

"I won the 15-lap Sheldon Cup race on Saturday with the C," Hill
says, "although I had a little trouble getting around Phil Walters in
Allen Guiberson's 2.6 Ferrari coupé. He'd keep weaving on the
straight to keep me from getting a tow, but I downshifted to third
out of the back stretch, mashed the pedal and got by. Finally finished
almost a minute ahead of him."

On Sunday, Hill's Jaguar was swamped by three monster Cun-
ninghams in the hands of Fitch, Walters, and Briggs Cunningham,
though he managed to pass Briggs and close on Fitch until a hole in
the exhaust pipe allowed deadening fumes to leak into the Jag cockpit. Drugged by these exhaust gases, Phil was forced to angle his head
into the stream of fresh air outside the car, and this dropped him to
fourth overall at the flag, just ahead of George Weaver in the other
C-Type.

John Fitch gave Hornburg's C a whirl at Watkins Glen that same month, with Hill piloting the sister car, but engine trouble slowed the Californian and Fitch drove to a solid win in the Seneca Cup. The main event was called due to an accident involving spectators, after which Phil agreed to drive one of the Cs from New York back to Los Angeles.

"Photographer Jerry Chesebrough drove back with me," relates Hill, "and we didn't have any muffler or top. No weather protection at all. I remember getting sick en route and paying a visit to a hospital in New Mexico. These simply weren't highway cars."

· · · · ·

Back in California, at Madera (an airport circuit near the gateway to Yosemite Valley), Hill again faced his tenacious Coast rival, Bill Pollack, who was reinstalled in Carstens' always-potent Cadillac-Allard. The C-Type seemed more than a match for the growling Allard, and Phil took the lead on the initial lap, pulling smartly away from Pollack. However, as he was moving up to lap a slower Lincoln-Allard, the C began to fishtail. The tank cap had popped open on the Lincoln Special and the car was dumping a stream of gasoline in Hill's path. He spun the Jag trying to get around and, passing the pit area, Phil gestured frantically to attract the attention of officials. His signals were interpreted as meaning brake fade, and Pollack's crew held out a board reading: PHIL'S BRAKES!

"It was really a rather amusing situation, when you look back at it," says Hill, "because when I finally got past the Lincoln I found Pollack right on my tailpipe. He was convinced I didn't have any braking power left, so was throwing that Allard insanely into each turn, pressing me very hard. Well, pretty soon my brakes *did* begin to fade—and two laps from the finish Bill got by to win!"

· · · · ·

A week and a half later Hill entered his first international event, the third annual Carrera Panamericana Mexico, a brutal five-day marathon in which many of the world's finest drivers were set to compete.

"I'd never driven in a city-to-city open-road sort of thing," says Hill, "and I didn't know what to expect. Here were most of the Europeans I hero-worshiped at the time: Villoresi, Manzon, Kling, Lang,

Maglioli, Bonetto, Chinetti, Bracco, and even Ascari, the '52 World Champion. Jean Behra was in it, too, although he was known then mainly for his motorcycling exploits. John Fitch was down there in Mexico with one of the team Mercedes 300SLs, an open-cockpit job, and Jack McAfee had Parravano's 4.1 Ferrari. So the competition was by far the roughest I'd ever encountered."

Hill's international racing debut was further complicated by his poor state of health. His sinus condition was aggravated by extreme nervous tension and he could not keep solid food on his stomach.

"I was forced to eat like a damn baby," he says. "Allen Guiberson, whose Ferrari I was driving, had to bring along practically a truckload of baby food for me. And I had no control over a lot of weird muscles. Heart muscles and all sorts of odds and ends were having little convulsive spasms — and most of this stemmed from my basic uncertainty about life. I just didn't feel that I belonged down there in Mexico driving against all these professionals. My system rebelled, and I recall almost blacking out a couple of times before the race was over."

Hill's mount was a well-used 2.6-liter coupé (which Guiberson had purchased that year from Alberto Ascari when the Italian champion raced at Indianapolis) much like his own open-bodied Ferrari, with a top speed of just over 130. This was the same machine Phil had recently beaten at Elkhart Lake, when it had been driven by Walters, and it was out-powered by all of the factory entries. Arnold Stubbs had accompanied Phil to Mexico and would ride as co-passenger in the small Ferrari.

Divided into eight legs (split over the five days, with overnight stops), the long race began at the jungle town of Tuxtla Gutiérrez, some 100 miles north of the Guatemalan border, proceeded over the jagged spine of Mexico, following the Pan-American highway (little more than a goat trail in many spots) to end 1933 miles later in Ciudad Juárez, a plains town just south of the U.S.–Mexico line. Mercedes had the edge, with their new SLs, but Ferrari had sent three powerful 4.1 models, backed up by two Lancias and McAfee's very fast private Ferrari. The Germans would be hard-pressed.

The Hill/Stubbs Ferrari was ninth off the line on the morning of November 19, 1952, and almost immediately moved up a notch in standings when Manzon's Gordini snapped a rear axle just beyond Tuxtla. The next casualty was the World Champion, Alberto Ascari, who overturned his 4.1 Ferrari in a 90-mph bend. Hill described the scene of the crash.

"We saw Ascari's mechanic rushing toward us down the highway, waving excitedly. The road disappeared into a sharp cut and as we slowed going through we saw this battered Ferrari rolled on its side, with Ascari standing calmly beside it. This shook our confidence, but then we saw two of the Mercedes [Fitch and Lang] undergoing tire changes by the edge of the highway, and this really cheered us up."

Behra's light French Gordini was leading, with Bracco pressing for second. Kling almost left the road in the third Mercedes when a low-flying buzzard smashed through his windshield, injuring his co-driver. Bonetto's Lancia dropped out with mechanical troubles and McAfee blew a tire at speed.

"The road was not too mountainous into Oaxaca, our first stop," relates Hill. "The pavement was blacktop, mixed with crushed volcanic rock. Very smooth, but hard on rubber. We had a hole cut in the fenders so we could watch tread wear, but at high speed this was difficult to determine. Three-quarters of the way into Oaxaca the thread started to show on one wheel, and we made a four-minute tire change. We saw the other tires were bad also. For the rest of the way in we were forced to take it easy around the turns because of this condition—and we arrived ninth."

After an overnight stop, the contest was resumed, the next leg ending in Puebla. Hill's shock absorbers began giving him trouble on the winding highway, and the coupé became tricky to manage. Several times in the course of the afternoon their 2.6 became airborne, due to a bump in the road surface, and Phil could not risk hard cornering.

"We were just getting accustomed to this when we came steaming into a tiny village called Acatlán," he says. "The main street led us through a kind of shady tunnel between buildings rather tall for this part of Mexico—and suddenly here was a raised plaza in the center of the town, with the road twisting sharply around it. McAfee had gone off here and dented the tail of his 4.1, and we heard later that several other cars came to grief there. Anyhow, the *policía* and the crowd had been waving us on and we sailed into the corner, slid on the wet clay and smacked the plaza, wrecking our left front wheel and bending our left transverse spring. Took us 10 minutes to get the 2.6 hauled off that stupid plaza and a new wheel installed. But, at that, we were a heck of a lot luckier than Behra."

Gusty winds were harassing the drivers, and near Atlixco, after a 7000-foot rise into the mountains, Jean Behra was still setting a hot pace with his Gordini. But here his lead ended. The Frenchman's wheels locked on an abrupt turn and the Gordini skidded violently down the steep incline, bulleting off the cliff edge to bury itself in a deep crevice. Pulled from the crash, Behra had suffered a concussion and was hospitalized.

Hill left Puebla, after a 30-minute layover, still riding in ninth spot, well behind the Ferrari/Mercedes battle. The 80-mile stretch into the second night's stop at Mexico City climbed to the highest point in the race, nearly 10,000 feet.

"This was like California's Lake Arrowhead road, very twisty and full of 30- to 60-mph bends, so top speed didn't matter. Our car handled peculiarly with the bad springs, but we made good time. We got into Mexico City just behind McAfee, having held our overall position."

Mexico's capital was in the midst of a gigantic anniversary celebration, and all the competitors were escorted into the heart of the city, past a tall monument to the revolution, and the vast crowd closed around the cars with immense enthusiasm, thumping the fenders, drumming hoods, and howling with delight as the angry drivers attempted to wave them aside. The death of one of their countrymen, Santos Metona Díaz, who had smashed into a bridge near the city in his red Jaguar, had no effect on the spirited populace. Eventually the cars were safely garaged.

"That night was a busy one for us," says Hill. "We pounded out the dented body as best we could, fixed the springs and the leaking radiator—and got away the next day half-exhausted, headed for León."

Early-morning fog slowed the race, but soon it was dissipated under a hot Mexican sun, and speeds increased. The road, dropping from its high plateau, was hilly, with long straights, and McAfee began blowing tires at 130. He could no longer hold Hill's 2.6, and Phil also found that he was gaining on a supercharged Lancia.

"Our shocks had failed completely by then," Hill relates, "but we were on these long straights and the car could be steadied. We saw the Lancia way up ahead, and we gradually closed on him, *crawling* past at 133 with the tach reading 7000. At León we took on fuel and put larger tires on the rear wheels. Then we took off for the run into Durango, only to discover, just a half hour later, that we couldn't get over 5500 rpm. The Lancia zoomed past as we checked the carburetors. Sure enough, they were full of dirt! We were in eighth place that night when we made Durango, but we *were* still running."

Many others were not. Villoresi's gearbox had packed up and he was out. Kling was now first in the Mercedes, and Bracco a minute behind him, yet still retaining an overall timed lead in the race. The Ferrari/Mercedes battle had not yet been decided.

On the fourth day's run Hill picked up another position. Over the Durango-to-Parral leg, the 2.6 again caught McAfee's 4.1, which had sustained a splintered windshield.

"Jack was crouching down in the seat, peering through a tiny spot of clear glass," says Hill, "and this gave us the advantage. But as soon as we hit the next straight we had to drop back behind him. By then his whole windshield had blown cleanly out and he could see again."

The Parral-to-Chihuahua stretch was disastrous for Ferrari, as Bracco's transmission exploded, handing the race to Mercedes. Kling was now in firm command, with his teammate, Lang, also going strong.

"We moved out in seventh position on the final day's run into Juárez," Hill relates. "Our car was now in its best condition and had the nicest balance of tire pressure, size of tires and fuel load. We'd done a lot of work on the suspension that night and it was finally okay. The road was straight and flat, with an occasional 80-mph turn over the railroad tracks, and we were able to unwind the 2.6 in relative safety."

The finish line, at Ciudad Juárez, was a scene of great excitement as the race neared its close, and although John Fitch, in the Mercedes, scored fastest time over this stretch it was revealed that he had been officially disqualified for turning back to effect suspension repairs. Thus Hill was automatically moved up into sixth overall, where he finished just behind McAfee's larger Ferrari. Kling and Lang had made it 1-2 for Mercedes, with Chinetti's Ferrari and Maglioli's Lancia finishing third and fourth.

"We were sorry about John, after his fine job," says Hill, "but it was a wonderful feeling to know we'd finished well up in such superior company. Beating Jack would have been fun, but that engine of his just had too many inches for us."

Hill capped the year with a runaway victory at Torrey Pines that December, in a Hornburg C-Type, and made plans for an attempt at Le Mans in 1953. His performance in Mexico had encouraged him; if his health did not fail he determined to try his hand in Europe.

CHAPTER SIX

Of Danger and Death

T HE home-built blue-and-white cars of Briggs Cunningham had been dominant on the U. S. sports car scene for many months, but their superiority was seriously threatened by Ferrari, as Phil Hill dramatically proved in February of 1953 when he took over Bill Spear's fast 4.1-liter model at MacDill Air Force Base in Florida. On the 93rd lap of the six-hour endurance event, as John Fitch made his scheduled pit stop in a Cunningham, Hill took the lead, but a collapsed wheel sent him limping in on the brake drum for repairs. Returning to the fray, he blistered through the time traps at 140 mph in his pursuit of Fitch, cutting the American car's lead to just eight seconds—when another wheel gave way and Hill was forced to settle for second on overall distance and a first in class.

Two weeks later Hill entered the international 12-Hour race at Sebring, again sharing Spear's Ferrari, but their car was destined not to finish. Spear took the initial stint at the wheel, handing over to the Californian at the end of three hours. Hill lasted just 45 minutes. The brake lining on the left front wheel came adrift, causing the hydraulic piston in the master cylinder to abruptly release its fluid. Phil rocketed into a tight corner, stabbed the pedal, and it snapped to the floor. Brakeless, the Ferrari disemboweled itself on the stone foundations of a deserted army barracks, bouncing high into the air as it struck. Hill was shaken, but unharmed; and Fitch again won for Cunningham.

"In April," Phil says, "I had a real go with Jim Kimberly at Bergstrom Air Force Base in Texas. We were nose to nose on the straights at 135, but he nailed down first by a few seconds. Masten Gregory was third in his C-Jag."

.   .   .   .   .

Anxious for a victory in '53, Hill arranged to sell his used 2.6 Ferrari and pick up a new 250 Mille Miglia 2.9-liter V-12 model from Chinetti.

"This one was a real honey," he says. "It was a New York show car. Had triple four-barrel Weber carburetors, a synchromesh four-speed gearbox, and the engine developed 240 hp at 7200 rpm. It could reach 60 in just five seconds and get 160 in top with the right ratios. Of course, it was geared lower for a shorter Stateside circuit like Pebble Beach, which is where I began racing it."

Pollack was again the top favorite at Pebble, with the Carstens Allard, but Bill Spear had brought out his 4.1, and the car looked as though it could catch the big Allard. These two drivers, in fact, battled fiercely through the opening stage of the main event—but Hill was on the move in his razor-tuned 2.9, disposing of the Manning Mercury Special (as it slid into the hay bales) to scream up on the front-running pair. Spear tried to hold off the Californian with his 4.1, but Hill snarled past, hot after Pollack. By the end of the race he had taken sweet revenge on the Allard, passing and opening up a full lap's lead on his old Coast rival. Hill therefore scored his first seasonal triumph with the new Italian car, and his chances seemed excellent at the upcoming Golden Gate Park races in San Francisco.

"I started way back on the grid," he says, "but by the third lap I had the lead sewed up. I'd lapped all but four cars by the 15th tour, and then—powie! The 2.9 dropped its rear axle, spilling oil all over the road. Gregory took the flag in his white C-Type. This was Masten's first major win."

.   .   .   .   .

It was June, time for Le Mans, and Hill was set to co-drive a small Italian Osca with SCCA prexy Fred Wacker. Here, amid the glitter and excitement of the 24-Hours, Hill was amazed at the attitude toward the sport. "In Europe, as I discovered that year, professional auto racing was not shunned as some kind of wild man's hobby; it was considered a respectable existence, and the star drivers were treated like gods — much as our baseball idols are treated in the States. I gained a whole new perspective at Le Mans."

The Hill / Wacker Osca was leading its class after eight hours when the differential failed, putting them out, but Hill watched with avid interest as John Fitch and Phil Walters brought a Cunningham into third overall at the windup (behind a pair of C-Type Jaguars). However, at dawn, the popular Anglo-American driver Tom Cole was killed when his Ferrari skidded off the road at the treacherous White House S-bend at 100 mph, throwing him into the path of another machine. His death cast a shade of gloom over the event.

"I was beginning to be very much aware of the risks connected with fast driving at this time," says Hill. "At first, I seemed to have built-in filters in my brain which minimized danger and amplified safety. But, despite the filters and my innate belief that somehow I could not be injured in a car, I began to brood over the whole business. Cole's death intensified my feelings in this regard, and while I could appreciate the new attitude I had found in Europe it did not cancel out the extreme tension and anxiety which was building up within me. Now it came home to me that I was deeply involved in a sport in which people were crashing and killing themselves. Díaz in Mexico, now Tom Cole. I became hypersensitive to danger, but I wouldn't allow myself to quit. A month later I was at Reims."

Luigi Chinetti had arranged to have Hill co-drive his 4.1 Ferrari at the French sports car race at Reims, in July, and they were plagued with brake trouble and wind buffeting.

"We lasted four hours," Hill says. "Our brakes were terrible, and the windscreen was so poorly designed that Chinetti's helmet was blown off on the second lap! We'd go flying down the hill at 7700 rpm in that 4.1, better than 150 mph, and the wind would be so bad it would blur our vision. That race didn't do my peace of mind any good, and I was just as happy to pull out when we did."

• • • • •

Phil returned to the United States for the Moffett Air Force Base meet in mid-August, but he dropped in the clutch too quickly on the starting grid with his 2.9 and wiped out the rear axle assembly. He had it repaired by the first week in September, when he took the car to Santa Barbara for the Labor Day event.

"I took the main there when Stroppe put his Merc-powered Kurtis in a ditch," says Phil. "Then Bill Devin let me drive his 2.9 Ferrari coupé down at Madera and I won again. Then it was off to the Stead Air Force Base, in Reno, with my own 2.9 for a class win and a second overall to Edwards' 4.1. I was going strong, driving wherever I could, working on the car between races, trying not to think about the possibility of a crash. But, sometimes, that's just when it happens. Which may partially explain what occurred down in Mexico that November."

•   •   •   •   •

Allen Guiberson had offered Hill another Ferrari for the fourth running of the Pan-American Road Race, a 4.1-liter coupé, and Richie Ginther had agreed to ride as co-passenger for the five-day grind across Mexico. In this latest edition of the rugged classic, Juan Fangio of Argentina led the competition, driving for Lancia. Also on hand: Taruffi, Bonetto, Castellotti, Bracco, Maglioli, Chinetti, Behra, Rosier, Kling, Herrmann, plus a contingent of top Americans, many running in the stock car class.

Hill tells the full story of his participation in the 1953 Carrera: "Our 4.1 was beautiful, but unstable. It had a very long chassis, no limited-slip and almost too much power. The engine had been hotted up considerably by Guiberson's boys in Dallas. Richie and I went to Texas to help them finish the car, and it was a hassle from the outset. We were trucking the 4.1 coupé to Mexico City when the truck broke down, so we had to tow it the rest of the way by trailer. Then we had an awful time trying to get the engine to run properly at that altitude and on the available fuel.

"Just as we'd done the year before, we drove from Mexico City to Tuxtla Guitérrez, sort of using this as a shakedown trip, but saving top revs and tires. As we rode we tried to make strip maps and notations regarding kilometer posts and bends, but since we were going in the *opposite* direction we had to keep turning around and asking ourselves, 'Does that look like a bad curve, or not?' It was quite confusing. Now, based on my runs down there, I would say there were about 50 very rough spots really worth knowing about in advance. If a man is driving so hard that his natural instinctive appreciation of what's coming up next can't take care of the rest of the trouble spots, then he's off the road anyhow. But any driver in a car capable of 150 mph and upwards was going to get into plenty of trouble if he didn't know about these 50 places.

"Everything seemed to go wrong the day before the race. Our truck took off back to Oaxaca, leaving us alone with the wrong fuel. And we didn't have spark plugs hot enough to keep from sooting up on this fuel they'd left us. But we had to make do. Next, a shock absorber broke and we had to weld it. So we got just an hour's sleep before we had to get up at 4 A.M. and prepare for the start, had to completely reject the whole carburetion, set the float levels over again and so forth.

"We finally got the car up to the line — and we were scheduled to be the third competitor away. It was still dark, and we had to warm up the engine and change the plugs. Just as we finished this I noticed that the whole battery box was haywire. The battery was just sitting there on a little ledge all by itself with nothing holding it in. We'd been fooling with it earlier, trying to keep it from shaking so badly, and the two T-bolts that held the thing to the frame had slipped out. We knew that it couldn't last 20 miles over that road from Tuxtla to Oaxaca unless it was properly held down.

"Richie ran back into town, which was a mile, then ran back to say he couldn't find a thing to use on the battery. I yelled, 'Try again!' and back he ran. We went through this routine twice, until I was beside myself with nerves. I even attempted to tie the battery in with some old cow fencing — and the Lincoln boys were taking off their belts, hoping to strap the damn thing in. I remember Chuck Daigh broke a buckle, trying to help. Then we decided to wire it up, so I tried to insulate the battery, then wrap the wire around the outside — but at the last twist one of the wires touched a terminal, and the whole works just melted!

"By this time the number one car had been flagged away and we were supposed to take off a couple of minutes later. In that space of time I ran down the line and found Bill Doheny's lovely 4.1 coupé parked beside the road. I clawed open the hood, tore the bolts and frame off his battery and rushed back. We got the new frame installed and slammed down the hood as they were screaming at us to get our car up to the starting area.

"I drove it up there—and here comes Richie, back from town again, crawling on all fours because he was so exhausted. I just pulled him into the car and we took off. By that time I was so upset I couldn't even talk. My judgment was just plain shot—and within five minutes, here we were seeing the number two car in front of us which was a real hot Chrysler with Imperial brakes and a chopped chassis, running in the sports category with the 300 prototype engine. And he was just behind the number one car.

"Well, I managed to gobble up both of them in one sweep, taking them on the outside and sliding practically down the entire length of a hill to do it. *That's* how I was driving! As bad as the first Pebble Beach run!

"For the next half hour we were in fog, and I was cooking up to 6000 rpm in that stuff. Richie had his eyes glued to the windshield, but that didn't help much because the wipers were sort of flopping around in the wind, not touching the glass. Every so often Rich would yell 'Left!'or 'Right!'—and I'd get all over the brakes and scramble down three or four gears and we'd just, by the grace of God, make it around the turn. Once I slid completely across the road and out onto the dirt shoulder and at the last split second, just as the car was sort of hesitating at the edge of the drop, I punched the gas and we were off and away again. I told Richie we'd been saved by Providence, and slowed down a bit. Five minutes later we went into another bad slide—and I realized that this was, in large part, the fault of the car. It was just *not* handling.

"By the time we got down to the long Tehuantepec straightaway we were still in the lead. And we continued to make good time until the tires started popping. We changed our first one, jacking up the car with a little Mickey Mouse-type jack, pounded out the fender where the tread had half wiped it out, and not a soul passed us! And we were there for at least five minutes.

"We got going again and *pop* goes another tire. Then along comes Maglioli in one of the new 4.5s, and he was having his troubles too. Every time he hit a bump in the road his radiator twisted and the hose would work loose. Well, we were the first car into the mountains, after passing Maglioli again. We changed all four tires at the next checkpoint, then discovered we'd forgotten to bring along the key to the padlock on the gas tank. Richie had to take a hub mallet and knock off the lock in order to get the fuel in.

"On the next stretch we got passed by three other cars, because we began breaking wheels. This was a bad characteristic of this 4.1-model coupé; it was so long and top-heavy that it would overload the wheels, even though we had an extra dozen spokes in each one. Anyway, we pulled off the road with a wheel running like a Saturn moon, spokes sticking up every which way. I think we finally ended up about tenth after that first day's run.

"The next morning we took off for Puebla, going easier, trying to save the wheels, since we'd worn out *nine* tires by then. The car now seemed to have a tremendous aversion to going around a corner. You either forced it through or went around slowly, with the front end plowing. Anyhow, we ended up breaking another wheel — and when we got this one fixed I started to push harder, trying to make up some lost time.

"On the twisty, mountainous stretch between Puebla and Mexico City they had the road lined with big white boulders and I knocked a couple off the edge, as you do burros down there. We were really going hard.

"We'd just topped a steep rise and here was a mean, curling downhill turn, a right-hander. My foot was on the brake pedal, but we had a lot of fade and not enough brake left to do the job. We began to slide toward the edge, and I was mentally considering how far down we'd fall — because at our speed we were sure as hell going over. Now, some drops are sheer, down hundreds of feet, and you don't stand a prayer — and we didn't know about this one.

"We slid off backwards, bouncing end over end down the jagged rock slope of the mountain, for maybe forty or fifty feet — *boom, bang, bong!* When we stopped bouncing, the Ferrari's top was caved in. I shouted, 'You okay, Rich?' and he said yeah, he was, and we got out fast. We were remembering Stagnoli who burned to death in his car the day before. But luckily the coupé didn't catch fire.

"When we'd climbed back to the road we found black skid marks all over it, and one of the soldiers told us that Fangio had nearly gone off at this same spot. Someone had removed the turn sign — and we saw a crowd of Mexican spectators, a whole pack of 'em, keeping just out of sight beyond the curve, so the approaching cars couldn't see them and slow down. We knew how deadly this spot was, so Richie and I shook off the guards who were trying to drag us into a first aid tent and went on up the road to flag down the approaching cars. I had my bright red coveralls on and they could see us clearly; we'd wave as the guys came in, and we must have saved at least a dozen from going over the edge.

"The crowd didn't like this at all; we were spoiling their fun, and the soldiers told us they'd shoot us down if we didn't get off the shoulder of the road and stop waving. The whole crowd booed and yelled insults, then the soldiers started poking us with bayonets and we had to move back. But the fast cars were all past by then, so it really didn't matter.

"We ended up spending 17 hours on the top of that damn mountain until the last car had gone by and we could hitch a ride into Mexico City. Later we found out that Bonetto had been killed when he crashed his Lancia into a lamppost on the Mexico-to-León run. Fangio won the race."

• • • • •

In an attempt to momentarily erase the stress and strain of motor racing, Phil and Richie journeyed to Acapulco for some sailfishing prior to their return to California.

"We just didn't even *think* about cars," says Phil. "It was great out there on the water — and we had some luck, too. I managed to haul in a nice sailfish measuring nine feet two inches which weighed 103 pounds. This break relaxed both of us, but my nerves were in lousy shape and the minute I got back to the States it was the same thing all over again. Only this time I had a crash behind me, and I began to think about the possibility of really injuring myself in a racing car. That Mexican crash, I realized, *could* have been fatal."

———————

CHAPTER SEVEN

El Batallador

HILL'S SHATTERING EXPERIENCE in Mexico, coupled with his increasing sensitivity to the dangers connected with the sport, further affected his system; and his condition did not improve in the opening months of 1954.

"In January I went down to Buenos Aires, with Gregory, Bob Said, and Carroll Shelby, representing the Sports Car Club of America," he relates. "None of us did anything. My car only lasted a few laps. Shelby got 10th overall."

In March he was back in Florida, co-driving Spear's 4.5 Ferrari at Sebring. Hill took the wheel after Spear's opening run, and within a half hour he led the race, only to retire shortly thereafter with a broken oil seal. His declining physical condition was apparent at Sebring.

"I was in terrible shape," Hill admits. "Used to get an awful heart flutter on the grid. So bad I'd have to get out of the car and walk around. Then I had these stomach spasms, and I still couldn't eat proper foods."

Hill consulted his family doctor, who told him that he had ulcers and that if he didn't quit racing he might hemorrhage. He needed a relief from the tension of competitive driving. Would he quit?

"I said I would, and agreed to go on an ulcer diet," Phil relates. "I knew that I wasn't *really* quitting, that this was only a temporary layoff, but immediately my mind was eased. That tranquil state didn't last long, though. Within a week I'd tackled the incredibly difficult job of restoring my Aunt Helen's old Pierce. Jerry and I went at this hammer and tongs!"

•　　　•　　　•　　　•　　　•

The Hill brothers had often discussed the possibility of stripping down the stately, blue, 1931 Le Baron Pierce-Arrow town cabriolet and restoring the car to its original showroom splendor. They had even purchased a similar "parts" model in 1951, but the project had languished for three years. Now, armed with the necessary spare time to do the job correctly, Phil and Jerry began to dismantle the big machine.

"I really tied myself up in a snit with that Pierce," says Hill. "Took us seven days to get it stripped completely down. The rafters of our garage were covered with scribbled notes, telling us what part went where — and I boxed all the various tiny pieces, stuck a label on each box, and set these on the shelf. The place looked like a botany lab."

Lifting the massive body from the chassis required the muscle power of two dozen men, recruited (so Hill tells it) from a local bistro. The bare chassis was brushed and sanded, then towed to Rich & Jones Custom Shop for painting. Several boxes of parts were rechromed by a plating firm in Glendale, while the Hill brothers were busy with the 132-hp straight-8 engine.

"Five interior carpets also had to be replaced," says Phil. "These included a leather-bound snap-over pile carpet for normal weather, a leather-bound rubber carpet for wet days, a rug of baby lamb's wool, and a heavy lap robe made from the skin of a beaver."

For months the work progressed, and slowly the car assumed its showroom elegance. New wiring was installed, all the interior wood was restored, the leather refinished, weather molding on the windows covered with top-grade black cuff velvet. Finally, the outer paint was carefully applied, blue lacquer for the body, enamel for the undercarriage.

"We had Art Summers, who was a master brushman, do the detailed white striping," Phil says. "When it was done we knew that the whole Pierce was perfect, down to the tiniest nut and bolt deep inside. And that's a feeling no one can describe; you have to experience it."

After months of work on the Pierce, plus his duties as a mechanic at Brentwood Motors, Phil could not resist a go at Torrey Pines, over the Fourth of July weekend. He accepted a ride in a small, production Triumph TR-2, winding up first in class and 10th overall.

"I stayed well clear of the main event," he says, "and so you might say I was still in retirement. At least I didn't race again for the next four months. In August I joined *The Racers* company out at Twentieth Century-Fox as their technical adviser. This was the picture made from the racing novel by Hans Ruesch, and John Fitch was hired by Fox for the European scenes. The studio had a camera crew in Europe in the spring of '54 equipped with 12 Cinemascope lenses. They got more than 90,000 feet of color film, most of it at events such as the Mille Miglia, French Grand Prix, Nürburgring and Spa."

Part of Hill's job on the West Coast involved keeping the competition machinery in running order. The cars used for the film in Hollywood included two four-cylinder Grand Prix Maseratis, a trio of sports Ferraris and one HWM Special.

"The stars, Kirk Douglas, Cesar Romero and Gilbert Roland, did very little actual driving," Hill reports. "On the Fox back lot they'd duplicated the pit areas at Reims, Nürburgring, Monza and Spa, and in these sequences Douglas and the others would roll in for a tire change, or accelerate out of the frame. I taught them how to take off without spinning the car or stalling, and with those GP Masers this was no cinch. Doubles were used for all the long-distance stuff."

Hill describes a hazardous bit of stunt driving connected with *The Racers,* in which an old friend, Dave Sykes, also participated.

"The shooting took place on a stretch of closed canyon road at Rincon Springs, near San Diego. Before we got started the director showed us stills of a crash and told us this is what he wanted to end up with. Two smashed cars! We took off down the canyon, following the camera car, which was an old KB Lincoln with a full-house Chrysler engine. Sykes was told to move over on the road and pinch me off as I tried to pass. We began rubbing tires at about 60 mph.

"Now, when anyone's tire touches mine my natural instinct is to get away fast. But we had to keep this up — until suddenly my front tire caught Dave's rear tire and climbed right up his wheel. Locked together, both our cars spun beautifully off the road at 55, wiping out a post as we slid into a ditch. The camera caught all of this in Cinemascope and color, but we were later told that none of it could be used because it didn't fit the script!"

• • • • •

As the 1954 season drew to a close and his part in *The Racers* was completed, Phil began chafing under what he termed "the strain of inactivity." Then, from Texas, he received a letter. Inside was a glossy photo of a fierce-looking white 4.5-liter Ferrari, with a shark-like tail fin and huge air vents cut into the body. This was the car with which Ascari had won the Nürburgring in 1953, now completely re-built. Stapled to one corner of the photo was a brief handwritten note from the oil-rich Texan enthusiast Allen Guiberson: *Guaranteed not to cause ulcers.*

These five words put Phil Hill back into major-league racing.

"I just couldn't resist that car," he says. "I was *compelled* to see what I could do with it — and I first drove it at March Field in early November."

Phil's ulcer had calmed, and his nerves seemed somewhat less strained. He lined up on the airport grid in Riverside with no less than eight other Ferraris, along with a host of Allards, Jags and Kurtis Specials. At the checkered flag only one other driver finished ahead of him: Bill Spear in his fleet 4.5 model. Hill's second place verified the fact that he had lost none of his speed or skill, and Guiberson immediately entered the Hill/Ferrari combination in what was to be the final running of the annual Pan-American Road Race in Mexico.

· · · · ·

Although several of the larger European factory teams had de-clined to subject their cars to the five-day punishment of the 1954 Carrera, more than 150 entries, representing 14 nations, filled the various classes, stock and modified, driven by luminaries such as Chinetti, Chiron, Bracco, Herrmann, Mieres, Macklin, Taruffi, the fast-rising Alfonso de Portago, and the chief threat, Umberto Maglioli, who had a new factory 4.9 Ferrari capable of 180 mph. Jack McAfee also piloted a 4.9, and Carroll Shelby had contracted to handle an Austin-Healey 100-S. The usual array of Indianapolis aces added color and competition to the stock-car lineup.

Richie Ginther again accompanied Hill as his riding companion, and they were among the favorites in the large sports car class. Un-fortunately, the Guiberson 4.5 was three years old, and would give away 20 mph on the straights to Maglioli's 4.9, but Phil hoped to outcorner the larger car in the mountains.

Roaring out of Tuxtla Gutiérrez under a lazily rising sun, Hill took an early lead with the white Ferrari, making excellent time around the more than 3000 curves on the first leg into Oaxaca.

"We were able to pass Maglioli in the mountains, because our acceleration was damn near equal to his up to about 100," says Phil. "Then we dropped down to the long Tehuantepec straight, and it began to rain. Well, I just stuck my foot into the floor and left it there, feeling reasonably certain that the rain would keep the tires cool. Heat will fling the treads off, and you're in real trouble when that happens. And nothing could be more conducive to flinging off treads than Tehuantepec, some 50 kilometers of dead-straight road, the surface black and corrosive. Since we were down at sea level our engine got full power and I wound up the 4.5 to around 160, maybe a little better. But here comes Maglioli, going by us like a shot at 180, and nothing we could do but wave at him. Back in the mountains we nailed him again, and made it first into Oaxaca by four minutes. That was our best run, because the brakes were holding."

Tragedy struck in the mountains, when McAfee's 4.9 shot off the road, killing Jack's passenger and close friend, Ford Robinson. The next morning Hill boomed out of Oaxaca ahead of Maglioli, but trailed the Italian by six seconds into Puebla. Shelby, running behind the two Ferraris, crashed in the mountains, surviving with several broken bones. Hill's brakes were gone, and he and Richie worked through most of the night relining them. They subsisted on two hours of sleep.

Over the third leg, into Mexico City, Hill again finished first, 45 seconds ahead of his Ferrari rival. ("We hit a fog patch out of Mexico City and I let Maglioli pass, staying just far enough back so that I could follow his taillights.") But the speed of the 4.9 was soon unleashed and Maglioli led into León by more than three minutes. Hill was hanging on, fighting hard to stay with the factory machine, but his brakes had faded again under the constant pressure and he was gradually losing ground. The fifth leg saw him six minutes behind, as Maglioli blistered through Durango's main street at 150 mph.

"A weird thing happened when we came into Durango," says Hill. "We were both exhausted after the day's run, and quite worried about the differential holding out. It had been making unhappy sounds! Anyhow, when I tried to get out the door on my side wouldn't open. Furious, I *kicked* it open. Then I went around to help Richie who was also having trouble with his door. We fought and struggled with the damn thing, determined to make it open. Now, Richie *could* have jumped out without using it, but by then it was a matter of principle; the dumb door *should* open! Finally we took a bar to it, and all at once the whole rear section of the car, from the doorjambs on back, fell crashing to the ground! Simply rolled right off the rear of the frame. The weight represented by the extra spare wheel we carried out at the very tail end had been too much for it, and the only thing that was left holding the tail section on were the two door pegs which sheared. All the usual welds holding the body to the frame had broken due to road vibration. Richie looked at me and I looked at him and we both began to laugh like fools. By the next morning we had the rear end welded back in place."

Maglioli's lead increased to 10 minutes on the next stage into Parral, and he gained another four minutes over Hill on the seventh leg to Chihuahua, aided by the fact that Hill's rear-axle assembly was working loose, his valve timing was off and he was having magneto trouble. Nevertheless, on the final 222-mile stretch, to the finish line at Juárez, the Californian made his last supreme effort and sliced under the flag at full revs, bettering the 4.9's time by 53 seconds. It had not been fast enough. Phil Hill, who earned the nickname *El Batallador* (The Battler) from the local Mexican press, lost the five-day race to Maglioli by just 24 minutes after almost 2000 miles of speed.

"We'd beaten Fangio's previous record," says Phil, "and I was satisfied to have taken second. In fact, my performance in this event convinced me that I should continue to drive. It seemed to be the only area where I could be really successful, and the temporary layoff had only intensified my desire to compete."

•   •   •   •   •

Phil campaigned extensively in 1955, beginning at Sebring. There he was teamed with the genial Texan Carroll Shelby, who appeared with one arm in a cast (as a result of his Mexican smashup). Shelby had the doctor fit the cast around his arm in "driving position," and claimed that it would not affect his speed.

Apparently it did not, for the Hill/Shelby Ferrari engaged the Mike Hawthorn/Phil Walters Jaguar in a wire-to-wire 12-hour battle for first. The Jag was the new D-Type, a sculptured bit of wheeled dynamite which was destined to challenge the all-mighty Mercedes that season. Allen Guiberson had just purchased one of the sensational new "Monza" Ferraris (a four-cylinder 3-liter masterpiece from Modena) derived from the Formula 2 car on which Ascari had won the 1953 World Championship. Enzo Ferrari's son had designed the sharklike body, and this was the car piloted by Hill and Shelby.

Building a full lap's lead, the D-Type suffered from dropping oil pressure plus other ills, and was forced back into the pits on several occasions. The Monza then took over, according to the scorers, and won the race at 10 P.M. as the flag fell. But immediately the decision was reversed. The D-Jag was declared victor by the narrowest of margins: 10 seconds after 12 hours! Ferrari protested, but after debating for a full week the official AAA judges upheld the decision. Hill and Shelby had to content themselves with a class first and the Index of Performance prize. (As Shelby later remarked: "Ah jes dunno *who* won, but it shore was a hell of a good race!")

．　　．　　．　　．　　．

Returning to Pebble Beach in April, Hill pitted the Guiberson 3-liter Monza against his indefatigable West Coast rival, Bill Pollack, now at the helm of a 4.7-liter Mercury-powered Special. The main event, for the Del Monte Trophy, was contested in blinding rain, and Pollack had the lead by the fifth tour of the pine-and-cypress-lined two-mile circuit. ("I'd driven the Monza up from Carmel Valley before the race," says Phil, "and I couldn't even go 30 miles an hour without sliding. It was just fishtailing over the highway and it was all I could do to keep the front end ahead of the back. But in the race we had new rain tires put on, and the circuit was very clean. This made a big difference, and I began to relax.") Hill dogged the second-place Buick-Kurtis until it broadsided a stack of hay bales on the rainy macadam surface, then powered up to ride Pollack's tailpipe, almost lost to view in the drenching spray from the Special's rear wheels. By lap 22 Pollack was out of the race, and Hill came home winner, after a superb display of wet-road driving in which he was clocked at almost 100 mph on the short front straightaway.

Hill made it a twin-victory weekend when his meticulously pre-pared 1931 Pierce-Arrow was declared Best of Show at Saturday's Pebble Beach Concours d'Elégance held on the emerald-green lawn of the Del Monte Lodge. Three judges, led by the popular Lucius Beebe, resplendent in top hat, long coat and white gloves, picked over the many gleaming machines with the patience and exactitude of watchmakers before giving the final nod to Phil's Pierce.

· · · · ·

On May 26, tragic news from Italy: the great Italian champion Alberto Ascari had died in a practice run at Monza (only a week af-ter he had escaped from his Lancia when it plunged into the harbor at Monte Carlo during the Grand Prix of Monaco). And four days later, on May 30, Bill Vukovich was dead in a crash at Indianapolis. He had been trying for the "hat trick"—three victories in a row at the Brickyard. These deaths cast their long shadow toward Le Mans, soon to become a scene of carnage unrivaled in the history of motor sport.

"I got my first factory ride at Le Mans that year with the help of Luigi Chinetti," declares Hill. "Ferrari invited me over to share Maglioli's new 4.4-liter six-cylinder job. I'd met Ferrari when I was in Europe the previous season, and I recall I was very much in awe of him at the time. This offer seemed like a dream come true. I felt that if I could do well in France I might get an offer to drive in Eu-rope for a full season."

Hill's performance at Le Mans that year was lost in tragedy when Pierre Levegh's fast new Mercedes 300SLR plunged into the crowd two hours and a half after the start, killing 83 spectators in addition to Levegh himself.

"Before it happened I was feeling great," Hill says. "I'd made sixth fastest practice time with our 4.4 and Maglioli was due to come in and turn over the wheel to me. He was holding fourth overall, a fine position at that point, so our chances looked excellent. Then I heard the terrible screech of tires as Levegh hit Lance Macklin's Healey, and I rushed out to see what had happened. Our pit manager held me back, wouldn't let me get a close look, because he knew I had to drive and thought it would be a dangerous thing to let me know the real ex-tent of the crash. Our car finally quit us at 9 P.M. when we were holding third, but nobody really cared. The Levegh accident had depressed all of us. Bueb and Hawthorn won in a D-Jag."

. . . . .

Hill had intended to line up further competition overseas, but the Le Mans disaster changed his mind. In the States he'd met wealthy George Tilp, a New Jersey businessman who also owned a Monza Ferrari, and Hill drove this car over the Fourth of July at the Beverly Airport some 20 miles north of Boston, birthplace of the Sports Car Club of America.

Millionaire sportsman Jim Kimberly was the favorite at Beverly, with his massive 4.5 Ferrari. "Gentleman Jim" was the No. 1 SCCA pilot, definitely the man to beat. Phil did just that, passing on a curve with his smaller Monza and opening up a 35-second gap by the checkered flag.

"A week later at Torrey Pines I found myself in Johnny von Neumann's Monza," Hill says. "He suddenly pitted on lap 21 and said, 'Here, Phil, you take it!' I was standing around without a car, just spectating — so I hopped in and set out after Shelby, who was leading by a full lap in the same 4.5 I'd driven in the last Pan-Am race. Picked up two places, nailing second, but Shel won. He beat me again that same month at Seafair, but I gave his 4.9 Ferrari a nice run with my Monza and closed to within four seconds at the flag."

Santa Barbara was next, and Hill wound up buried in hay, after his brakes locked coming into a fast curve. Ernie McAfee carried away the trophy that afternoon.

"Then, in mid-September I took George Tilp's Monza to the new Road America circuit at Elkhart Lake. And, boy, what a race *that* turned out to be!"

CHAPTER EIGHT

From Wisconsin to Argentina

WISCONSIN'S ROAD AMERICA was designed in the classic European tradition, as a severe test of man and car, and its builders had capitalized the venture by selling shares of stock over a 15-month period. By April of 1955 they had sold enough to begin the bulldozing, grading, leveling and surfacing which took another five months. In September the course was finally ready for its trial by speed.

It was fast and deceptive, four miles of smooth blacktop, 27 feet wide, rolling, climbing, dipping through a series of kettle moraine depressions which formed natural amphitheaters for an estimated 50,000 spectators on hand for the inaugural. The circuit contained six 90-degree corners and eight curves, one of which was a downhill 180-degree affair of diminishing radius, demanding close attention to avoid the waiting roadside woods. In short, Road America was not for children.

Spin-outs and crashes became the pattern of the day in practice. One driver lost control of his Maserati and was severely burned.

"Look, Fellas," warned starter Ben Harris before the initial race began, "this is a real hairy track. Get wise to it or you'll get sent home in a box."

Phil Hill was wise to it. In Tilp's Monza he had racked up an unofficial 3:02, four seconds faster than his best competition, but he knew that mistakes could be costly here. This circuit invited trouble.

Twenty-six cars lined up for the main event. They included a half-dozen Ferraris, a pair of D-Type Jags, two Maseratis and Cunningham's Offenhauser Special. Spear and Kimberly and Gordon Bennett were on the grid, but New York's Sherwood Johnston, driving for Briggs Cunningham in a white D-Type, was Hill's chief worry. He was fast, very capable, and with his disc brakes he could outlast Phil's Monza into the turns.

Hill got smartly away at the flag, gunning through the first turn with a clear track ahead of him. Johnston took up the chase in his white Jag, hanging tight to the Ferrari. By lap 10 only four seconds separated them. Phil kept increasing the pace, leading Johnston by 13 seconds on the 18th tour, having brought his own time down to 2:58.8 in an effort to leave the D-Jag behind.

Abruptly, without warning, an Allard spun off the course, and under the yellow caution flag Johnston moved up to close on Hill. At the all-clear, the D was squarely framed in the Monza's rearview mirror, and both cars screamed past the third-place D-Jaguar on the 23rd round, having already lapped the entire field in their two-man duel. It was here that Johnston registered an astounding 2:55.5, out accelerating the Monza in traffic and taking the lead away from the fighting Californian.

But Hill would not concede the victory. Lap 25 saw Johnston take to an escape road; Hill passed. Johnston repassed on lap 27 as Hill dove too deeply into turn 5 and skidded into the bales, scattering hay. Feeding power to the Ferrari, he tire-squealed back into the race, but Johnston now had eight seconds' advantage. Phil knifed the Monza around the circuit, cutting away the gap, until Johnston found the shark-snouted machine directly behind him. The Jag's disc brakes helped into the turns; out of them the Monza's quicker acceleration made up the difference.

Lap 32, past the stands in a dead heat. Lap 33, another dead heat past the stands. Lap 34, again this nose-to-nose run down the front straight!

On the final tour, lap 37, Hill was weaving to either side in an attempt to get past, edging along the Jaguar's rear deck on the straights, then dropping back a hair through the turns. One more mile to go. Johnston drifted the treacherous diminishing-radius turn leading to the wide S-bend under the bridge. Seven-tenths of a mile to the checker.

As Johnston executed a precise, lightning-fast downshift from third to second, setting up the Jag for the last right-hand turn leading up the slope to the front straight, he glanced into his mirror. The Ferrari had disappeared! Off the road? No. This could only mean that Hill was in the blind spot, to the right, making his bid.

The crowd pressed forward against the protective fencing, a rippling sea of tense faces, eyes locked to the struggle taking place on the coal-black strip of road in front of them. Hill was taking a desperate chance: if Johnston continued his normal outward high-speed drift through the corner the two cars would clash in an accident that might prove fatal to both drivers. But then again, Hill *might* ease off at the last instant, letting the Jag through. Johnston shot a quick glance at his grim adversary. No, Hill would not ease off.

In the last split second before contact, when the decision had to be made, Johnston lifted his foot from the pedal, and the white Monza howled past, riding the ragged edge of traction. Phil Hill roared up the slope at 8000 rpm to blur under the checkered flag a scant two car lengths ahead of Sherwood Johnston to win the 148-mile main event at Road America. He had turned the final lap at a nerve-shattering 2:54.2, for the race record.

"I was utterly exhausted after that duel," says Phil, "and not just because of the strain. I just didn't know how to eat properly prior to an event in those days — without sending my stomach into a tailspin — so I just wouldn't eat anything. Of course this meant that I ran out of energy. You know, after Wisconsin, the rest of the Stateside season seemed pretty dull. I drove with Paul O'Shea at Torrey, in the six hours, and we got second; I won the main at Sacramento, got a second at Hagerstown, Maryland, and won again at Glendale in November. Then things livened up—when I took Chinetti's new 3.5 Ferrari down to the Bahamas and dueled with Portago in three events during Speed Week at Nassau. That Portago—he drove like a demon!"

Don Alfonso Cabeza de Vaca, 17th Marquis de Portago, was a swashbuckling sportsman who gloried in the Good Life. He was an expert fencer, swimmer, horseman, skier, jai alai player, Olympic bobsledder and polo ace—a connoisseur of fine wines and beautiful women. In 1955 road racing was his prime passion, and when he

69

came to Nassau in December of that year he was twenty-seven, a long-haired, lazy-eyed adventurer who coldly defied superstition by flaunting the "unlucky" number 13 on his coffin-black Monza Ferrari. He had won the semi-main the previous year at Nassau, for the Governor's Cup, and now he wanted to add the Nassau Trophy to his laurels.

• • • • •

The island circuit at Windsor Field reverberated to the jungle roar of 17 Ferraris during Bahamas Speed Week, the largest assemblage of these potent Italian machines to run at a single non-European meet, and Hill knew he would have to work hard for victory. Sherwood Johnston was down in the Cunningham D, and made his intentions clear when he stabbed into the lead at the outset of the Governor's Cup race on Friday, hard-pressed by Hill. Portago wedged his Monza between them for a three-way duel. On lap 15, at the halfway point, Johnston tapped the brake pedal, readying a downshift, when he felt a solid thump from behind. Portago, at over 130 mph, had been riding too close, and both machines spun wildly, leaving 750 feet of black tire marks in the center strip, with Johnston narrowly avoiding a crowd of spectators. Off again, the two drivers resumed speed, with Hill challenging from third. Lap 18 saw Portago leading the D, as Johnston fell back with a damaged axle stabilizer. Phil dogged the damaged Monza to the wire, losing to Portago by a second.

The main event, Sunday's 60-lap Nassau Trophy Race, would settle the issue. Masten Gregory, with a 3-liter Maserati, was also in the lists and would give a good account of himself.

Seventy cars got away for the big 210-miler, and Hill forged ahead of Johnston, with Portago and Gregory moving up rapidly. But no one could catch Phil Hill that afternoon, and he took the flag over Portago by 25 seconds, with Gregory in for third. The rapid Californian had notched his first international victory.

"Had myself a shunt in that race," says Hill. "I was coming around the dogleg in a long, swooping approach. There, directly in front of me, right in the apex of the turn, is this little Osca who is attempting to avoid a Porsche. The Porsche was spinning, and the Osca pulled right into my line of approach. I was committed, so I couldn't possibly avoid hitting him. Well, my Ferrari was the cue ball—and when I hit him he just sailed! I flattened out the side of my car a bit, but I must have moved him up at least three places in his class."

. . . . .

With a total of 9500 points, Hill was declared 1955 National SCCA Class D-Modified Champion, winning out over 25 other drivers, in a year darkened by the tragedy at Le Mans and the death of Ascari.

. . . . .

"They ran Torrey Pines for the last time in January of 1956," says Hill. "The place was being turned into a golf course, so everyone sort of trooped down for the final meet—because we'd all had fun at Torrey, and wanted to give it a good send-off. I had nothing but rotten luck that weekend. On Saturday I was in the six-hour race, driving a tired old 2-liter Mondial Ferrari, and by the end of the second hour I'd moved up to within a few seconds of the lead D-Jag when, *boom,* the rod lets go and puts a hole the size of your fist in the block! Next day, in the main, I'm in a Monza and out in front, with Gregory chasing me. Then I see that the engine is overheating and I pit for water. Another lap and I'm done—with the radiator boiling like a volcano."

. . . . .

Again Luigi Chinetti set up a factory sports car ride for Hill, on this occasion in Buenos Aires, Argentina, in the Thousand Kilometers. His mount was a 3.5 model, and his co-driver was the canny Belgian, Olivier Gendebien—who was later to become Phil's international teammate in many victorious races around the world.

Proudly bearing the name of a knighted family in Belgium, the debonair Gendebien, whose independent wealth placed him in the class of "gentlemen drivers," was already famous for his skill in long-distance rallies and for his superb performances with a Mercedes 300 SL. He had signed with Enzo Ferrari in '55, and despite a serious crash at Dundrod (in practice for the Tourist Trophy) he was once again serving as a Ferrari team member in 1956.

The 5.9-mile course in Buenos Aires was formed by the perimeter of the city Autodrome with fast dual roads outside forming a freeway, at the end of which the cars swept around a 180-degree three-quarter loop and reversed direction. The event counted toward the Manufacturers' Championship for sports cars and Ferrari wanted his marque to win this honor. He therefore sent two powerful 4.9-liter machines for Juan Fangio/Eugenio Castellotti and Luigi Musso/Peter Collins. Against them, the Ferraris faced the smaller 3-liter Maseratis of Stirling Moss/Carlos Menditeguy and Jean Behra/Froilan González. The battle would be among these cars. The Hill/Gendebien 3.5 was sent to "back up" the two faster team Ferraris and to harry the opposition.

Gendebien got to his job by jumping the 3.5 into a lead, but Fangio soon nipped past along with Musso. At 20 laps it was still the Argentinian, Musso creeping up and Moss in third. Gendebien held fourth.

"I got the wheel on lap 35," says Phil, "and Castellotti took over for Fangio. He overdid things a bit taking Moss, hit the bales and blew a tire. By lap 60 we were up into third, behind Musso and Menditeguy. But I didn't feel at all comfortable, certain that I was doing a sloppy job—but pretty soon the Musso/Collins car was out with a broken differential. So we were then running second."

Fangio was back in, storming up to regain the prime slot, which led to some fiercely competitive driving between Moss and the World Champion. It ended on lap 90, with the two cars all but tied together, when Fangio's transmission burst. Moss coasted to a solid victory with the Hill/Gendebien Ferrari in for second (despite their having lost nine minutes in the pits with a broken oil pipe). Behra/González took third in their Maserati.

"Despite my own self-doubts as to how well I had done," Hill says, "I was approached in the pits after the show was over by Ferrari's team manager. He calmly asked me if I would like to join the official factory drivers that season in Europe. I wasn't nearly as calm in accepting. This was the chance I had been waiting for since Le Mans, in '53. That day in the pits at Argentina changed my life. Now I would find out just what potential I *really* had against the best in Europe."

Checking the spark plugs of the C-Type Jaguar with Charles Hornburg at Madera. (Bob Canaan)

In December of 1952, Phil Hill drove the C-Type Jaguar of Charles Hornburg to a win at the 2.8-mile circuit of Torrey Pines, 17 miles north of San Diego. (Ralph Poole)

Racing to a win at Pebble Beach in '53 with a new 2.9 Ferrari 250MM. (Bob Canaan)

Phil is pictured seated in the Vignale-bodied Ferrari 250MM. (Griffith Borgeson)

Two views of the hard-cornering 2.9 as seen at the airport circuits in '53. (Bob Canaan)

The 1953 Carrera Panamericana was Phil's second run in the Mexican road race. Richie Ginther joined him as copilot in the 4.1-liter Ferrari 340 Mexico coupé of Allen Guiberson. *(Dave Friedman Collection)*

The Ferrari 340 Mexico of Hill/Ginther north of Oaxaca, during the second leg of the 1953 Carrera Panamericana. On the third leg, to Puebla, they went backwards off a dangerous curve. The locals had removed a warning sign in an effort to increase the entertainment provided by the racers. *(Lee Render/Ferrari Market Letter Archives)*

In 1954 at the fifth-annual Carrera Panamericana, Phil Hill and Richie Ginther again entered with a Ferrari, this time the 4.5-liter 375 MM of Allen Guiberson.

This same car had been entered in the 1953 race by Luigi Chinetti.

(Bob Tronolone Collection, Cliff Trussel photos)

At Pebble Beach in 1955, Phil won the Del Monte Trophy at the road races, and his Pierce Arrow garnered the coveted Best of Show award at the Concours d'Elégance. Famed driver of the board track era, Peter DePaolo, is pictured in hat.
(Ralph Poole / Road & Track)

The last races before Torrey Pines became a golf course took place in January of '56. Phil drove an old 2-liter Mondial 500 Ferrari in a six-hour race. Mechanical failure put him out after two hours. The next day, in the main event, Hill drove John von Neumann's Monza till it overheated. A bad weekend. (Jim Sitz)

Hill at speed in the No.20 Ferrari Monza of George Tilp at the 1956 Sebring 12-hour. Juan Manuel Fangio won the event; Hill and co-driver Masten Gregory did not finish. (Jim Sitz)

At the Nürburgring 1000 Kilometer in 1956 with a factory 3.5-liter Ferrari. (Bernard Cahier)

Phil Hill with "El Maestro," Juan Manuel Fangio, at Kristianstad, Sweden in 1956. Phil won the sports car race, his first for the Ferrari team, and at the same time, locked up the Sports Car Championship for Ferrari. (Bernard Cahier)

A delighted Phil Hill receives the checkered flag in front of his fans on a sunny day at Palm Springs in 1957. He won by a full 49 seconds with Tony Parravano's 4.4-liter Ferrari 121 LM. *(Dave Friedman Collection)*

On Saturday, January 19, Phil drove John von Neumann's silver Ferrari Monza to a win at Pomona in '57. For Sunday's event, drenching rains turned the Fairgrounds into a skating rink. After a number of spins, Hill retired the bent car. *(Jim Sitz)*

In 1957 Phil joined MG to run their streamliners at the Bonneville Salt Flats. Hill assisted David Ash and Tommy Wisdom to achieve a number of Class G records with the 58 cubic-inch EX179. (BMIHT/Rover Group)

Hill's primary function at Bonneville was to perform shakedown runs with MG's mid-engine EX181, pictured with stabilizer fin. He reported shifting into high gear near 200 mph. While slowing down, the wheels acted like pumps, drawing deadly nitrobenzene fumes in the cockpit, and the canopy could not be opened until the streamliner was near a standstill. (BMC/Griffith Borgeson Collection)

CHAPTER NINE

A Brisk Introduction to Europe

H ILL'S FIRST EUROPEAN RACE of the '56 season was set for late May, at the Nürburgring, in Germany, but he competed in a trio of Stateside contests prior to this debut on the Ring. In the first of these, at Palm Springs, his Monza failed to make the starting grid, sidelined with mechanical problems. He therefore drove a 550 Porsche Spyder in the under-1500-cc main, and was running with the leaders when a bent shifting fork put him out of action. At Sebring, in March, his 3.5 Ferrari, co-driven with Masten Gregory, lasted just 61 laps before being retired with a sick engine. (This race was notable in that an all-American Chevrolet factory team, comprising three works Corvettes and two private entries, took to the field for the first time against international competition, the Fitch/Hansgen entry finishing ninth.)

. . . . . .

Phil was back at Pebble Beach in April with the Ferrari in which Fangio and Castellotti had won Sebring, and, on paper, his chances for an overall victory seemed excellent. Actually, the car, which had been set up for the Sebring airport course (with its long straights), was wholly unsuitable to the tight Pebble Beach circuit.

"I found the car so unstable during practice that I almost decided to switch to the Monza," says Phil. "But the crowd had come to see me drive the Fangio 3.5, and pre-race publicity had stressed this, so I felt I should stick with it. We finally weighted down the rear end with a 100-pound chunk of lead, strapping it to the frame to keep the rear wheels on the ground, and this seemed to help some. But the car was never right for that course from the beginning."

Hill's main competition stemmed from Shelby's 3-liter Monza and a big 4.4-liter Ferrari in the hands of Ernie McAfee. On Saturday a Triumph TR-2 had slammed into a tree, seriously injuring its driver, and Hill was concerned about the fact that this narrow, tree-lined circuit might prove too dangerous for the power-brimming Ferraris. On Sunday morning he met Jean McAfee, Ernie's wife, in the pits and told her he was worried about the race. (Phil and Jean were old friends, and had, in fact, been engaged during one period prior to Jean's marriage to McAfee.)

The race itself proved that this concern was well founded. Hill's 3.5 stormed into an early lead, shattering previous lap records, but Shelby and McAfee were both moving up to challenge. Hill's car became a handful as the gas load lightened, and Shelby got by, with Ernie slowly closing on the two front runners. His powder-blue 4.4 boomed down the back straight at full bore. Suddenly he was skidding. He'd missed his shift, locked up the brakes, and was out of control. At 100 mph, the big Ferrari swiped a hay bale, then lashed into a pine with sickening force. McAfee was killed instantly in the crash.

"I'll never forget the sight of his blue car, wrapped around that tree," says Hill. "I was numb. All I could do was drive and try not to think of anything but shifting and braking and accelerating. It was a terrible afternoon. Shelby won the race and I came across for second. But nobody was smiling."

•　　•　　•　　•　　•

When Hill journeyed to Europe for the 1000-kilometer sports car race at the Nürburgring he was joining a legendary team.

Ferrari is a derivative of the Italian word for iron—and certainly the man behind the marque, Enzo Ferrari often demonstrated a will of iron in creating the red cars bearing his name, the first of which he ran late in 1940. Born at Modena, in 1898, Ferrari served as a mule shoer during World War I, became a racing driver in 1919, finished second in the Targa Florio in 1920, and won his first overall victory three years later on the Circuit of Savio at Ravenna driving for the newly formed Alfa Romeo team. Witnessing his triumph, the parents of the renowned Italian air ace, Major Francesco Baracca (who was finally brought down in flames after destroying 34 enemy aircraft) presented young Ferrari with the great sky fighter's personal crest: a prancing black horse rampant on a field of yellow. They asked Enzo to carry this coat-of-arms into motorized battle in memory of their son, and Ferrari assured them that he would bear the crest proudly on his machine wherever he drove.

Graduating to team manager for Alfa, Enzo took complete command when the factory retired from competition, forming his own Scuderia Ferrari in 1929. All the greats of this period drove for him, and by 1939 he had designed his own racing car, an eight-cylinder 1500-cc model which Alberto Ascari drove in the 1940 Mille Miglia. Awarded the title of *Commendatore* by King Victor Emanuel III, Ferrari established repair shops at Modena and a factory in the village of Maranello (10 miles south of Modena) on farm property owned by his family.

During World War II, in a daylight raid, Allied bombers destroyed his small factory, but he was able to rebuild and, by 1947, the marque of the Prancing Horse had achieved its first victory at Piacenza. Ferraris amassed over 500 wins by 1956, despite the fact that the Commendatore's factory at Maranello employed only some 300 workers and produced just 200 cars each year. (General Motors, in 1955, employed 624,000.)

Supported mainly by his victories, Ferrari admitted that his prize money kept him in business and that racing was his main concern. Passenger Ferraris were secondary. Although in close contact by phone with his team during each major race, Ferrari made it an early rule never to watch his own cars compete.

"When a man has taken something," he said, "and transformed it with his own two hands into something else, he has not made a machine of it but a soul, a living, breathing soul. When he goes to a race and sees this soul being mistreated, it makes him suffer. A man cannot bear it. I do not go to races because I suffer too much."

A haunted, withdrawn individual, wholly absorbed in his machines, working up to 15 hours a day including Sundays, Enzo Ferrari's goal is plainly stated: "I build cars for champions to win championships in."

And, indeed, in 1956, when Hill came to Europe, the great World Champion Juan Fangio himself headed the powerful Ferrari team, backed up by Italians Eugenio Castellotti, Luigi Musso and Britisher Peter Collins in the first string lineup. "Fon" Portago and Olivier Gendebien were also signed, with the Belgian journalist-driver Paul Frère and the French veteran Maurice Trintignant in for special events.

"I was at the end of the bench," admits Phil, "and I felt very inferior to most of my competition over there in '56. Fangio was a god to me, and most of the others were also in the idol category. My self-confidence completely disappeared. As a result of this attitude, my lap times were affected. In a sense, I was still a fan in Europe driving against the famous professionals. I found it quite difficult to adjust, mentally, to this situation."

The Nürburgring event was a confusing one, in that several driver changes were made in the lead Ferraris. Hill had originally been teamed with Ken Wharton in a factory 3.5, and he started the race, with Wharton due to relieve him. At the end of the first long 14-mile lap Moss was pacing Hawthorn, with Fangio riding third. Then came Collins, Musso and Hill. By lap 5 Musso was out of contention, having rolled his Ferrari, and Portago had also crashed. Behind the three front runners, Hill and Taruffi were battling for fourth.

The Moss vs. Fangio duel continued, but Hill was doing a remarkable job on this exceedingly difficult circuit. The Californian was only a minute behind the two leaders, with Behra (having replaced Taruffi) chasing him in the factory Maserati.

"Then they called me in to hand our car over to the Portago/Gendebien combination," says Phil. "Fon got in and kept up the pressure, with Gendebien in turn relieving him at the wheel. At the windup, our Ferrari got third overall, with only the Moss and Fangio cars ahead of us. I felt pretty good about this, but my jubilation didn't last long. At Monthléry, in France, the best our car could do was a poor fifth. Fon co-drove that one with me. I managed to break the sports car lap record nine times before Behra set the fastest time of day on the last lap. We fractured a fuel line, and this dropped us back during the final three hours of the race."

•   •   •   •   •

The Grand Prix of Oporto, Portugal, for sports cars was run in June, with Portago wrapping up the race in his Ferrari. Hill notched second behind the Spanish marquis, holding off Benoît Musy's Maserati which took third. It was a fierce 40-lapper.

"I might have done better in Oporto, except for my feelings regarding the circuit," says Hill. "There was one fast downhill stretch through the trees that really had me bugged. I kept losing the tail of the car, and my adrenal flow was something awful. I'd heard about two drivers who'd gone into those trees the previous year and were in asylums, and that little bit of information sure didn't help to settle my nerves."

At Monza, in June, Hill was set to drive with Peter Collins, but when Mike Hawthorn's Lotus-Climax broke its gearbox and Mike was available, Enzo Ferrari switched the blond Englishman to Hill's cockpit, depriving Phil of a chance to compete. The Collins/Hawthorn duo went on to win the race.

. . . . .

In a 12-hour event at Reims, on June 30, Hill got a ride with Stirling Moss, co-driving the Britisher's Cooper-Climax, but they were plagued with mechanical troubles from the outset. Stirling's mechanic, Alf Francis, had been forced to rush the car to Reims from London, where it had undergone a quick teardown, and although Moss set fastest time of day in practice, he complained about the machine. Just 30 minutes before the race, Francis noticed that one of the hydraulic brake pipes had broken. He hurriedly replaced it, and Moss was away into an easy lead.

Within a half hour the car had pitted for the first of many stops. When Stirling turned the wheel over to Hill the engine was very rough, and it was clear the car would not finish. Phil soon brought it in with overheating problems, caused by a water leak in the combustion chamber.

. . . . .

A week later, for the Grand Prix of Rouen, Phil was in the lists as an independent, handling George Tilp's 3-liter Ferrari Monza. In a warm-up event at Rouen, prior to the GP itself, Hill tried out a factory Cooper-Climax with disheartening results. (A rod came through the side of the engine, abruptly terminating his race.)

"I was strangely relaxed for the Grand Prix," relates Phil. "I knew that beating the factory teams was impossible, so this meant that I could concentrate on the private entries and not really worry too much about my overall position. I drove very well at Rouen because of this."

Indeed, Hill drove splendidly, being the only independent to keep up with the works cars. However, as the contest drew to its close his shock absorbers failed; a sticking throttle slowed him further and he was forced to cede fifth overall to Salvadori's works Aston. Even so, in finishing sixth, he had beaten all the private entries, prompting the British editor at *Motor Sport* to remark: "Phil Hill drove his Monza so rapidly at Rouen that several Ferrari drivers took a poor view; it made the other customers think he had better attention from the factory than they did. Actually he was just driving faster."

* * * * *

"The next race was something of a hassle," says Phil. "It was at Bari, Italy, and I made up my mind to compete there at the last minute. Mac Fraser and I got in my Volkswagon and screamed off, driving that little thing flat out for maybe 800 miles, from Genoa to Bari. Then, in practice over this really hairy road circuit, I managed to blow up the Monza, so I never even made the grid!"

* * * * *

The 24-Hours of Le Mans wound up the month of July, and Phil was teamed with André Simon in a factory 2.5-liter Testa Rossa, with two other similar Ferraris in the hands of Portago/Hamilton and Trintignant/Gendebien. New Le Mans regulations required each car to have a full-width windscreen, which tended to obstruct the driver's view, particularly in the rain which fell during most of the race. A gradual rivalry had sprung up between Portago and Hill, and the Spaniard seemed determined to prove to Ferrari that he was a faster man than his American teammate. In practice, he was the quickest of the Ferrari drivers, although Portago's style was still far from polished.

Hill tells his own story of the race: "I was set for the first stint at the wheel, and lined up across the road for the running start. Stupidly, I missed the countdown, and was winding my watch when all the other guys took off for their cars! But I got away okay, moving up from maybe 15th to a position right behind Portago. It had just begun to rain, and a kind of dark haze hovered over the circuit. Fon and I charged past a packet of cars on Mulsanne, and when we went by the pits I was about 50 feet behind him. Hawthorn and Moss were leading, with three of the D-Type Jags following. Then came our two Ferraris. We sailed under Dunlop Bridge, really going all out, and topped the hill—to see two of the Jags losing it in the Esses. Frère had spun into the bank. The circuit was as slippery as a bar of soap that year, and both Fon and I began to climb on the brakes, desperately trying to cut down our speed before the Esses. Immediately Fon got out of shape; he couldn't slow up enough, and he wrote off both Jags, hit both of 'em and split his own tank in the bargain, spilling oil all over the track. Well, I was braking, sliding, nearly losing it, braking again, and it looked as though I wouldn't make it through. I was still trying to get things sorted out when the other cars scattered at precisely the right second and I nipped by cleanly.

"Next, the clutch started to seize in the first hour, and this was deadly in the wet. People were crashing all over the place, and we were holding down fourth overall despite our trouble. When the springs wouldn't return the pedal we just shifted without the clutch, hoping to last it out. I was exhausted when I turned over to Simon. After more than 100 laps we were still holding onto fourth when the rear axle broke and *that* did it. We were out in the ninth hour, joining an incredible number of non-finishers. In fact, only 14 cars out of 49 crossed the line that year. The Scottish Ecurie Ecosse D-Jag, with Flockhart and Sanderson up, finally won. Moss and Collins were second for Aston Martin."

• • • • •

Phil was, of course, very much interested in handling a Formula 1 car for Ferrari, since only in the faster Formula events could a driver reach for the ultimate goal in road competition, the World Championship. The brash Portago had already been given a seat in a Formula car and was proving himself fast, but predictably erratic.

"A week after Le Mans came the Grand Prix of Germany at Nürburgring," says Hill. "I'd remarked to Mike Hawthorn that I thought I might get a chance to drive in the race, but he shook his head. 'Phil, whatever you do, *don't* drive a Grand Prix car for the first time at the Ring. Just take my word for it—don't!' So when Ferrari's manager asked me if I wanted to be part of the Formula 1

Team in Germany I hesitated, mumbling some bad Italian, and he withdrew the offer, figuring I wanted to stick with sports cars. This wasn't the case at all, really, but I felt that Mike had been sincere in warning me not to begin at the Ring. I respected his judgment."

• • • • •

When Enzo Ferrari sent his factory team to Kristianstad in August, for the Grand Prix of Sweden, he was well aware that the results of this contest would decide the 1956 Manufacturers' Championship for sports cars. Maserati and Ferrari were tied on points, and victory at Kristianstad would settle the issue.

The four mile rectangular circuit was generally fast, but due to three extremely slow corners it was noted for its severity. Almost every top driver in Europe had turned out for this 1000-kilometer race: Moss, Behra, Taruffi, Schell, Maglioli, Villoresi, Musy, Godia, Bonnier and Simon were with Maserati; while Fangio, Castellotti, Collins, Gendebien, Portago, Trintignant, von Trips, Manzon, Hawthorn, Hamilton and Hill were in the stable of the prancing horse. The Le Mans-winning D-Jags of Ecurie Ecosse were also on hand, with Flockhart and Sanderson up. Private entries filled out the large field.

"Trintignant had asked for me as co-driver after Le Mans," Phil relates, "and we were handed a 12-cylinder 3.5 which Maurice found suitable, but which I hated. The front end plowed badly and it required great chunks of steering to get it through a corner. Even so, I horsed it around for seventh fastest qualifying time, 2:28.7, just a tenth of a second behind Villoresi. But I wasn't happy with our car."

Trintignant began the race, getting away smoothly, and was riding in sixth position after the first hour. The rate of attrition was high, and Collins, in the lead car, was being sprayed by oil from a leak in the tank. At the end of the second hour pit stops were made, and Hill took over from Trintignant, still in sixth position.

When the last driver change had been made (in the initial series of pit stops) a Maserati was leading, Behra at the wheel, Fangio was in second for Ferrari, and Hill had moved into fifth overall. But Jean Behra's brakes began to fail, and Hill motored into fourth as the Frenchman pitted.

"Near the third hour of the race I had passed Portago and pulled away from him," says Phil, "and when Behra pitted I saw a chance for us to possibly place in the top three. This race was full of surprises!"

On lap 78, with half the contest remaining, Manzon's Ferrari skidded on the tricky Rabelov curve, breaking an oil line. The hapless pilot ended in a wheat field, his car effectively out of action. Collins and Hill, unprepared for the oil-slick turn, followed Manzon into the wheat. Hill was away first, while Collins lost a great deal of time regaining the road.

"I simply turned right in the field," explains Phil, "and bumped along almost standing up in my cockpit to see above the wheat. I drove about 200 yards in this manner, parallel to the road, before I found a way to get back onto the circuit. Peter made the mistake of trying to get out the same way he'd gone in."

In the fourth hour, when the race had once again settled down, Fangio was leading in the Maserati with Hill running second for Ferrari, 90 seconds behind the World Champion. Phil relinquished the wheel to Trintignant, who got away nicely, still holding their position.

"I couldn't imagine anyone catching Fangio at this point," says Phil, "and Maurice and I would have been delighted with a second overall—but when Castellotti took over from Fangio in the final stage their engine blew, and Maurice brought our car in 40 seconds ahead of the Collins/von Trips Ferrari. Seeing that checkered flag drop was a wonderful moment."

Against the finest competition in the world, Hill and Trintignant had won the Swedish Grand Prix, giving Enzo Ferrari the sports car Manufacturers' Championship for 1956.

* * * * *

Phil's final race in Europe that season took place at Messina, in Sicily, on August 25. His mount was a 2-liter Ferrari, and he chose to drive solo for the entire five-hour event.

"This was a night race," he states. "We were flagged off at 8 P.M. with the windup at 1 A.M. the next morning. You could see the lights of the other cars sweeping down the long hill and the bobbing lights of the ships in the harbor as you drove past. It was a very satisfying race for me, and I won it rather easily, breaking the previous lap record by 15 seconds. Only had to make one fuel stop."

About 2 A.M., after the victory, Hill returned to his hotel. A group of angry-looking Sicilians was waiting for him at the entrance, blocking his passage. One of them, who had driven in the race, accused Phil of forcing him to scrape a wall when the Californian passed on a tight turn. He demanded money in payment for the damaged car.

"I didn't know what the hell he was talking about," admits Phil. "I tried to calm him down, but this didn't help. He had all of his buddies and relatives with him, egging him on. Next thing I know his brother is poking a lighted cigarette in my face and another guy is hitting me over the head from behind with a board. Just then a friend rushed up, waving a gun at the crowd. They scattered back and we made it into the lobby, bolting the door. Finally the local cops arrived to see what was going on. If we hadn't brought along that gun I might still be in Sicily, buried in the local churchyard."

. . . . .

Hill returned home, driving two more races in the States that season. At Wisconsin's Road America he took a class first with Paul O'Shea in a Mercedes 300SL, then engaged Carroll Shelby in a relentless 35-lap duel at Palm Springs, finishing just a few feet behind the Texan's 4.9 Ferrari with a smaller 3.5 model. Although he was able to pass on the turns, Hill could do nothing to offset the 4.9's superior horsepower on the long straights. A determined Shelby, armed with the necessary cubic inches, had captured the laurels. As one journalist remarked: "At least Hill had the consolation of winning the Palm Springs Concours d'Elégance with his surgically clean, stately 1931 Pierce-Arrow."

. . . . .

Nassau, in December, ended a long, instructive year of international competition for Hill. ("I learned more about racing that season than in all the years in the States put together!") Tires proved to be the big headache at Nassau in 1956. As Phil tells it: "The surface of Windsor Field was very abrasive, and this chewed up rubber at a fierce rate. I got a third in a warm-up event, in George Tilp's Monza, then took off in the Governor's Cup Race, moving up from 14th on the first lap to third. Then things began to happen!"

Shelby was leading with Portago running second when Hill spun wildly on the first turn. A jagged piece of coral, thrown up by his tires, shattered his goggles, and he gunned into the pits, blood stream-ing from his face.

"I couldn't see out of my right eye," he says. "At first I thought I'd been blinded, but the doctor looked at it and told me not to worry, that it was okay, that I just had some minor scratches on the surface, but that my sight would not be affected. But it was enough, of course, to put me out of the race."

In the final day of island competition, for the Nassau Trophy, Hill suffered another poor start when his engine refused to fire. He got off the line in 21st place.

"Knowing that tire wear would be the main factor, I swore to myself that I wasn't going to *fight* my car around the turns," he says. "So I babied the tires all the way, moving gradually up among the leaders, being very cautious about the whole affair. By the halfway point, due to all the tire stops the others were forced to make, I was riding in second behind Moss. I hoped that when Stirling pitted, as I assumed he eventually would, I could then take the lead and hold it to the end. But, instead, I goofed."

Hill's "goof" occurred just 10 laps short of the finish, when he got off into some sand and struck one of the heavy, tar-filled steel drums marking the course. The impact split his gasoline tank, and he was forced to drop out while Moss went on to win.

"Sometimes too much caution can foul you up," he admits. "I was thinking about saving rubber instead of properly negotiating the turn. When I won the race in '55 I had practically no rubber left on my tires—one was clear down to the cord—and I knew the circuit was even more abrasive in '56. I saw this haze of black rubber thrown up by Portago's rear tires whenever he cornered, and so I took it that much easier. Still, I was so busy thinking, 'Don't fight the wheel at any cost', that I neglected to pay enough attention to other items. So I ended up saving my tires and losing the race—a pretty stupid way to wind up the year."

CHAPTER TEN

Rain, Reims, and a Run on the Salt

EUROPE HAD PROVIDED Hill with a fresh perspective on racing. He saw, for the first time, that the life of a professional driver could be considered respectable, that it could provide much more than mere personal satisfaction and silver trophies.

"I found that racing drivers were highly regarded in Europe," he says, "and that the sport was not considered a wild man's game as it so often is in the States. That first season overseas gave me an entirely new kind of outlook, knowing that auto racing was a means to earn a decent living and respected way to exist. Until then, I had never fully realized how strongly I had felt this lack of conformity as far as an occupation was concerned. Europe's mature attitude toward the sport was a real incentive to continue."

•   •   •   •   •

For the 1957 season, Enzo Ferrari had assembled an incredibly strong team: Hawthorn, Collins, Castellotti, Musso, Portago, von Trips, Gendebien, Trintignant and Hill. Fangio had gone over to Maserati, joining Moss and Behra for the marque of the trident.

Bypassing the Grand Prix of Buenos Aires on January 20, Hill remained in California for the West Coast's first seasonal event at Pomona, piloting John von Neumann's silver Ferrari Monza to victory on Saturday, January 19, while his U.S. rival, Carroll Shelby, spun out his 4.9 with locking brakes. On Sunday, a drenching rain turned the Pomona Fairgrounds circuit into a skating rink, with treacherous pools of water collecting at each turn. Shelby lost the 4.9 on the back straight, wrapping the car around a tree, and retired for the day. Hill's luck was no better; after gunning the Monza into an early lead he spun furiously on the wet track and crumpled a rear fender against a hay bale. Taking up the chase, he spun again, losing more ground. Further gyrations convinced him that his car was unstable at speed on the circuit and he pulled into the pits with the sour comment: "I'm tired of making an ass of myself out there!"

· · · · ·

At Havana, Cuba, in late February, Phil's luck did not improve. After rectifying some brake trouble, in Tilp's battle-weary 3.5, he qualified in the front line, only to be disqualified for a push start when his engine failed to fire. Fangio won in a Maserati, while Shelby took second ahead of Portago.

Enzo Ferrari lost one of his top stars, Eugenio Castellotti, who was killed testing a car at Modena shortly after the Cuban race. Hill automatically moved up a notch in the team.

· · · · ·

"Sebring was next," says Phil, "and we had nothing but grief there too. 'Taffy' von Trips was co-driving a year-old 3.5 with me, and we had battery trouble from the outset. This was an unpleasant surprise, actually, since we had worried most about our brakes. The pedal pressure was murder on this car. You needed real strength in order to stop properly. For six weeks before the race I did deep-knee bends each day with a hundred-pound weight on my back — just to build up my leg muscles. Then this battery trouble knocks us out. At one of our pit stops, after about six and a half hours, the car simply refused to start. I don't think we were ever higher than sixth anyhow."

· · · · ·

Phil returned to Palm Springs in early April to tackle Shelby, hoping that he could turn the tables on the affable Texan and win at the desert spa, avenging his November defeat. Win he did, taking the main with ease in Tony Parravano's growling 4.4-liter Ferrari, while Shelby trailed him under the flag by a full 49 seconds. The Shelby fans were quick to point out that Carroll's Maserati was only a 3-liter machine, which meant that Shelby was giving away almost a liter and a half. (The Hill rooters happily reminded them that when Phil lost to Shelby in November his Ferrari had only 3.5 liters under the bonnet, as compared to Shel's 4.9 — and that Hill had lost by only .05 of a second.)

· · · · ·

The tragic 1957 Mille Miglia claimed the life of swashbuckling Fon Portago, who crashed in his Ferrari on the final stage to Brescia. Several spectators and Portago's co-driver also perished in the accident, most probably caused by a blowout. The nerveless Spaniard had ignored a plea to change the wheel at an earlier checkpoint. This decision cost him his life.

• • • • •

Before leaving for Europe and his second season for Enzo Ferrari, Hill took a 4.9 Ferrari to Santa Barbara, where he was once again plagued by rain.

"This was even worse than Pomona," he admits. "On Saturday, I couldn't do a thing with the car. It would hit water and spin like a top. I didn't even finish in the first ten. It was terrible. Then, on Sunday, one of my brake liners came loose inside the drum and every time I'd punch the pedal the liner would stop but the aluminum drum would continue around on the outside of the liner! The minute I'd try to brake, the car would dart to the right, so I didn't dare use the brakes at all in the closing part of the race. I didn't want to risk driving right through the crowd to win. Actually, I was fortunate to finish third."

• • • • •

In Europe, for the Grand Prix of Portugal at Lisbon in June, Phil dropped a valve and was a non-finisher. Assigned a potent new 4.1 Ferrari at Le Mans, he watched co-driver Collins take a first-lap lead, only to pit just two laps later with a seized engine. Their run was over before Phil had been given a chance at the wheel.

Hill was equally frustrated over the fact that he was not allowed to try out for the Ferrari Formula 1 team. He wanted to be the first American driver to win a Championship event, and since Masten Gregory was now driving a Formula 1 Maserati for Centro Sud (snaring a third at Monaco), Hill felt that it was time he also had a chance to prove himself in Formula racing. At Reims, in mid-July, during a practice session, Phil was asked if he wished to have a go in one of the works Ferrari/Lancias, and he immediately accepted.

"I don't know to this day exactly why, but they called me in after a couple of laps," relates Hill. "Maybe I was trying too hard and looked wild. Anyhow, I didn't get any further offers to drive Formula cars that season."

Hill had gone to Reims to co-drive a 250 GT (Gran Turismo) Ferrari in the 12-hour event on the famed Champagne circuit. He got off to a fine start, leading for the initial two hours, then handed the car over to his co-pilot, Wolfgang Seidel. Unfortunately the German could not maintain Phil's hot pace, and was passed by racing journalist Paul Frère, who had taken over for Gendebien. Phil was unable to regain his position in the closing hours and finished second, with the Gendebien/Frère GT Ferrari winning decisively.

"Any elation I felt at having done well at Reims was canceled out by the death of Mac Fraser," Phil declares. "In the Formula 2 event following my race Mac was in a very fast Lotus Mark XI. On lap 27 he spun on a patch of oil, flipped the car and was thrown into a pole. This was an awful shock to me, because we were close friends — but when you race you accept the hazards along with the rewards. You simply *cannot* allow another fatality, however personal, to make you doom-conscious. It's difficult for the average racegoer to understand this necessary state of mind, this seeming callousness, but a professional must rule out all destructive emotions if he wants to continue. When three drivers such as Castellotti, Portago and Fraser die in the same season it isn't easy, but you learn to adjust to the danger or you quit. And I wasn't ready to quit."

•   •   •   •   •

On August 11, a week after Fangio had driven to a stunning Formula 1 victory at the Nürburgring in what many observers considered the greatest race of his fabled career, the Grand Prix of Sweden for sports cars was again held at Kristianstad. And again, as in 1956, it was scheduled to be Maserati vs. Ferrari, with the Manufacturers' Championship in the balance. If Ferrari could win at Sweden the points would guarantee them the title; if Maserati won, then the issue would be decided at Caracas in November.

With the exception of Fangio, who was taking a richly deserved rest after his German victory, all the ace team drivers were on hand for the battle. In Maseratis: Moss, Behra, Schell, Bonnier, Scarlatti. In Ferraris: Collins, Hawthorn, Musso, Gendebien, Trintignant, Gregory and Hill. The Ecurie Ecosse D-Jaguars filled out the entry list, though they were never a serious threat.

In the Le Mans start Hill accelerated away first with the 4.1 Ferrari, but was almost immediately passed by Mike Hawthorn in another 4.1, obviously the Ferrari pacesetter. Mike's job was to "burn up" the Maseratis, allowing Hill (with co-driver Collins) to lead later in the six-hour grind. But Moss would have none of this; he sailed by in the thundering 4.5 Maser (which had won so impressively at Sebring) and Mike fell back, soon to be passed by Behra in the second 4.5-liter. Hill was riding behind the leaders, conserving his brakes, yet staying close enough to take advantage of any mistakes or breakdowns among the opposition. In his desire to close on the two Maseratis, Hawthorn spun off the road, giving away third to Hill. At the two-hour mark, Moss pitted to turn over his car to Schell, putting Hill in second. The Californian was driving one of his smoothest races.

"Within a half hour Schell had retired one of the 4.5s with a broken transmission," relates Phil, "and this meant that we still had second tied down. Peter was in the car then, and if the leading 4.5 went out I felt that we had a good chance of winning. A lot of fast cars were falling by the wayside."

But the big Maserati roared on, pulling away. The Ferrari pits waved in Collins and handed the 4.1 back to Hill, in the hope that the American could close the gap.

"Our car was rapidly losing its brakes," Phil says, "and so I just tried to hang onto second. At the checker, the brakes were nonexistent, and the Behra/Moss 4.5 Maser won, a lap ahead of us. Another Maserati was third, and Mike and Luigi Musso were fourth in our other 4.1. I'd driven for nearly five of the full six hours, and I felt that this was one of my most satisfactory efforts to date."

As European correspondent Bernard Cahier summed up: "It was clearly evident that the American was the best man on the Ferrari team that day."

In 1939, driving a streamlined MG Magnette in Germany, Major A.T. Goldie-Gardner set several international records in Class G and Class F. Top speed attained was 204.2 mph. Eighteen years later the men of Abingdon were ready to shatter these records with a pair of teardrop-shaped Specials which were shipped to the Bonneville Salt Flats in Utah for an all-out record assault. MG's EX 181 was to be entrusted to England's Stirling Moss, who would go for a new Class F mark. The Class G machine, dubbed the EX 179, was in the hands of David Ash and Tommy Wisdom.

"The MG people flew me out to Bonneville after the Swedish GP as alternate for Moss," says Hill. "My main job was to break in the EX 181 and find out if it had any bugs. Moss would do all the official driving with it when he arrived after the shakedowns. This turned out to be an entirely new experience for me, and quite a frightening one."

When Phil arrived at the immense white expanse of open salt flats he carefully inspected the proposed record breaker. The four-cylinder supercharged 91-cubic-inch powerplant was situated behind the cockpit, and a plastic canopy fitted over the driver's head for complete streamlining. The thin aluminum body shell sported a sweeping tail fin for lateral stability at top speed, which was rumored to be in the neighborhood of 250 mph. The driver handled the wheel from a semi-reclining position, and his movements were limited since every inch of space was utilized within the torpedo like machine. Under the MG emblem on its gleaming blue nose the flags of Great Britain and the United States were crossed, signifying an international effort. The EX 181 looked as though it could get the job done.

"I was impressed," says Hill, "but I was also naturally apprehensive. The car had never been opened up prior to this run, and you never know what will happen in a high-speed attempt with an untried vehicle. They told me that they'd be clocking me, but that I wasn't to try for any all-out marks, and risk breaking the car. Still, they wanted me to go fast enough to surpass the old '39 record just in case Stirling didn't make it to the flats. Which meant around 210 or so."

Hill eased himself into the cockpit, and after final instructions the canopy was closed over him. He'd been warned not to correct for a skid if the car got out of shape on the black timing strip, to give it free rein and not hold it on a line it did not wish to follow, to ease it gradually back in the proper direction in order not to disturb the machine's basic thrust. He was also instructed to brake very gingerly; at record speeds the tires could let go under sudden braking and this would almost surely spell disaster. With a popping of exhaust, Hill was away for his initial dash over the ice-hard salt.

"Driving this thing was very strange," Phil relates. "Just imagine it. Here you are, up there in the nose with the front wheels under your knees, with no part of the car visible in front of you, only this great white plain. You feel as though your head is suspended about three feet above the ground which is tearing along under you at lightning speed! The whole long body of the car is *behind* you, which creates this weird sensation. Steering was felt only in the sense of a peculiar wagging effect, as though you had a great, long tail.

"Everything seemed okay, and I recall shifting into fourth, or high, at around 200 mph. I saw the speedometer needle climb sharply and decided to ease off a bit, but nothing happened. I'd been told not to leave my foot on the accelerator for longer than five seconds at a time — since the engine would not withstand this extreme power over any length without damage. I discovered that in order to begin slowing down even slightly I had to lift my foot way back off the pedal. And the minute I did this the back carburetors began to react strongly. Now, the wheels were only separated from the cockpit by a little sponge-rubber strip that pressed against the coachwork when the shell of the car was lowered down over it. It was by no means airtight, and so the wheels themselves began working like pumps, and this meant that deadly swirls of nitrobenzene exhaust fumes were being pumped into the cockpit. Well, when they suddenly rushed up into my face I damn near lost consciousness. All I could do was hold my breath and try to get the car stopped.

"I used the brake as rapidly as I dared, keeping the tires in mind. The brakes were on the rear wheels only, one spot on a locked rear axle, and it seemed as if it was taking forever for them to cut down my speed. I knew there was no way for outside air to reach me — and that I couldn't possibly get the canopy open until the car had almost stopped because the wind held it down. I must have been trapped in there for a good 30 seconds — though it seemed like an hour — and I was in a panic. My respiration had increased terrifically and my heart was pumping, which made it all the more difficult to hold my breath.

"Finally, I got the car stopped and the canopy open. After that we cut a hole in one of the radiator ducts which passed by the driver's head, and this guaranteed a stream of fresh air. Then I took out the car again and made several more runs."

No other bugs were found, and when Moss arrived on the night of August 20 the EX 181 was ready for him. He proceeded to officially shatter the old Class F record, posting a top speed of almost 246 mph, commenting after the runs: "Steering a car such as this is like keeping your balance while walking a rail, not terribly difficult, just tricky."

Phil stayed on at Bonneville to share the wheel of the EX 179, setting a hatful of Class G marks. In a six-hour run, Hill and Ash set 44 National records plus six International Standing-Start records. Wisdom then joined them for a 12-hour assault which netted an average of 118.13 mph, another world mark gleaned from the small 58-cubic-inch Morris Minor powerplant.

The trip to Bonneville had been an unqualified success for MG of England, and Phil Hill had contributed substantially to it.

CHAPTER ELEVEN

Many Crashes in Caracas

IN SEPTEMBER of 1957 Hill drove in three events. The first of these was a six-hour affair at Road America, the Elkhart 500, and his mount was a factory-prepared 318 Ferrari owned by Gene Greenspun. The classic Hill vs. Johnston duel at this circuit in '55 was still fresh in the minds of many observers, and although Sherwood Johnston was not on hand to resume the battle, Hill's old rival, Carroll Shelby, elected to drive a 3-liter Maserati. The larger class cars were officially handicapped in this event, and Shelby would get a 45-second head start on Hill's 3.8, which the Texan hoped would bring him victory. Another top threat was Walt Hansgen in a Cunningham-entered D-Type Jaguar.

"I practiced in a tired old 3.5," says Hill, "because Greenspun's 3.8 was still at Modena. The race was to start at 10 on Sunday, and the factory didn't ship out the car until Thursday. They had it flown into New York, then expressed it over 1300 miles out to Wisconsin. It reached us Saturday morning. It was fast and well prepared, but right away I found that I'd have to baby the brakes to make them last out the full six hours."

Utilizing his 45-second advantage, Shelby stormed the Maserati into an early lead, with Hansgen's D-Jag holding down second. Moving up fast from his handicapped start, Hill passed 35 cars in the first 10 laps, and took second behind Shelby on lap 11. He was driving hard, yet saving his brakes for the long run ahead. On lap 27 Shelby gave way, and Hill passed him into an undisputed lead. The Texan was never able to regain prime position for the remaining five hours, though he finished second ahead of Ed Crawford's RS Porsche.

Hill had notched another victory on Road America.

· · · · ·

"I went back to Europe to handle a 250 GT Ferrari in the Tour de France," says Phil. "This was a kind of rally and race combined, over the French Alps, involving seven stages on a 3800-mile route. Very rugged and demanding, and not the kind of thing I really enjoy. Wolfgang Seidel, who had taken second with me at Reims, was assigned as my co-driver."

Several GT Ferraris were entered in this event, and a special Trophy de Portago was to be awarded by the Parisian Los Amigos Club for the most meritorious performance. (Portago had won the Tour de France in 1956 for Ferrari in a GT machine.) The Italian cars were heavily favored and only Stirling Moss in a Mercedes 300 SL stood an outside chance to defeat them.

Hill relates the details of his participation in the sixth Tour de France: "The worst thing about this whole business for me was having to sit beside another driver while he handled the wheel at racing speeds. I'd never done this before — and I began to appreciate how Richie Ginther must have felt down in Mexico when we were after Maglioli. The Tour was basically a rally from point to point, and you drove against the clock, not really having to push too hard. But, once each day, you had a road race over some famous French circuit en route — such as Le Mans, Reims and Montlhéry. Also, you had hill climbs which were also races, and which had to be driven all out.

"I told Seidel that I would drive the circuit races if he would drive the hill climbs, since racing up a hill I'd never seen just didn't appeal to me. He agreed to this. We would alternate on the rally sections. Well, as it turned out, Seidel did quite a good job but it took me a day or so before I could get over the feeling that I had signed my own death warrant. I was literally sick. Then, when I got over this, I began to go through the guilt of being such a selfish person — for wanting him to sit beside me and die, but damned if *I'd* die alongside him. But I finally forced myself to accept the situation, concentrating on our overall chances.

"We were fourth at the first stage, then moved up to third, then dropped to fifth after the Le Mans stage, due to the fact that when I was getting ready to pass Gendebien, who was leading us all, the windshield on our GT coupé just burst, exploded in my face—and since I wasn't wearing any goggles I was very lucky to escape uninjured. This was on the regular Sarthe circuit. So we dropped back to fifth, just ahead of the Moss Mercedes.

"On the next stage, after Rouen, we moved back into fourth, then into second, behind Gendebien's GT Ferrari. But that was the end of it for us. At Montlhéry I hit a hay bale and part of the coachwork buckled down into one of the joints on the steering column. The car was suddenly all over the road, and so we pulled out for good. Gendebien went on to win with Bianchi, and Moss got fourth behind two other Ferraris."

. . . . .

Hill's final race that September was at Bridgehampton, in the U.S., where he drove Tilp's old Ferrari Monza, his '55 Nassau winner. The Monza couldn't stay with the faster D-Jaguars, and Hansgen took the checker, followed by Chuck Wallace. Phil tooled the Tilp Ferrari into third, after a spirited duel with Wallace on the opening laps.

"Then I had a month's rest," says Hill, "while the factory got our cars ready for the Grand Prix of Caracas in November—which turned out to be one of the most dangerous races I've ever driven. It's a miracle no one was killed down there!"

. . . . .

This contest in Venezuela was slated to decide the 1957 Manufacturers' Championship for sports cars as once again Ferrari and Maserati reached the end of the season locked in combat for the coveted title. Ferrari had won at Buenos Aires and in the Mille Miglia; Maserati had captured Sebring and the Swedish GP. Caracas, therefore, would settle the issue.

Both teams showed in force. Maserati was there with a pair of their fast 4.5-liter giants plus a 3-liter, with Masten Gregory's bored-out 4.7 completing the lineup. Ferrari sent two 4.1-liter cars and two 3-liter models. Driver combinations were all potent, with Moss and Behra each in a 4.5 Maser, against Hill (with Collins) and Hawthorn (with Musso) in the 4.1 Ferraris. The main battle was expected to take place between these four brutish machines. (America was in the lists with a token entry of three Corvettes, but they were never competitive in this league.)

The 6.1-mile circuit, laid out over long boulevards and freeways, embracing cloverleaf overpasses, contained some very fast bends and an almost-full-stop hairpin. On the straights a top speed of 175 mph could be reached, and the big Maseratis of Moss and Behra were able to average 100 mph during their practice laps.

"The whole circuit was ridiculous," says Hill, "like some kind of surrealist nightmare. It was very easy to go the wrong way down ramps and so forth. The road was unmarked, except for people standing at the side and pointing in various directions. These men, who were supposed to show you where to turn, weren't posted where your eye would naturally pick them out. That is, when I'm hitting 100 my eye is well down the road where I can deal with whatever might come up. So here would be this little man off the road, somewhere down on the side, pointing out a turn. If you missed seeing him you missed the turn! I recall a bunch of people all gesturing and waving frantically at me on the first day of practice. I figured they were just excited spectators and ignored them. Next thing I know a big tanker truck is heading toward me, honking like mad! And I see passenger cars with drivers staring at me aghast. Sure enough, I'm *miles* off the circuit and going maybe 100 down one of the city streets in my big red Ferrari."

Peter Collins shared Hill's discomfiture; he also found the Caracas layout quite unusual, remarking (in a published report): "There was a very brave fellow who stood at the end of one straight, waving two large yellow flags. Now on this stretch you'd be doing perhaps 170 mph — and this intrepid man provided the only clue that, so far as racing was concerned, you were at the end of the straight and should turn right. The road carried on, die-straight, for another 15 miles, and this little character simply placed himself in the middle, waved his flags, and *hoped* you'd turn."

The race was set for 1000 kilometers, or 621 miles, and when the cars got away from the Le Mans start Masten Gregory had boomed his 4.7 into the lead. He held it for just one lap. Looking over his shoulder to check on Hawthorn (who was coming up very fast behind him), he misjudged an 80-mph bend and rammed some sandbags. The Maserati rolled over, trapping Gregory beneath it, while gasoline drenched his clothing from the split tank. Well aware of what would happen if the gas ignited, Gregory kicked the door from its hinges and pulled himself free, suffering only minor facial cuts. The roll bar he'd insisted on having installed the previous night had saved his life.

Now, with the biggest Maserati out of action, Hawthorn, Collins, and Behra engaged in a fierce duel, swapping positions from one lap to the next. Moss soon joined the party, and the four drivers blistered around the circuit, disputing every inch of ground. Collins, who had been passed by Moss, was running second when a Porsche whipped off the road, scattering sandbags in its wake. The Ferrari struck several of these, ripping off most of its exhaust system, then continued as Collins discovered that no real harm had been done.

On lap 33, leading his Maserati teammate Jean Behra by a full two minutes, Moss was bulleting down a fast straight at something over 150 when an imprudent AC-Bristol suddenly cut in front of him. Moss rammed the AC, slicing the car in half and destroying his own Maserati. Both drivers escaped, with the AC pilot taken to the hospital and Moss to the pits; Stirling was shaken, but otherwise sound.

Behra pulled the leading Maserati in for a routine stop, only to have the whole car burst into flames. The petrol had ignited. When the fire was put out the French ace could not continue, his arms having been singed by the blaze. Moss jumped in and roared away in pursuit of Hill, who now led, having taken the wheel from Collins on lap 34. Within one tour Stirling was back, bouncing uncomfortably up and down in the cockpit, his pants aflame. Again the fire was quenched, but Moss was in no condition to operate a car, with the entire seat of his coveralls burned out. He limped away for medical aid as Schell leaped aboard the last of the big Masers and accelerated after the Ferraris.

Hill and Musso were pacing the field, but Schell was gaining rapidly. At 140 mph, he pulled out to pass Bonnier's 3-liter Maserati on a fast section when Bonnier's inside rear tire exploded, sending the Swedish driver's car into a skid.

"I saw the whole thing," says Hill, "because I was just about to lap Bonnier as Schell attempted to go by him. The 3-liter Maser sideswiped the 4.5 and Schell went right into a wall, his car in flames. He was able to get out in time. Bonnier's machine rammed a tall power pole, but Joe leaped out at the last second just as the pole collapsed and fell across the cockpit. Both drivers were incredibly fortunate—but it was the end of Maserati. All of their cars were smashed up. Peter and I won, with the Hawthorn/Musso and von Trips/Seidel Ferraris second and third. We all took the flag abreast, in team formation."

For the second consecutive season, Hill had cinched the Manufacturers' Championship for Enzo Ferrari. Thus, his place on the team for 1958 was guaranteed.

But Hill had one more victory to achieve before the year ended— as he headed back to the scene of his first international triumph, Nassau in the Bahamas, for Speed Week.

• • • • •

"Masten was at Nassau with the same 4.7 he'd rolled at Caracas," says Hill, "and Moss had a factory 3.7 Aston Martin DBR2. Shelby was along in a 4.5 Maser and I had the 4.1 Ferrari from Venezuela. Richie Ginther was in John Edgar's old 4.9. The main competition would be among these cars."

As indeed it was. Gregory won the week's opener, the Tourist Trophy Race (prior to Hill's arrival), and when practice began for the next big event, the Governor's Cup, Moss achieved some very impressive lap times with the green Aston. Phil borrowed a Volkswagon to learn the course (switched, in '57, to Oakes Field, over which a 5-mile circuit had been laid out). He found that it was wide and fast, and that tires would not be the problem they were in past years.

"If there is one thing which American drivers must learn it is the fast bend," says Phil. "We don't have many of them in the States, where the corners are sharper, but in Europe and here at Nassau a fast bend quickly separates the men from the boys. At Caracas, for example, about three-quarters of the way down one of the long straights you'd run into a last bend. How well you got through that bend depended on just how fast you could go on the remaining part of the straight. In other words, if you lost say 100 rpm through here then you were that many revs down for the rest of the time into the next corner. That's the art of high-speed motoring, taking these fast bends as quickly as possible without losing engine power. The acceleration up in these high ranges is such that if you lose much in the bend you simply won't be able to get it back before reaching the corner.

"Let's say you've got 20 seconds worth of straightaway left beyond the bend. Now, if a driver such as Moss manages to get through the bend at 5800 rpm, and I have to drop to 5600, then by the end of the straight he'll have a few car lengths on me — amounting to a second or so at the end of each lap. Learning how to handle a fast bend is not easy, though to the spectator it seems as though no problem whatever exists as the driver drifts serenely through. The story is told in that rev counter, and a race is won or lost there. In my first two European seasons I found out quite a bit about high-speed motoring."

Hill put his knowledge to good use in Nassau that year, winning the Governor's Cup in dramatic fashion. Leading on the final lap, his right rear tire blew out. The 4.1 swerved, threatening a spin, but Hill corrected, reduced his pace just enough to hold off Gregory's onrushing Maserati, and crossed the finish line on the rim at 80 mph. Shelby was third, Moss fourth, Ginther fifth.

For the Nassau Trophy Race, ending Speed Week, Moss made one of his rare appearances in a Ferrari (a 3.5-liter model) and won the race in masterly fashion, taking the measure of Shelby and Hill, who finished behind him in that order.

I headed home for California," says Phil, "and I *should* have been feeling fine. I'd done well in '57, and knew that a team spot would be open for me in '58 — but I felt a gap opening in my career. It had to do with Formula racing, and the fact that I had never had a chance to enter any Formula 1 events in Europe. I began to feel that perhaps I was not *ever* going to be a really first-rate driver, that something in my makeup might prevent me from reaching the ultimate stage in motor racing. There are several drivers who do well in sports cars but can't seem to do well with a GP machine. I was beginning to be haunted by the fear that maybe I'd be one of them. I *had* to find out."

CHAPTER TWELVE

Team Triumphs – and a Cuban Kidnapping

T HE '58 SEASON'S initial championship event for sports cars was set for January 26, in Buenos Aires, and Hill was due to handle a factory 3-liter Ferrari there with Peter Collins. After the practice sessions ended, it was revealed that Hill had made fastest time (3:27.5) with Juan Fangio second (at 3:28.2). Collins was fifth fastest around the circuit at 3:32. These times reflected the pattern of the race itself, in which Hill twice broke the course record and turned the fastest lap, a blistering 3:25.9, near the end of the contest.

"We had eight other Ferraris and seven Maseratis against us," says Phil, "but we only really worried about Fangio and Moss. I watched Peter take an early lead, with Fangio chasing him in the 3-liter Maserati. They were running right together when Fangio tried to pass on a curve and overdid things, sliding into a fence. This bashed in the front of the Maser and it never ran properly after that, pulling out for good on lap 25. Stirling's Porsche wasn't fast enough to threaten our Ferrari and we won, with Gendebien's Ferrari in for second. During the closing stage, having lapped the other cars, I held off Moss who was trying to pass Gendebien into second, thus assuring our team of a few more points. That was a very successful afternoon for us."

Hill remained in Argentina for another week, on the promise that he would be allowed to practice in a Formula 1 Ferrari for the Grand Prix of Buenos Aires, set for February 2 in that city.

"I was afraid they'd flag me in after just one lap as they'd done at Reims," says Phil, "but this time they let me have a real go at finding out what a GP car could do. And I certainly didn't put on any display of precision driving. I was really hanging it out down there, and without any knowledge of the car I couldn't judge just how far I could go without getting into trouble. So I just went and did what was obviously too much. The turns rushed up at a far greater rate than I was accustomed to, and it required a new kind of perspective to deal with this. I was spinning around, sliding off the road and so forth—all quite safely because there wasn't anything to hit. After a few laps I began to get the hang of things, and started to enjoy myself immensely. It was a genuine pleasure to drive a car with such direct responses. After you handle a GP machine a sports car seems rather clumsy and sluggish."

Hill's debut in the swift single-seater was most impressive, and he got his time down to 2:21.2 after six laps on Friday. He was back on Saturday to cut this time by almost four seconds, to 2:17.3, tying with von Trips. (Only six other drivers qualified ahead of them from a 19-car starting field.)

"They told me that when Trips came in after the first heat I could then take over the car," says Phil. "But this didn't work out. Trips passed Fangio on lap 15, and was so astonished at the fact that he looked back over his shoulder to see if anything was wrong with the World Champion and spun off the road, bending up the car and putting *both* of us out of the running. Fangio won this event, which was incidentally his last Formula 1 victory. He was then just a few months away from announcing his retirement."

The Grand Prix of Cuba for sports cars, run in late February in Havana, was a catastrophic affair from the outset.

The day before the race, in the lobby of Havana's Lincoln Hotel, a tall, fever-eyed young man thrust the barrel of a big .45 Colt automatic into Fangio's left side and told the Argentine champion to accompany him to a waiting car. If anyone tried to stop them the four machine guns outside would go into action. Thus, in the full blaze of a Cuban sun, Juan Manuel Fangio was boldly spirited away.

President Batista instantly threw a cordon of police around the entire city, but the World Champion was not found. A cryptic phone call informed the authorities that Fangio had been kidnapped in the name of the revolution by a band of Fidel Castro's rebels, and that he would not be allowed to enter the Grand Prix. Otherwise, he was safe.

Maurice Trintignant inherited Fangio's car, and the race began as scheduled, although a "bomb scare" of the previous evening, combined with the kidnapping, had an unsettling effect on many of the drivers. Guards were posted at the garages, and police patrolled hotel hallways to prevent further incidents. The 3.1-mile course, running along Havana's shoreline on Malecón Boulevard, then into the city itself, was slick with oil, spilled in previous warm-up races, and the 200,000 spectators, unprotected by hay bales or fencing, crowded every turn and straightaway. Disaster was in the air as the field roared off.

Moss led past the pits at the end of the first tour, with Gregory and Shelby hounding him. Von Trips was next, with Hill behind the German.

"We had seized two pistons during practice," relates Phil, "and so I was driving back in fifth, knowing my only chance at a placement was to stroke around and try to outlast the competition. The course was impossible, slick as glass with all the spilled oil, and when the red flag came out on lap 6, stopping the race, I wasn't surprised. A car had gone into the crowd, killing six or seven people."

Armando García Cifuentes, a Cuban amateur who was driving a Ferrari for the first time, had lost control on a turn and crashed. Ambulance teams sirened onto the course, taking casualties to the local hospital, while Moss was declared the winner (based on F.I.A. regulations which stated that five full laps constituted a race).

Fangio was returned, unharmed, several hours after the ill-fated Grand Prix, and he was quick to assure reporters that he had been treated "with extreme kindness" by his captors, and that the whole incident had been designed to attract public attention to their revolutionary movement. However, the World Champion admitted that he had never been certain just what they intended doing with him. "I had unhappy visions of myself, bearded and wearing a forage cap, being forced to drive arms trucks up and down those mountain trails!"

Hill summed up the general feeling among the drivers: "I think we were *all* glad to get out of there, especially Fangio!"

.   .   .   .   .

Back in California, Hill polished up his 1939 Packard with the intention of entering it in a concours and gymkhana for classic cars to be held at Sebring prior to the annual 12-hour endurance race. He then drove the Packard across country from Santa Monica to Florida, cleaned off the road grime, and won his class in the Concours d'Elégance.

"I was foolish enough to accept a challenge to drag out with a Mercedes 540 K," he grins. "As a result, I stripped all gears except high in the Packard—which was damn stupid and embarrassing."

Hill's performance in the big Sebring contest was far from "stupid and embarrassing." Again teamed with Peter Collins, in a 250 TR (Testa Rossa) Ferrari, their main competition was the potent Moss/Brooks combination in a sizzling 3-liter Aston Martin DBR1. Another works Aston, several Ferraris, D-Jags and Lister-Jags were also very much in the running. In all, 65 cars were lined up for the Le Mans start at 10 A.M. on March 22, 1958.

"On the first lap I got away into the lead, but was passed immediately by Moss, Hawthorn's Ferrari, and Salvadori in the second Aston. I was taking it easy with a full load of gas, figuring we had a long way to go. The Astons had disc brakes, which meant they could dive much deeper into the corners before shutting down. We were still struggling with the old drum brakes, and they had to be carefully conserved in order to make them last the distance."

At the end of the first hour Hill got a pit signal demanding a hotter pace, and he passed Hawthorn in the process of obeying these orders. Hawthorn repassed, then Hill passed again, with both drivers fighting off Salvadori's attacks in the green Aston. Moss was steadily pulling away from the whole field, driving superbly.

"Then Stirling blew a tire and limped into the pits to have it changed," says Hill. "Brooks took over their car at this point, and I came in to turn the wheel over to Peter. We were then running second behind the Moss/Brooks car. When Pete came in at the end of his stint we were in first, because Brooks had been having a bit of transmission trouble and was in the pits. I took off, with Stirling after me. It looked as though they'd cured their troubles because Moss was closing at the rate of several seconds per lap. By then our brakes were *really* suffering, since I started having to hurry in a way I didn't want to do, but I was trying to hold off Moss, and had no choice. Suddenly, just as he was about to catch me, his transmission finally let go—and the pressure was off. I eased down, slowing about five seconds per lap, mighty relieved to see that Aston in the pits for good."

Eight hours remained in the race, and the Ferrari's brakes were almost gone, but the Hill/Collins team had some luck as the D-Jags, the Listers, and Salvadori's Aston all dropped from the fight.

"During the final hours I had to use a special technique to get around the course," says Hill. "It took about seven full strokes of the brake pedal in order to get the shoes out to the drum, and I had to spend half the straightaway in slowing, changing down at very high revs—maybe 7500—in order to get some stopping power from the engine. Hawthorn's transmission broke near the windup, allowing Musso and Gendebien to bring in the other team Ferrari to second overall behind us."

Phil Hill and Peter Collins had scored their third straight championship victory for Enzo Ferrari, and were now recognized as the most potent two-man combination in sports car competition. Their triumph in Florida rated world-wide press attention, and in covering 200 laps at an average speed of 86.7 mph they had shattered the previous Sebring record set in '57 by Fangio and Behra in the larger 4.5 Maserati, their Ferrari giving away 1.5 liters and 100 hp to the Maser.

"I got into the old '39 Packard for the drive on into New York," relates Hill, "and since I only had top gear left, my acceleration was ridiculous. I was passing through this small Florida town, called Waldo, with a huge truck in front of me just crawling along at maybe 10 mph. I dropped back, calculated how much time I'd need to get around him, then moved out to pass, doing maybe 25 at the most, my foot to the floor. Just as I got alongside the truck a car popped into sight ahead of me, but I was able to get tucked in ahead of the truck before he reached us. But the guy does a fast U-turn and heads back, lights blinking like crazy. Turns out to be the town marshal, who pulls me over and gets out his ticket book. Told me I was speeding and that I'd almost caused a head-on crash with my wild driving. When I explained that speed was the one thing I *couldn't* do in this car, he just growled and handed me the ticket, telling me that if I wanted to drive like a maniac to go join 'them nuts' down in Sebring."

· · · · ·

The world's last surviving open-road race, the Targa Florio, was run through the rugged mountains of Sicily in May, and Hill was paired with Peter Collins once more (their last race together) in this

630-mile affair. The endless, twisting circuit was 45 miles long, rising and descending through the remote Sicilian countryside like a nightmarish roller coaster, and was studded with uncountable hazards. In practice Hill ran into a scooter, Gendebien wiped out a Fiat, von Trips hit a dog, Moss a chicken.

"I'd never driven the Targa," says Phil, "and found it quite a job to get around with any degree of safety. I had grown to hate uncalculated risks, and this race was full of them. You never knew when a mountain or a marker stone was going to jump out at you, and loose gravel made the roads quite dodgy. And with 700 curves per lap to get around, this kept you worried. Peter was quicker on this circuit than I was, and he started the race for us."

Collins was running in second behind Musso at the end of the first long lap, with Moss already out of contention. (His Aston Martin had slammed into a stone marker.)

Hill took over on the third lap, but lost their second overall position during his stint when he left the road on a turn, damaging a wheel. He changed this, dropping to fifth as Collins again took over. Of 41 starters, only 13 completed the tortuous Targa, with the Hill / Collins Ferrari taking fourth overall, beaten by two Ferraris and a Porsche.

. . . . .

"They teamed me with Musso who'd won the Targa when we went to Germany for the Nürburgring 1000-kilometer race in June," says Phil. "I liked the Ring, as difficult as it was, and felt we had a good chance there, but I had a blowout as I came out of the Karussell, and had to stop on course to put on the spare. Moss won with the Aston in fine style and two other of our team Ferraris finished behind him. We were fourth, beating out the Porsches."

The storied 24-Hours of Le Mans followed the Nürburgring in late June, and it was here, on the fast Sarthe circuit, that Phil Hill was due to put in one of the finest drives of his career.

Peter Collins and Phil Hill are surrounded by the international press after their record-setting 1958 Sebring victory. Sadly, that August, Peter would lose his life at the German Grand Prix at Nürburgring. *(Bernard Cahier)*

In 1958, Phil won Le Mans with co-driver Olivier Gendebien in the No. 14 works Ferrari 250 Testa Rossa. Hill displayed masterful wet driving on a circuit that was drenched for 20 of the 24-hours. He was the first American to win Le Mans, and Hill's efforts assured Ferrari the Manufacturer's Championship for sports cars. *(LAT)*

At the second Monza 500 "Race of Two Worlds" held in 1958, Phil was given the No. 14 Ferrari, using a 3-liter V-6, angled in a GP chassis. Due to magneto trouble he retired the 296 "Monza Special" 10 laps into the 63-lap heat.

In the second and third heats, Hill relieved Luigi Musso and Mike Hawthorn in the 4.1-liter 412. They gained a third for the three heats with the No. 12 Ferrari special.
(Bernard Cahier/ Ferrari Market Letter Archives)

The 18-car field consisted of America's top Indy 500 cars and drivers, pitted against the European GP and sports car aces.
(Publifoto / Ferrari Market Letter Archives)

Tired of waiting for a Grand Prix ride from Ferrari that was not materializing, Phil gained attention by driving a two-year-old Maserati 250F of Joakim Bonnier's at the French Grand Prix at Reims in 1958. (Geoffrey Goddard / GP Library)

Hill is pictured in his Formula I debut following the Ferrari of Mike Hawthorn. He earned a respectable seventh in the two-year-old private entry at Reims. (LAT)

Hill gained a Formula I drive with Ferrari at the Italian Grand Prix at Monza in September of 1958. After a great start and leading the opening laps, he was forced to pit with a punctured tire. After working his way back up to third place, he held that position behind the No. 14 Ferrari of Mike Hawthorn. Stirling Moss in his Vanwall is following Hill and Hawthorn into this bend. *(Bernard Cahier)*

A couple of sports car events preceded the next GP race at Casablanca. The first at Watkins Glen, followed by the West Coast's first FIA-approved event, the Times Grand Prix at Riverside. Hill drove the 4.1-liter Ferrari 412MI of John von Neumann in these events, but mechanical difficulties forced retirements in each. *(Bob Tronolone)*

Mike Hawthorn is interviewed after the Moroccan GP at Casablanca, where he became the first Englishman to win the Driving Championship of the World. Phil Hill was instrumental in assisting his teammate gain the points required to best Stirling Moss' bid for the 1958 title. Mike would announce his retirement at season's end. Tragically, he would die three months later in a road accident. (Peter Coltrin)

Mike's fiancée, Jean Howarth, listens while the drivers confer. Ferrari technical director, Carlo Chiti, in necktie, oversees preparation of the cars. (Peter Coltrin)

The first event of the '59 sports car season was held in heavy March rains at Sebring. Four hours into the race, the team of Phil Hill and Olivier Gendebien was forced to retire the No. 8 Testa Rossa because of a bad pinion bearing. The pair was then assigned to the No. 7 car of Dan Gurney and Chuck Daigh. They brought it home for a win.
(Flip Schulke)

Hill also drove to a win that October at the Riverside Grand Prix for Sports Cars. The Testa Rossa is bent from an encounter with a guardrail during a practice run.
(Bob Tronolone)

Back with the MG group at Utah's Bonneville Salt Flats in October of 1959 for an attempt at several Class E records. The photo of Phil Hill standing next to EX181 gives a sense of the record car's size. (BMIHT/Rover Group)

The tight-fitting cockpit situated between the front wheels of the mid-engined streamliner offered no shoulder harness, or roll bar for protection. (Griffith Borgeson)

MG EX181 was run at Bonneville in 1959 without the stabilizer tail fin used in 1957. The fastest of the new Class E marks Phil set in the streamliner was a record two-way average of 254.91 mph over the flying Kilometer. (BMIHT/Rover Group)

Phil Hill and Cliff Allison were co-drivers at Buenos Aires, Argentina, for the first sports car race of the 1960 season. Former Ferrari teammate Dan Gurney pictured next to them in his helmet, was teamed with Masten Gregory in one of the new Tipo 61 "Birdcage" Maseratis for the American Camoradi team. (Bernard Cahier)

Hill handed the 250 Testa Rossa over to Allison, who brought the 3-liter TR home to take first place in the 1000-Kilometer event. (Bernard Cahier)

Chapter Thirteen

Masterful Driving at Le Mans

S INCE 1923, when the first Le Mans round-the-clock race was
run, men and cars from many nations have annually battled the
famed French road circuit, located some 120 miles from Paris,
searching for the magic combination of talent, luck, speed and per-
severance which would bring victory after the long day-and-night
grind. Winning at Le Mans has a special heady flavor, and many fine
drivers stubbornly compete there year after year, ignoring the odds
against fatigue, mechanical failure, accidents and ill fortune, not only
unable to win but unable to finish. Until 1958, Phil Hill had been in
this luckless category.

"In '53,'55 and '56 the machines I drove folded up, ending in the
dead car park," says Hill. "Then, in '57, when Peter went out early,
I was left sitting on the pit wall. But you forget all the past grief when
you come to Le Mans each year. You arrive full of hope, ready to
tackle the circuit and defeat it. The challenge is always there."

In 1958, for the 26th running of *Les Vingt-quatre Heures du Mans,*
Enzo Ferrari sent three V-12 3-liter Testa Rossas (deciding, at the
last moment, not to enter a pair of still-untested prototype machines).
These TRs were manned by Hill/Gendebien, Hawthorn/Collins and
von Trips/Seidel. Ferrari's chief rival, Aston Martin, had sent along
a trio of DBR1s, for Moss/Brabham, Brooks/Trintignant and Salvadori/
Shelby. A factory-supported D-Jaguar, driven by Duncan Hamilton
and Ivor Bueb, plus two of the Ecurie Ecosse D-Types, also figured
as potential winners. The Porsches were there, always in the fight
as the larger cars fell by the wayside, and a host of smaller machines

filled out the 55-car starting field. A lone 3-liter Maserati, in the hands of Bonnier and Godia, represented the marque of the trident.

"We didn't want the new, front-mounted synchromesh gearbox," says Phil, "because this had given us trouble at Sebring, so we asked for the old crash-type box mounted at the rear. This meant using a de Dion axle, which weighs more and gives no advantage on the smooth Le Mans asphalt, and it also means an extra pair of spur gears in the drive train, which consume more power—but we accepted these limitations to insure reliability. The old crash box juddered, but it held—and we wanted to make sure we could depend on the gearbox for a long race like this one."

Practice, over the 8.3-mile Sarthe circuit, proved what nobody needed to be told: that Stirling Moss and Aston Martin were very, very fast. The Briton posted a lap of 4 minutes 7 seconds, while the best Ferrari time was 4:13 (Hawthorn). And in the brief Le Mans footrace, across the track into the car, Moss also proved his unquestioned speed. He was accelerating briskly away in the green Aston DBR 1 while the other drivers were still fumbling with ignition keys.

"At the end of the first lap Moss had the bit in his teeth," says Hill. "Our car, with Gendebien up, was holding down fifth behind Hawthorn, Brooks and Trips. We had agreed before the start that this race could be won by two drivers in a fast car with guts enough to go *slow* in the opening stages. You have this terrible tendency to forget that there are 24 hours to go—and you just blaze away down those smooth roads. Well, we determined to let someone else do this and stay close enough to inherit the lead when the front runners wore themselves out. Riding in fifth, we were all right."

Indeed, the flying Moss was forced to retire his car after two hours of utterly dominating the opposition. The Aston had not stood up to the pace, and Hawthorn, in attempting to stay close to Moss, had also strained his car too severely. A slipping clutch told the story. Von Trips and Tony Brooks were now moving up to dispute the lead, with Gendebien hanging on behind them, ahead of Duncan Hamilton's D-Jaguar.

As Moss gave up for the day the elements seemed in sympathy. The sky darkened, releasing a thick mass of rain which swamped the circuit. Seidel took over for Trips, and led the race as the rain continued. Accidents and mechanical failures began to deplete the ranks:

both Ecurie Ecosse D-Types were out with burned pistons, and crashes had already claimed four of the private entries. The course was extremely tricky to navigate, with mud and spray thrown up by wheels biting for traction.

Hill replaced Gendebien in the No. 14 Ferrari at the end of two and a half hours (since regulations limited the number of laps any single driver could take), and shot away after the Seidel Ferrari, only to come in after just one tour wearing a most unhappy expression and pointing to a rear tire. It was almost flat, and the pit crew hurried out a replacement. When Hill saw that they were not using the spare wheel he began to shout at them in Italian, gesturing wildly. According to Le Mans rules, the first wheel change in the race must be made with the spare carried on each car. Hill feared disqualification on this basis, but the dilemma was solved when a French official allowed the spare wheel to be removed and replaced again, in token compliance with the regulations.

"I got back into the cockpit and took off," Phil says, "and by the third hour we were in the lead. I'd caught Seidel and passed him. The Brooks/Trintignant Aston was then third. The frustration of that pit stop probably caused me to drive faster than I'd planned, because we still had almost 21 hours to go. But the rain had slowed most of the others down and I felt we could afford to take the chance of leading this soon in the race."

Rain and darkness form a deadly combination, and the nightmarish road conditions affected every driver. The misted glow of taillights was lost in the opaque downpour, and Hill fought for vision. "I'd try peering over the windscreen," he says, "but my goggles got covered with mud and dirt. I changed them, using a visor on my helmet. I tried angling my head back and sighting over the top of the screen with my eyes screwed up into slits. We were driving so blind that we could hear the small Panhards before we saw them. With their twin-cylinder motors and open exhausts they had a sharp bark to them, and were actually noisier than most of the big cars. Which was a blessing under the weather conditions."

Before 10 o'clock that night a dozen drivers had been involved in serious crashes, and 21 cars were out after just six hours of racing. One crash was fatal, claiming the life of Jean Brousslet, driving under the nom de plume of "Mary." Just beyond the Dunlop Bridge Brousslet's D-Jaguar slid out of control into the banking, rolling over and killing its driver. American Bruce Kessler could not avoid the wreckage and his Ferrari also crashed. The dark curtain of rain blinded many drivers, and on the long Mulsanne straight the smaller cars doing a top of 90 were all but invisible in the downpour as the bigger cars rushed upon them at 160 mph.

Hill describes one such chilling encounter: "I was boiling down Mulsanne, trying to see through the darkness and the rain, when suddenly two cars appeared directly in front of me, side by side, doing maybe half my speed and blocking the whole road. I was too close to use my brakes and I couldn't risk going off the course at speed. So I just tromped the gas pedal and, somehow, passed *between* them."

Bueb had replaced Hamilton in the D-Jaguar and was relentlessly overhauling the leaders, passing the Seidel/Trips Ferrari into second. Gendebien was then at the wheel of the No. 14 Ferrari, while Hill tried to sleep in the bunkhouse-restaurant provided for the drivers by Shell Oil. Phil awoke to the unsettling news that his teammate was being rapidly overtaken by Bueb's Jaguar, and by the time Hill had donned his heavy black rain suit and gloves the D-Jag had snatched the lead from Gendebien.

"Olivier repassed again just before he pitted," says Hill, "but the D was back in first and pulling away fast when I got into our car. It was almost midnight and the rain wasn't letting up. I knew I had to catch the Jag or we might lose it entirely by morning."

Hill thundered the Ferrari onto the treacherous course and struck out after Bueb. Clustered loudspeakers conveyed the news that an all-out chase was in progress, and the soaked spectators trudged back to the fences, squinting into the night as the red Ferrari growled past, closing on the finned Jaguar.

Within seven laps the hard-driving American was at Ivor Bueb's tailpipes, and he slammed past in a whirl of spray to regain the pace position. Once by the Jaguar, Hill kept pushing, widening the gap to a full lap, then to a lap and a half before wearily bringing No. 14 back to the pits at 2:30 for Gendebien to take over. It had been a brilliant display of wet-track driving, and it had effectively broken the back of the opposition. Hamilton had replaced Bueb in the D, but had been unable to gain on Hill. Their lead, barring a crash or mechanical troubles, was now secure.

At dawn the sky was still overcast, and the weather remained nasty, with blowing squalls of rain reducing the surrounding terrain to a sea of mud. The road was lined with wrecked, abandoned cars, and in the early-morning mist the No. 14 Ferrari roared on, holding the field at bay. Seidel had crashed in the wet with the other remaining factory car and Ferrari's hopes rested entirely with Hill and Gendebien. A win here would clinch the 1958 Manufacturers' Championship.

"Around noon I was following Hamilton, just short of lapping him for the second time," says Phil, "and I got some 'back-off' signals, which meant 'don't try to pass.' I was well aware of their meaning, since Hamilton was thrashing that Jaguar through the corners in a very wild fashion, trying to pull away from me. If I had attempted passing he might have tangled us both up, and I certainly didn't want to risk anything like that. So I just kept him in sight. He was accelerating away from Arnage in third gear, and coming up on a left-hand bend with a slight hump in the middle. The rain was pouring down, and a Panhard had slowed to what amounted to a dead stop in this bend. The car loomed up right in front of Hamilton, and he had no time to brake. His Jag spun onto the grass verge, clouted the bank, flipped over and threw its driver out, then whiplashed across the road again just in front of me. At one moment it was broadside and I saw it silhouetted across the road. Then I saw the underside as it flipped, and I figured it was going to hit me. I couldn't do much except keep straight on, and slipped by without a scratch. I never realized a car could travel so far out of control. I thought it was never going to stop bouncing! They took Hamilton to the hospital and he was all right, but that Jag was sure a mess."

By noon, with just four hours to go, the last of the factory Astons had retired, and the Hill/Gendebien car had a clear run to the flag. Under a darkly clouded sky, at 4 P.M. on Sunday, June 22, their mud-spattered red Ferrari claimed the coveted victory.

In a race in which rain had drenched the circuit for 20 of the 24 hours, in which three dozen cars had retired (15 of them having been involved in accidents), Hill and Gendebien had maintained an average speed of just over 106 miles per hour to win what many observers termed "the toughest Le Mans in history." Their nearest competitor at flagfall, the privately entered Aston Martin of the Whitehead brothers, was a full 100 miles behind them. In the heart of the rainswept darkness past midnight, when he had been battling the tenacious D-Jaguar, Hill had been clocked in a trio of consecutive laps at 4:17—only four seconds slower than the best Ferrari lap time (posted, on a dry track in practice, by Mike Hawthorn).

Here at Le Mans, Enzo Ferrari had won the Manufacturers' Championship for sports cars for the third straight year, and Phil had been largely responsible, once again, for this annual achievement. In becoming the first American to win this classic race, Hill's superb performance placed him among the sport's elite. In a single season he had won at Buenos Aires, Sebring and Le Mans.

Yet, the ultimate challenge, that of a Formula 1 Grand Prix, still lay ahead of him.

CHAPTER FOURTEEN

A Battle and a Beginning

IN THE DINING room of the Hôtel de Paris at Le Mans the afternoon following the race, Hill was drinking tea with a number of friends and well-wishers, when the subject of the French Grand Prix arose. Phil was asked if Ferrari intended providing him with a ride in this Formula 1 event Phil shook his head, ruefully remarking that he was still waiting for Enzo to give him a chance in Formula racing. As Denise McCluggage, who was there that afternoon, tells it: "We all chimed in with what a fool he was to wait, how unappreciative Ferrari was, how Phil was stupidly loyal hanging around year after year with no guarantee of a ride in the Formula cars, how he would never get anywhere with Ferrari if he didn't *rebel*, if he didn't force Ferrari to recognize his potential talent in Grand Prix racing."

The Swedish driver Joakim Bonnier then offered Phil a chance to drive his private two-year-old 250 F GP Maserati at Reims, and Hill accepted, even though he was well aware that Enzo Ferrari would strongly disapprove.

"I felt that a decisive step had to be taken," says Phil, "and if I drove Joe's old Maser it would prove that I was serious about wanting to break into Formula racing. At least I'd call some attention to myself. I was tired of waiting in the wings for an onstage call."

•   •   •   •   •

Prior to the French GP, Hill was committed to drive a Ferrari at the banked Monza oval on June 29. The factory had entered two single-seat "specials" in this 500-mile event, billed as the second annual "Race of Two Worlds."

The high-speed banking had been built at Monza in time for the 1955 Italian Grand Prix, and the organizers had hoped that the spectators would appreciate the fact that in adding this banking to the existing road circuit the cars would be visible more often (since they could be seen twice up on the banking and twice along the straight). However, the '55 race was not a success, and although the banking was again used with the road course in '56 the combination inspired a host of complaints, involving broken chassis frames, dangerous tire wear, etc. In 1957, therefore, only the road circuit was used for the Italian GP.

In order to pay for their investment, the Monza organizers invited the top Indianapolis drivers to come to Italy for a special race on the banking against the top Europeans. Unfortunately, most of the European drivers felt that the contest would be too dangerous and declined to compete against the track-bred Indy cars. By 1958, however, since a huge purse of $80,000 was at stake, the situation had changed, and the event was truly a "Race of Two Worlds," though designed to favor the Indianapolis cars and drivers.

"The car I was to drive was not really competitive in all-out speed," explains Hill. "I was supposed to try to outlast the Indy boys and aim for a placement based on overall distance. My Ferrari was a 3-liter, with a V-6 sports car engine mounted at an angle in a Dino GP chassis, with beefed-up suspension. My best practice time around the Monza oval was 161 mph, well below most of the other cars."

Luigi Musso and Mike Hawthorn were on hand to drive Enzo's second "Monza Special," a very fast 4.1-liter, V-12, with a reputed horsepower of "something above 440" (in contrast to the Indianapolis cars, whose 4.2-liter Offenhauser powerplants delivered just over 400 hp). The 4.1's body was a cross between the early Grand Prix Super Squalo and the current Formula 1 machines, while its outdated suspension, which was to prove entirely unsuitable for the rough Monza banking, harked back to that used on the GP Ferraris of the pre-Lancia days. The Indy cars were far more stable at speed, and were expected to set the pace.

Musso, therefore, astounded everyone by posting the fastest practice time around the 2.6-mile oval in the brutish 4.1 Ferrari, a blazing 174.67 mph, giving him the pole position. Veith was next with

173, beating out Fangio (driving the '57 Monza winner from Indianapolis, the Dean Van Lines Special) who recorded 171 mph.

Although there were two D-Type Jaguars and a Lister-Jaguar entered, in addition to an ancient private Ferrari (for Harry Schell), the only other possible threat to the Indianapolis machines was a $21,000 Maserati Special provided for Stirling Moss by the Eldorado ice cream company of Italy. This 4.2-liter car, rated at 400 hp, had been built especially for Monza, and its suspension was far superior to that of the large Ferrari.

As the 18-car field got away for a rolling start for the first of three heats (of 63 laps apiece, with an hour between each heat for repairs) the American cars and drivers were highly favored to repeat their victory of the previous year. (Only a trio of brave, but hopelessly outclassed, Ecurie Ecosse D-Jags had challenged the Indy machines in '57.) Last year's Monza winner, tough, cigar-chomping Jimmy Bryan, in his Belond AP Special, was rated as favorite, although Monza newcomer Jim Rathmann, in his bright orange Zink Special, was showing great form and speed. (Bryan had flashed over the line to win the Indianapolis 500 just a month before coming back to Monza, and he brashly predicted that the Indy cars would "blow all them foreign junkboxes off the track!" Masten Gregory, handling one of the slower D-Jags, assured Bryan that he would happily move over for him to pass, and should he stay high or low on the banking? The big man removed his cigar and snorted: "Look, Masten, it don't make a damn to me *what* you do. I'll go by you so fast it won't make any difference at all!")

With the first heat well under way, Musso was furiously battling the Indianapolis contingent, his bellowing Ferrari bouncing about in horrifying fashion at over 170 mph on the concrete joints of the steep Monza banking. It was obvious that Musso's suspension and tires were taking a severe beating, and the brave Italian was forced into the pits after 26 laps for a new set of rubber. He staggered from the cockpit, sick and exhausted from his struggle with the plunging Ferrari. Mike Hawthorn took over, with unconcealed reluctance (since the Englishman clearly had no taste for high-speed oval racing). He failed to match Musso's fiery pace, and the big car dropped to sixth position by the end of the initial heat.

Hill, meanwhile, was having magneto trouble, and had been forced to retire the smaller V-6 Ferrari after 10 laps. He told Hawthorn that he would be willing to take out the 4.1 as relief for Musso in the second heat, and Mike happily agreed to this plan.

Jim Rathmann had captured Heat 1, ahead of Bryan, with Veith in third, Moss in fourth. As the second stage of the battle began Rathmann was still firmly in command, but Moss had engaged Bryan and Troy Ruttman in a spirited duel for second, with Musso also back in the thick of things with the Ferrari.

"After 19 laps Luigi brought in the car," says Phil, "and I took over after a wheel change. I got the 4.1 back up to seventh, but another tire stop dropped us to ninth by the end of that heat."

Fangio, whose car had been a nonstarter in the first two heats, took a slow lap in the final stage, only to retire with a malfunctioning fuel pump—while Jim Rathmann continued to extend his impressive lead. The Maserati challenge ended abruptly when Moss had his steering break at the top of the banking. At 160 mph, he cannoned into the rail, blowing two tires, slid viciously down the length of the banking and spun into the infield, shaken but unhurt.

Hawthorn had taken the 4.1 Ferrari into the pits after 25 laps, putting Hill back at the wheel. The Californian was determined to make a respectable showing. He vigorously threw the heavy car into the fray, moving steadily up in the closing laps, thrashing the red giant over the choppy banking, climbing from eighth to a solid third overall as the race ended.

Rathmann had won (at a sizzling average of 167 mph), with Bryan second, but the Hill/Musso/Hawthorn Ferrari had finished in the money for third (ahead of Crawford and Reece) in the final ratings, based on the sum of all three heats. Only half a dozen cars were still running at flagfall.

This had been the fastest race in automotive history, and in taking over the lion's share of driving in the massive 4.1 Ferrari (over 70 laps to Musso's 45), in fighting the "battle of the banking," Phil Hill had split the Indianapolis ranks and earned the respect of the track-tough boys from the Brickyard.

"Driving that monster around the Monza banking was the hardest job I ever tackled," Hill declared after the event. "This type of oval competition is just a case of how much physical discomfort you'll put up with. To my taste, it could never replace genuine road racing."

.   .   .   .   .

Pressure was mounting against Hill's Maserati entry for the upcoming French Grand Prix. He was asked not to drive the Maser at Reims by Ferrari's pit manager, Romulo Tavoni, who assured Phil that if he continued to be patient, a Formula 1 ride would soon be forthcoming. Hill said no, that he had waited long enough, and that he would not back out of his commitment to drive Bonnier's Maserati.

As race day neared, disturbing threats began to filter down from Ferrari himself, and Tavoni sternly warned Hill that he would never again drive a factory Ferrari if he went through with his plan to compete against his own team at Reims.

Actually, the two-year-old 250 F Maserati offered absolutely no competition to the fast new Formula 1 Ferraris, and Hill did not feel that any team disloyalty was involved in driving the tired machine. His battle would be fought back at the rear of the pack, against the other outdated private entries, and he therefore refused to withdraw from the race.

"To this day, I think I'm right in believing that they didn't really think I could drive a GP car," says Hill. "It was always 'next time,' and next time just never arrived."

An amusing pre-race incident, in which Phil was involved, helped ease the tension of Hill's first Grand Prix. It seems that Harry Schell, a great practical joker (who once donned the uniform of an airline stewardess in order to serve spiked drinks to his driver pals on a circuit-to-circuit flight), drove a perky Vespa 400 to France, parking the small auto outside his hotel, the Lion d'Or at Reims. Several of the drivers decided to carry the car through the hotel doors into the lobby, where they placed a huge vase of flowers on the Vespa's roof, leaving a message to the effect that Schell was wanted downstairs.

When he didn't appear, the group (composed of Moss, Musso, Troy Ruttman, Dan Gurney, Masten Gregory, Hill and Bernard Cahier) voted to carry the automobile to the floor above. Another dozen bystanders were talked into lending muscle power to the project, and the Vespa was transferred to the upper floor, where the vase of flowers was again placed on the roof. Then the whole group trooped off and left Schell to his night's sleep.

Early the next morning Harry discovered his flower-adorned car in the middle of the upper floor, and his expression of utter bewilderment was, according to witnesses, "worth all the sweat in toting that thing up those damn stairs."

Harry finally persuaded his tormentors to restore the Vespa to its rightful place on the street outside, but not before much debate on whether or not Fangio could *drive* it back downstairs. The smiling champion assured Harry that he was willing to try, but it was decided that the "road hazards" of a telephone booth and a big mirror by the last stairwell turn rendered the drive impractical.

Hill's first Formula 1 race turned out to be Juan Fangio's last. The five-time World Champion was retiring at forty-seven, and this event at Reims would end a brilliant career, during which the quiet man from Argentina had won a reputation as the greatest driver of his era. The master was stepping down from motor racing's throne after two decades of speed, to make room for younger talent, the Hawthorns, the Brabhams, the Hills. But his place in history was secure; Fangio was *Il Maestro,* and none could dispute his absolute mastery of the road.

．　　．　　．　　．　　．

The 44th running of the French Grand Prix began under a hot sun with Hawthorn (Ferrari), Musso (Ferrari) and Schell (BRM) occupying the front grid positions. Four rows behind them, on the outside, Hill had qualified the old 250F at 2:29.5 — for the fastest time among the privately entered Maseratis, almost a second and a half faster than Bonnier (in Scarlatti's newer '57 Maser), and well ahead of his fellow Americans, Carroll Shelby and Troy Ruttman (like Hill, making his Formula 1 debut in an older Maserati). Fangio had found the Ferraris, British Vanwalls and BRMs too swift for his '58 Maser, and he could do no better than row three with a time of 2:24, five and a half seconds faster than Hill.

As expected, the Ferraris took an immediate lead, Hawthorn battling to hold Musso at bay. On lap 9 the Italian was just a few car lengths behind the Englishman, and made the fatal mistake of diving too rapidly into a tricky right-hand bend, sliding out of control into a ditch, his car flipping end for end. Musso was rushed to a hospital by helicopter, but his injuries were too extensive, and he died shortly thereafter, the last of Italy's postwar driving greats.

Hawthorn won the race, stunned by the loss of this gallant competitor, with Moss and Trips filling out the top three slots. Fangio was fourth, never being able to challenge the leaders, Collins fifth, and Jack Brabham was sixth.

Hill had finished in seventh place, winning the "race-within-a-race" among the slower private entries, beating home the Masers of Bonnier, Geroni and Ruttman.

For Juan Fangio and Luigi Musso the race had provided an ending; for Phil Hill it was a beginning. The final phase of his difficult career was at last under way.

CHAPTER FIFTEEN

A Fast Start in Formula 1

IN THE FORMULA 2 race on July 7, at Reims (on the heels of the previous day's Formula 1 GP), England's Peter Collins had driven the recently completed Formula 2 Ferrari to a second overall behind Jean Behra's Porsche, proving the potential of the new Italian machine.

"I'd been promised a ride in that model at Reims," says Hill, "but after the dark threats about losing my place on the team if I drove the old Maser I'd pretty well abandoned any idea of more Formula racing for '58. But, after Reims, Ferrari turned around and offered me the Formula 2 car for the German Grand Prix at Nürburgring on August 3. Which was a very pleasant surprise."

Due to a smaller-than-usual Formula 1 entry at the Ring that year, the organizers decided to allow the Formula 2 cars to race in the same event, filling out the field, and providing an official race-within-a-race.

For Friday's practice, a mechanic drove Hill's new car to the starting line, and just as it arrived on the grid one of the rear wheels fell off! (The hold-on nut had been forgotten.) This embarrassing situation was corrected, and Phil set out over the tortuous 14-mile circuit. He came back complaining of brake trouble (a malady which was to befall him in the race itself), yet he *had* set the second-fastest Formula 2 lap time behind Jack Brabham. On Saturday Phil reduced this by a full 10 seconds, putting him in row three, behind the Formula 1 Ferraris, Vanwalls and Coopers.

Twenty-two machines took the starting flag (11 of each Formula), and while Moss whipped into an overall lead Hill was equally quick in demonstrating his firm command of the Formula 2 competition. As Moss dropped out (magneto) the two Ferraris of Hawthorn and Collins began swapping the lead. But the green Vanwall of Tony Brooks was moving up fast—and a high-speed duel was soon under way between the three British drivers.

Behind them, Hill was steadily increasing his class lead, and by the third lap he held a 34-second advantage over New Zealand's Bruce McLaren in a Formula 2 Cooper, who was trailed by Edgar Barth's Porsche. After increasing this to a full minute, Hill's chances for a class victory seemed excellent.

"I was coming down the winding section near Adenau," says Phil, "where the road twists and dips in bobsled fashion, and just at the beginning of a tight bend around a hedge my rear wheels encountered some spilled oil. Once you're into an oil patch you've had it; you spin."

Hill spun, slamming into an earthen embankment. He was about to get under way again when Seidel's Cooper zipped around the hedge, revolved on the same patch of oil and also hit the bank.

Hill finally got back into action, but his breather pipe had been broken in contacting the bank, and sprayed oil on his rear wheels for the balance of the event, forcing Phil to use extreme caution in cornering. Additionally, his brakes began to fail, and by lap 11 both McLaren and Barth had passed him.

It was on this same lap that Peter Collins overextended himself in his dedicated pursuit of Brooks' more agile Vanwall. The green car had passed by both Italian machines, and as Hawthorn dropped back slightly Collins gave full chase, refusing to bow to the Vanwall's superior roadability. On the tricky approach to the Pflanzgarten curve each car tops a brow in third gear, while the driver stabs at the brake pedal, shifts into second as the car is airborne, then takes the dip at the bottom still in second, accelerating around the right-hand bend. Brooks boiled through with Collins desperately trying to close the gap. The Ferrari sailed over the brow, then shot out of the dip leading to the fast bend at too great a speed. Collins' rear wheel hit the low dirt banking at the edge of the curve as he fought the car around, and the Ferrari rolled over, pitching the helpless Collins into a tree.

He died in the hospital in Bonn after the race without regaining consciousness.

"Brooks won," says Hill, "and I got ninth overall and fifth in Formula 2 — but Pete's death upset all of us. He was like a little boy in racing, full of fun and loving every minute of it. We still don't know *exactly* how it happened, but my theory is that he didn't or couldn't use his brakes before coming over the brow. By then he was going too fast to get around. Maybe his brakes failed... anyway he never had a chance on that bend."

. . . . .

The fortunes of motor sport decree that as one driver leaves the racing scene his place is taken by another. In the case of Peter Collins it was Phil Hill who was given his seat in a Formula 1 Ferrari for the upcoming Italian Grand Prix at Monza on September 7, thus providing the Californian with his initial Formula 1 factory ride after almost three years of warming the bench as a team member.

"Mike Hawthorn and Stirling Moss were locked in a tight duel for the World Championship in '58," says Hill, "and, at Monza, my main job was to try to set a blistering pace in the hope that Moss might break his car in attempting to match me. Then Mike could move up and take the lead. Also, either Mike or I would try to set the lap record — because, in those days, the FIA. granted one championship point to the driver who turned the quickest lap in each event, so fast time was an important factor."

Enzo Ferrari sent four cars and drivers to Monza. In addition to Hill and Hawthorn, von Trips and Gendebien were also on the team. The new Dino 256 engine, which increased the Ferrari's horsepower from 285 to over 300, had been installed in Hawthorn's machine. His was also the only Ferrari with disc brakes. With this more powerful engine, plus the discs, the Englishman hoped to overcome the advantage of the faster Moss disc-braked Vanwall.

"Our Ferraris handled much better with a full tank of gas," says Phil. "As the tank emptied, the cars would begin to oversteer, so I knew that my best bet was to go all-out from the start, since the Vanwalls tended to handle better as their tanks grew lighter. I would have a slight edge in the opening laps because of this difference. Actually, it would have been nice to have had a hundred-pound weight on board which could be cranked rearward as the gas load decreased. Anyhow, Moss qualified on the pole, with Mike just a bit over a second slower. I got seventh fastest time for row two."

Factory teams from BRM, Cooper and Lotus were also on hand, with several private Maseratis completing the Monza 21-car lineup. The rough, high-speed banking, used for the "Race of Two Worlds," was bypassed for this Italian Grand Prix, and only the 3.7-mile road circuit would be used. Despite this, tire wear was excessive, and was to plague Hill throughout the race.

As the Tri-color whipped down, Stewart Lewis-Evans put his green Vanwall neatly into the lead, but Phil stormed up from the second row to pass Lewis-Evans into the Curva Grande. (Hawthorn had slipped his clutch at the start—as he had done at Le Mans and in the GP of Germany—and this was to prove disastrous in the closing stages.) Moss was on Phil's tailpipe as the field headed for the always-dangerous Lesmo turn. Von Trips rammed Harry Schell's BRM at Lesmo, and both cars were destroyed in the crash, although their drivers escaped. The Trips Ferrari landed in a ditch after striking a tree, its chassis snapped in the center like a broken toy.

Hill was working desperately hard to hold off Moss as he maintained the lead, smoke pluming from his tires as he braked for the turns. Hawthorn was changing positions with Moss behind Hill's Ferrari, while Phil continued his role as team charger. On lap 4, however, Hill's left rear tire threw a tread, and he spun. Hawthorn inherited the front-running slot, Moss at his heels, while Hill pitted for a new wheel.

"I'd been so nervous at the beginning that I'd left my goggles up on my helmet," says Phil. "I pulled up the spare set which you're supposed to have around your neck. So there I was, with one pair up on the top of my helmet and the other pair over my eyes."

Hill's pit stop dropped him to tenth, but he was soon picking off car after car as he worked his way back toward the leaders, and by lap 15 he was seventh. Three laps later Moss was out of the contest with a seized gearbox; Hill—was sixth.

On lap 26, vigorously chasing Gregory's fifth-place Maserati, Phil set a new Monza lap record at 1:42.9—or 125 mph—which was to stand as the fastest time of the race. He soon passed the tiring Gregory, then moved into third on lap 30 behind the Vanwall of Lewis-

Evans. (Hawthorn was still setting the pace.)

"On lap 36, just past the halfway point, I had once more regained the lead," says Phil, "and Mike was in the pits changing tires. But my own tires were badly worn as a result of my having put such a strain on them, and within a couple of laps I was forced in for new rubber, which dropped me to fourth."

Gregory brought the Maser into the pits for tires (and to turn over to Carroll Shelby) on lap 47, and Brooks began putting the pressure on Hawthorn, with Hill closing behind them.

"After my second pit stop I kept getting all these signs about Brooks, and I was confused, figuring that maybe he was *behind* me instead of in front of me in overall elapsed time. First it was BROOKS–24, so I gave it a go. Next lap it was BROOKS–23, and I thought, Oh, hell, he's closing the gap!—and I *really* hung it out. Next lap it was BROOKS–21, and I thought, What's the use? and flubbed out a bit. Then, when I came around again, the pit gave me BROOKS–23, and I realized that Tony was up there ahead of me all the time. Pit signals can sometimes turn your thinking completely around!"

Lap 50 saw the Ferrari leading the Vanwall by only eight seconds, and Hawthorn found that he could do nothing to hold back Tony Brooks, since Mike was now suffering clutch trouble as a result of his starting grid error—and within four laps Brooks had nosed past the red Ferrari, dropping Hawthorn behind him.

Hill, in third, had been rapidly narrowing the gap which separated him from the two leaders when his foot slipped off the brake pedal just as he was entering the South Curve. His car spun, but he was soon away, without losing position.

In the closing laps, as Brooks consolidated his lead, Hill roared up behind the slowing Hawthorn, who threw out a hand to warn Phil not to pass. It was vital that Mike retain second in order to pick up the extra points against Moss, and Phil backed off sharply, almost stalling his engine, allowing his English teammate to cross the line four seconds ahead of him. Brooks was the victor, but in finishing with second position Hawthorn now led Moss in their fight for the World Championship by eight points.

The last Grand Prix of the season, at Casablanca on October 19, would settle the issue.

Hill's factory drive in Italy prompted the editor of *Automobile Year* to comment: "The real revelation of this race was the spectacular performance of Phil Hill. He showed us, here at Monza, that he has the makings of a great Formula 1 champion."

Enzo Ferrari was also impressed, and he guaranteed Phil a ride at Casablanca. A pair of Stateside sports car events intervened.

·　　·　　·　　·　　·

"At Watkins Glen, we ran what was called a *Formula Libre,* or Free Formula," says Hill, "and Joakim Bonnier brought over the ex-Fangio '57 Formula 1 Maserati GP machine. The rest of us had sports cars. Gurney had the 3.5 Ferrari Stirling had won with in Nassau, and George Constantine had an Aston DBR 2. I had a new short-wheelbase 4.1 Ferrari, and Bruce Kessler had the 3.8 I'd won Elkhart with in '57. Boy, that was a wild race!"

The 81-lap event began under cloudy skies, after a steady rain had soaked the tight 2.3-mile course. Hill gunned the 4.1 into an immediate lead, but the mud-and-water-slick road refused to provide a proper tire bite, and he slid into kneedeep grass before the first lap had ended, giving Constantine a chance to take the initiative. By the second lap Phil had worked up into fourth behind Bonnier. But the 4.1 spun off for a second time on the banked backstretch bend, dropping him to fifth.

By lap 12 Hill was up to the leaders, riding third behind Bonnier and Gurney, pressing hard to gain ground. On the next tour he nipped past Dan's 3.5, setting out to nail Bonnier's Formula 1 Maser. On lap 18 Phil had regained the lead, with the bearded Swede only inches behind him. Trying to establish a gap, Hill spun once more, allowing Bonnier to get past. Back on course, the Californian poured on the coal, yet spun again, giving second place to Gurney.

Within three laps he slammed by Gurney's Ferrari, eyes glued to the tail of Bonnier's Maserati. The talented Swedish pilot was opening up, breaking the lap record in his attempt to shake the dogged Californian.

But Hill could not match the roadholding qualities of the Grand Prix machine with his sports Ferrari, and on lap 53 he spun for the fifth time that afternoon, on the same banked bend, whirling tail-for-nose twice, then shooting off the road backward, just missing a solidly built fence, sliding for a full 75 feet down the muddy banking into the woods. Still, he would not abandon the chase. In a spray of mud from his churning wheels, Phil roared back onto the circuit, just ahead of Gurney. But his bid was over. What was later diagnosed as a loose bearing in the prop shaft retired the car in the 61st lap. An elated Bonnier won with a 97.45 mph average, a new closed-circuit road race record for the United States.

. . . . .

"Two weeks later I took the 4.1 to Riverside," says Hill. "This was touted as the biggest race ever to be held on the West Coast — and nearly all the top boys were there. Lance Reventlow had his Scarabs out, and Chuck Daigh in the five-and-a-half-liter job set a new course lap in qualifying at 2:04.3, which was damn fast. My best was 2:06, but it put me right next to him on the grid."

This FIA-approved event, the first of its kind on the Coast, was a joint venture of the California Sports Car Club and the United States Auto Club, and was backed by the Times-Mirror newspaper company, which arranged a purse of $14,500. Although Bonnier was on hand, with Salvadori of England, Behra of France, and an all-star U.S. roster including Shelby, Gurney, Gregory, Indy drivers Rathmann and Ruttman (trying their luck with sports cars), and young Lance Reventlow (who qualified third-fastest behind Hill), this affair turned into a two-man duel from the drop of the starter's flag: Hill vs. Daigh.

The desert heat was intense, hovering at 110 degrees, and the immense crowd flocked to the refreshment stands. (After the last paper cup was emptied the delighted concessionaires reported that they had sold 132,000 soft drinks and 84,000 bottles of beer!)

On lap 1 it was Hill by a coat of paint, then Daigh passed, Hill repassed, Daigh passed again. This process was repeated for lap after lap as the two cars thundered around the Riverside circuit, accelerating down the mile-long back straight at over 160 mph. The other competitors were lost behind them as their battle continued for 12 sizzling laps. Then Hill began to slow, his engine spitting mysteriously on the back stretch. On lap 24 he pitted to find out what was causing this sudden lack of power. As the hood was thrown open Hill stretched out on his back in the shade of the car while a pail of cooling water was thrown over him. Mechanics hurriedly checked his 4.1 Ferrari. Fuel pump! The engine was being starved out.

Phil took off again, but three more pit stops convinced him that the car was not operational and he retired it on lap 58, while Chuck Daigh scored an impressive victory with the all-American Scarab.

"The Grand Prix of Morocco was just a week after Riverside," Hill says, "so I took off for Casablanca to do what I could to help Mike cinch the '58 World Championship. Moss had to win the race and set fast time to get the title, but *only* if Mike finished third or worse. If Mike got first or second then he also got the title. Therefore, the Moroccan GP would provide the sport with a new World Champion, filling the vacancy left by Fangio."

•   •   •   •   •

The fast Ain-Diab circuit on the outskirts of Casablanca, almost five miles of sun-blistered, snaking road running along the beach fronting the white-capped Atlantic, then over the rolling hills and sand ridges, provided a dramatic setting for the tenth and last championship event of 1958. Arabs in long, flowing robes lined the course, adding a bizarre touch to the sight of the stark GP cars. It was again Ferrari vs. Vanwall, with BRM present to take advantage of any mistakes made, and it was again Phil Hill as Ferrari pace setter with orders to force Moss to overstress his Vanwall.

Practice was tense and hotly contested, with all five of the fastest drivers (Hawthorn, Moss, Lewis-Evans, Behra and Hill) within the same second. When King Mohammed asked to meet the competitors Hill was absent—swimming in the ocean, "loosening up" for the race — but he was in the cockpit and ready to go when the starting flag sent the field into action at 2:50 P.M.

The Moss-Hill battle, begun at Monza, was resumed at Morocco, as Phil stormed his Ferrari up from the second row to harry the rapid Englishman. As the pack streamed uphill, then down again along the Boulevard Panoramique, Hill was directly behind Moss, hugging the Vanwall along the Azemmour-Casablanca main road, maintaining the pressure as the road darted right toward the Sidi Abderhaman curve where the two cars were running wheel to wheel. As they streaked past the pits Hill had edged his Ferrari into the lead by a nose, but he could not hope to hold this position with his drum-braked machine against the disc brakes of Moss. On the second lap, at the end of the main straight, Phil braked too late and slid up the escape road, losing four seconds. Now it was Moss, Hawthorn and the BRM of Bonnier.

By lap 7 Hill had scrambled past Bonnier and his Ferrari team-mate to wedge his car into second behind Moss, who was stretching away at the head of the field. On lap 18, attempting to close on Moss, Phil set a new course record of 2:23.3 in his dedicated pursuit, but was unable to gain any ground on the flying green Vanwall. Still, if he could secure second position and cede this to Hawthorn as he had done at Monza, Mike could win the title.

Moss was going all out, and on lap 21 he set the day's fast time, 2:22.5, which was to stand, gaining him a vital point. His Vanwall teammate, Tony Brooks, had passed Hawthorn and it looked as though Stirling might pull it off by winning with fast time, while Brooks kept Hawthorn out of second.

Then Tony's Vanwall expired, his engine dumping oil on the circuit. A Cooper spun as a result, setting off a chain of accidents in which Gendebien's Ferrari flipped and was destroyed, injuring the Belgian. Lewis-Evans also crashed his Vanwall, and suffered fatal burns (dying in the hospital a week later).

On lap 35 the signal went out from the Ferrari pits: HAWT/HILL—meaning that Hawthorn, who was now 40 seconds behind the charging Californian, was to finish ahead of Hill. As it was still early in the race, with some 18 full laps to go, Phil misread the signal and failed to slow down. Tavoni grabbed the pit board and waved it frantically as Hill flashed by the pits on the subsequent lap, literally on his knees to the American.

Hill began easing off, and by lap 40 he allowed Hawthorn to pass into second, where Mike gingerly rode out the remainder of the race to become the 1958 World Champion, despite Stirling's Vanwall victory. In giving away second to his teammate, Hill had cinched the title for the blond Englishman. The final seasonal total: Hawthorn, 42, Moss, 41.

The year was over, and although Hill had firmly established himself as a superb Formula 1 contender (tying von Trips for seventh in point standings) the deaths of such stars as Musso, Collins and Lewis-Evans had proven that in the rarefied upper echelon of high-speed competition the risks are always very great.

Mike Hawthorn retired at season's end with a statement for the press: "I've accomplished what I set out to do in becoming the first British champion. And, in quitting, let me make a prediction: the combination of Phil Hill and Ferrari will be heard from over the coming seasons. I think Phil has an excellent chance of becoming World Champion—if his luck doesn't run out."

Three months later, in January of 1959, Hawthorn's own overstrained luck ran out on a narrow, rain-slick strip of public road near London. Mike's new Jaguar sedan slid out of control into a tree, claiming the speed king's life.

The World Champion's throne was again vacant.

CHAPTER SIXTEEN

Victory and Frustration

AWARE THAT HE had allowed a major talent to languish in the background, Enzo Ferrari quickly signed Phil Hill to a first-string contract for 1959. The American would drive in all championship Formula events as well as in the major international sports car races. And thanks in large part to Hill's active support, fellow Californian Dan Gurney was also added to the Ferrari ranks. Tempestuous and temperamental Jean Behra switched from BRM to the Italian stable, and the very fast dental surgeon from Britain, Tony Brooks, became Ferrari's No. 1 after Vanwall was announced as a nonstarter in '59. (Moss switched from Vanwall to Cooper-Climax). Talented Cliff Allison, also from Great Britain, completed the team.

"Our first go that season was Sebring in March," says Hill, "and this time all our cars had disc brakes. Still, we hadn't expected rain and didn't come with rain tires. This proved to be a serious error."

Practice sessions were conducted under appalling conditions, as the cars threw up long fantails of water around the circuit, wheels spinning in puddles as the drivers fought for control. In one of these sessions, after dark, a young auto salesman, E.P. Lawrence, who drove his Maserati strictly as a hobby, flipped and burned. Lawrence did not survive, and his fatal accident added to the general feeling of unease.

"Most courses drain," explains Phil, "but Sebring *held* the water, in puddles, and this made high-speed driving a gamble for all of us. Gendebien started in our No. 8 Ferrari, and when I took over we were in the lead. Then, at two o'clock, just four hours after the start, I heard a hell of a noise coming from the back end. The pinion bearing was shot — and there was nothing else to do but retire the car."

Tavoni, a wise race manager, realized that Hill and Gendebien were more experienced at Sebring than Gurney and Chuck Daigh, who were then leading in the No. 7 Ferrari. Rules permitted a driver change in an event of this kind, so Tavoni put out the COME IN signal for Daigh. Gendebien took over the Ferrari at 3 P.M. and rejoined the fight behind Moss, the second works Ferrari of Behra/Allison and the Porsche of Bonnier/von Trips.

"When I got the car Moss was no longer a worry," says Phil. "His car had been disqualified, and although he later took over one of Cunningham's Lister-Jags he was too far back to challenge. It had begun to rain heavily, and almost everybody began slowing down."

Hill didn't slow down; he overwhelmed the Porsche, then closed on Allison who was having a difficult time steering in the wet. By 5 P.M. Phil was leading, and when he handed back to Gendebien he had opened a full lap on the Behra/Allison Ferrari.

"I was pushing pretty hard," he admits, "and there must have been a dozen times when I felt the car skidding away from me. Every time it happened I was pretty frightened. The rain at Sebring was monstrous, worse than at Le Mans, and a hundred miles per hour on a course like this is like driving a standard car flat-out on ice. Anyway, we won, with our other team car second. Porsches were third, fourth and fifth."

As Gendebien flashed the car past the stands on the final lap Hill ran to the edge of the pit area, holding a board above his head. On it he had scrawled, in yellow chalk, BRAVO GEND!

This race had an amusing aftermath. When the winning Ferrari was wheeled back to the garage after its excursion down Victory Lane, mechanics discovered that overenthusiastic fans had taken a few souvenirs. Missing: the car's enamel nameplate, the oil-filler cap, the rearview mirror, the shifting knob, the fire extinguisher—as well as the spare wheel!

*   *   *   *   *

Phil's initial Formula 1 race of the season, at Silverstone in May, was not a points-counting championship event, serving mainly as a warm-up to the more important Grandes Epreuves, the first of which was scheduled for Monte Carlo a week later.

"Brooks had the other Ferrari at Silverstone," says Hill, "and neither of us had any luck. Tony didn't finish and I got fourth. Masten

Gregory piled up a Lister-Jag in the sports car race there, but managed to jump out as it hit the bank. Shelby drove one of the new F1 Astons, and blew the engine near the close of our race. Otherwise, he would have beaten me — but no one goes *really* fast at Silverstone except the Englishmen."

• • • • •

When the Ferrari team arrived at Monte Carlo, on the sunbright French Riviera, for the 17th running of the classic "round-the-houses" Grand Prix de Monaco, it was apparent that an all-out Italian effort was being made to win this difficult event. Brooks, Behra and Hill were each assigned a new coil-sprung, disc-braked, Dino-engined V-6 model, with the usual long Ferrari noses trimmed and larger radiators added to combat the heat of this tight circuit. Each car was equipped with a five-speed gearbox, which would be put to a severe test, since it is estimated that some 1800 gear changes must be made (one every five seconds) in this 100-lap "race of a thousand corners." Allison was there with the only Formula 2 Ferrari, ready to battle the F2 Porsche of von Trips and Halford's F2 Lotus.

"The main thing wrong with our cars at Monaco," Phil says, "was the incredibly poor cockpit ventilation. We sat deep down in these high-sided, wraparound cockpits, and the heat was *terrific* — to say nothing of the engine fumes which gathered in there as you drove. This was my first trip to Monaco, and I found this freak circuit took every ounce of my concentration. You'd never expect GP cars to run on a course like this anywhere in Europe. But this was Monaco."

Indeed, Hill was correct in dubbing this a freak circuit. Just under two miles in length, it begins with a short, fierce run along the quay, fronting the harbor. An abrupt right-hand hairpin turn at the Gasworks takes the field back behind the pits on the straight along Boulevard Albert I to Sainte Devote corner, then up the steeply climbing Avenue de Monte Carlo through a brief series of Esses to Casino Corner, downhill to the pretzel-shaped Station Hairpin, with the sharp descent ending at the right turn onto Boulevard Louis II, then a dip into the dark mouth of the Tunnel (where only the bravest maintain full throttle) to a fast chicane leading out along the quay again to the final, sharp left-hander onto the short pit straight. Wooden barricades, curbs, sandbags, stone walls, fencing and the waiting Mediterranean flank the circuit, exacting a heavy toll each year — and simply to finish at Monaco is a laudable accomplishment.

Moss (Cooper-Climax), Behra, Brabham (Cooper-Climax) and Brooks were the four fastest qualifiers, with Hill's Ferrari in for fifth, putting him in the second row of the 16-car grid. Prior to the race a 2-lap demonstration run was made (in new Formula Junior cars) by seven of "yesterday's champions," all retired, but more than capable of showing their splendid form. Chiron, Farina, Taruffi, de Graffenried, Prince Bira, Etancelin and Fangio seemed to thoroughly enjoy themselves in the little single-seaters, the happy crowd responding with enthusiastic acclaim.

Sunday's race, for 100 laps, began with the drop of the red-and-white flag of Monaco — and Behra forced the stub nose of his Ferrari around the Gasworks hairpin, with Moss, Brabham and Hill right behind him. The race quickly developed into a bitter two-man duel between Behra and Moss, with the Frenchman deliberately blocking the Briton in order to hold him back. Von Trips had written off all three Formula 2 cars when he spun out on the second lap, involving Allison and Halford, and the sad trio trudged back to the pits while the two-way battle progressed up front. After much fist-shaking, Moss took advantage of an opening on the 21st lap and snaked his Cooper into first. Three laps later, as a penalty for his over-revving, Behra's engine exploded and two of the four Ferraris were out. Brabham was then second.

Back in the field, Hill was riding third, learning the circuit, but already beginning to suffer from heat and cockpit fumes. Monaco-veteran Trintignant, in a Cooper, had been gradually overhauling the American, until forced to pit with a sticking throttle, allowing Tony Brooks to move up behind his Ferrari teammate. At 30 laps Schell had displaced Brooks into fourth, and was coming on quite strongly.

On lap 37 Hill overcooked things coming into the Casino Square at the rightangle turn just beyond the Hôtel de Paris and spun tail-first into the straw, stalling his engine. Shouting "keep back!" at the spectators who surged toward him (outside help was cause for immediate disqualification), he got his car rolling, leaped into the cockpit and fired the engine, getting away just as Schell and Brooks rounded the turn. Upset by his spin, Hill gave way to both drivers and they passed on lap 38. Six laps later he spun again, in the same spot, obviously affected by the rising exhaust fumes, his head lolling back and to one side, mouth open for air. Up front, Moss had things all his own way, leading Jack Brabham by a very healthy margin, with Brooks a distant third. Schell clouted the straw bales at the Casino, then abandoned the fight shortly thereafter, leaving a pool of oil behind him on the turn.

Hill came boiling around while dry concrete was being sprinkled over the oil, and the hapless Californian spun for the third time, bursting a large paper bag of powdery concrete in his wild passage and buckling both left-hand wheels. When he emerged from the pits with new ones Phil had dropped to sixth, just ahead of McLaren. Only seven cars were then left in the race.

Lap 81 saw a dramatic change in the standings, since Moss was suddenly out with rear-axle failure. Brabham inherited the lead which he held to the flag, winning his first Grande Epreuve. Brooks got second, despite the fact that he was vomiting in the cockpit during the closing stages, violently ill from the noxious fumes. The veteran Trintignant was third. Hill finished in fourth, driving to the limit in the final laps, but unable to catch the cool Frenchman. The Coopers of McLaren and Salvadori were the only other cars running as the checker fell, ending this race of surprises.

"I began doubting myself all over again after Monaco," Hill admits. "I was very depressed over my ragged showing there—and I wondered if perhaps Ferrari had not been right in keeping me out of GP cars for so long. Maybe I just wasn't capable of top performance in a Grand Prix machine. Also, what Mike had said about my having a good chance for the World Championship didn't help my state of mind. I function best when I'm doing something better than what is expected of me, as at Monza in '58. No one expected me to stay ahead of Moss for four laps in my first Ferrari F1 ride, so I just went out and did it, not thinking too much about who was watching me and who wasn't. But now it was different. I had become a full-time GP driver and every race counted."

On May 24 Hill was scheduled to drive in the Targa Florio, but sat out the entire affair in the pits when Gendebien was forced to retire their car on the first lap with a broken differential. Tavoni then decided to switch Hill and Gendebien to the Gurney Ferrari, but it too went out with rear-axle failure. Cliff Allison had demolished the practice car on a stone bridge, and Behra rolled the lead Ferrari into a ditch during the fourth lap of the race, ending all Italian chances. It was a sweep for Porsche, with the little German bombs finishing 1-2-3-4, scoring all the points in this second race of the season counting toward the Manufacturers' Championship.

The Dutch Grand Prix, at Zandvoort, was next on May 31, and all the factory teams were there to dispute the issue: Ferrari, BRM, Aston Martin, Cooper and Lotus. However, it was soon painfully evident that the Ferraris were not handling with the opposition. Behra managed to make row 2 and Brooks row 3, while an unhappy Hill sat in row 5 at the back of the grid. Despite involving himself in a brisk battle for fourth in the race, Phil was beset with an ill-handling machine, finishing in sixth behind Behra. After 11 years of unstinting effort, a BRM came home winner, with Jo Bonnier at the wheel. It was a very popular and long-overdue victory for the stubborn British marque, and also marked Bonnier's first major GP triumph. Brabham was second in the swift little Cooper.

. . . . .

Phil motored back to the Nürburgring, the scene of his international team debut in '56, to handle a new 12-cylinder Testa Rossa with Gendebien for the third round of the Manufacturers' Championship. Porsche led on points, as a result of Ferrari's debacle in the Targa, but the machines from Maranello promised to give a good account of themselves on the Ring, if properly set up for the tortuous circuit. Spring and shock absorber settings were of prime importance here, and much "chassis tuning" was done by Ferrari mechanics, with each driver lending his own opinion as to what was comfortable.

"On my car, the rear shocks were more powerful than the coil springs," says Phil, "so the suspension was staying compressed, as if on a rachet. On the fast bend near Flugplatz I lost it, spinning into a thick hedge at over 100. That hedge saved my life, acting as an absorbent, but bending up the car. Anyway, I had a guilt complex all the way back to the pits—until they verified this suspension problem. We had it rectified before the race, but the car never really handled the way it should have."

That evening, after the official teams had left the Ring, Hill took out a private Porsche for a quick lap or two, telling his companion that you can notice things at night you'd miss in the daylight, and that he wanted to see for himself if the long pit straight was smoother on the left than it was on the right—as he'd been told. It was, and Phil made a mental note of the fact. This might mean an extra split second in the upcoming 1000-kilometer race.

In addition to Porsche, the main thorn in Ferrari's side was a lone green Aston DBR1 in the hands of Stirling Moss. (Jack Fairman was listed as co-driver, but most of the wheelwork would be done by Moss.) The Aston had won last year's race on the Ring, with Moss up, and Stirling was out for a repeat victory. His usual lightning start got him off the line into an early lead, with Gurney and Hill trailing in two of the Testa Rossas.

Moss was taking full advantage of the Aston's superior roadability (though the Italian cars were a shade faster on the straights) and he built up a fat lead, flinging the green car around the circuit's 174 curves with the polished skill of a master. No one could catch him, though Gurney and Hill were certainly trying. Phil took over second on lap 11 of this 44-lapper as Gurney pitted to turn over to Cliff Allison. By lap 14 Hill was in for Gendebien—just as Tony Brooks arrived to hand over to Behra. Chaos reigned in the Ferrari pits with mechanics bowing under the shouted orders of team manager Tavoni.

On lap 17, after establishing a huge lead over the Ferraris, Moss pitted and Jack Fairman vaulted into the cockpit. After a wheel change he was away, still well in command, with no red cars in sight. Five laps later, however, after steadily losing ground, poor Fairman encountered rain and promptly slid off the road, putting the Aston in a ditch. It took him seven full minutes to extract the car and get back to the pits. Gendebien was then first, with Behra second and the Porsche of Maglioli in third.

Moss was desperate, and the moment Fairman arrived he took over the wheel and ripped away after Maglioli, passing the silver Porsche in short order. Lap 27 found Behra first with Moss already past Gendebien and closing. Within another two tours of the Ring the Aston once more led the Ferraris. Moss was in top form, driving superbly.

Hill rejoined the race, and on lap 31 scrambled past the Brooks/Behra car to move into second. Three laps more and Moss had given the wheel to Fairman, who was then 98 seconds ahead of Hill's car. Urged on by the pits, Phil began closing the gap, gaining no less than 50 seconds in one 14-mile lap! Fairman was no match for the Californian and Hill swept into the lead on the 35th tour as Jack obeyed pit orders and brought in the car for a frantic Moss. Before he had fully cleared the cockpit, Fairman was replaced by Moss, who gunned furiously onto the course, some 22 seconds behind Hill's disappearing Ferrari.

Phil was driving on the limit in his efforts to hold the Englishman at bay, but to no avail. On lap 39 the two cars were nose-to-tail, with Moss diving in to pass on the inside of the North Turn. Hill kept him back, but the green nose stayed glued to his rear deck. On lap 40, with just four more tours left in the race, Moss edged past the fighting American, holding his lead to the flag.

Moss had won in superb fashion, but the Hill/Gendebien car was just 41 seconds behind after more than seven and a half hours of speed, with the other works Ferrari of Brooks/Behra taking third away from Maglioli's Porsche.

Round four in the battle for the Manufacturers' Championship was due to be fought out at Le Mans, on June 20-21, and again Phil Hill was destined to be one of the stars of the show.

CHAPTER SEVENTEEN

Breakdowns, Behra–and a Bash at Lisbon

SINCE THEY HAD WON brilliantly in '58, Hill and Olivier Gendebien were the odds-on favorites at Le Mans in 1959, particularly in view of the fact that the Ferraris were quickest around the 8.3-mile Sarthe circuit (Dan Gurney having recorded fastest time in one of the factory 3-liter models). The Astons and Porsches were strongly in the lists, hoping to end the race with a points lead over the Italian cars, and Moss was naturally the man to watch in the British camp.

Handling problems were still the chief complaint in the Ferrari pits at Le Mans, but added to this was the fact that the Italian machines were undergeared; over-revving became a common problem on the long Mulsanne straight.

"The rev limit, in practice, was set at 7400 rpm," says Hill, "and when I got back from my session with the 'spy' needle reading 7900 Tavoni read the tach and exploded into furious Italian. I told him I hadn't over-revved, that the needle had been at 7900 when I got the car, and Gendebien backed me up, admitting he had been at fault in this case. Then one of the mechanics scratches his head and mutters something to the effect that he thought he had set back the needle after Gendebien's run and that I must have over-revved *this* time. Tavoni explodes again—and I just grabbed my helmet and walked away. Then Dan comes in with the tach at 8600. Said he missed a gear shift. Tavoni is furious, shouting at Dan. Then he starts to yell at Scarlatti who was also above the limit. Meanwhile Behra is going from one mechanic to another trying to explain what is wrong with his car. Nobody listens. They just tell him to get in and *drive*. It was a madhouse!"

At 4 P.M. the flag dropped and the 24-Hour race began—with Moss taking his usual lead from Gendebien. Behra, angry at his treatment in practice, got a late start and ignored Tavoni's careful instructions not to rev above 7500. He put his boot into the floor, and the needle jumped to 8800 as he howled past car after car in his pursuit of Moss. Soon the two drivers were running in close company, far ahead of the field, and by the 17th tour Behra had passed the green Aston to take the lead. But the aggressive Frenchman had asked too much of his engine, and the car eventually expired. Moss, too, suffered a similar fate when a cylinder let go in the Aston.

"I'd passed Fairman who was driving the Moss car into second before they retired," says Hill, "but I soon began having my own troubles. The carburetors were flooding and I pitted twice to have them corrected, dropping us to eighth. By midnight, though, with Moss out, we were back in second with the works Aston of Roy Salvadori and Carroll Shelby ahead of us."

At 2 A.M. the lead Aston pitted for fuel and brakes, moving the Hill/Gendebien Ferrari into the front slot. At half distance (4 A.M.), with 12 hours to go, Hill was two full laps ahead of the Aston. Another hour and Hill turned over to Gendebien, with a staggering *four-lap* lead.

The hours passed, and the Aston continued to fall back. It seemed as though a repeat victory was assured for the Californian and his Belgian co-driver— but a race is never won until the checker falls. Which proved to be true at Le Mans in 1959.

"I was sleeping behind the pits when Gendebien brought in the car at 11 A.M. with overheating problems," says Hill. "The fuel-pump pressure was increased, in the hope that this might take care of the trouble. Olivier took one lap, then pitted again, while the oil level was checked out and water poured on the fuel pump to cool it. This was all useless, and Gendebien went out, motoring slowly in the hope of finishing, while they woke me up with the bad news. I was there when Olivier finally came in at 11:45, shrugged, and got out of the car. He had no water at all in the radiator due to a leak in the cylinder liner, so—with just four hours to go—we were out."

Their gallant 20-hour battle had ended in defeat, but another American, Hill's old rival Shelby, won at Le Mans (with Salvadori) for Aston Martin. No works Ferraris or Porsches finished the event, and the steadily driven Trintignant/Frère Aston took second. Four privately driven GT Ferraris saved the honor of Maranello by finishing 3-4-5-6, thus putting the Italians ahead by two points. The Tourist Trophy, in early September, would decide the championship. A trio of Formula 1 races filled the two-month interim, and Enzo Ferrari turned his full attention to these.

·   ·   ·   ·   ·

The first, at Reims, was the French Grand Prix, and Ferrari hoped to cure his handling problems in order to win the day on this famed Champagne circuit. Actually, top speed was more important at Reims, and a GP car, properly geared and tuned, could climb up to 180 mph on the long three-mile back straight before having to brake sharply for the Thillois hairpin. The factory sent its largest F1 team, no less than five cars, to the French Grand Prix, backing up Brooks, Behra and Hill with Gendebien and "rookie" Dan Gurney. (Despite his having upended a GP car in practice just a week before Reims, the young American was entrusted with a new experimental-engined Ferrari, though warned to hold his rev limit well down in the race.)

The summer heat of July flared out of a burning sky, and since no shade was to be found on the circuit, flanked only by rolling wheat fields, the 100-plus temperature turned cockpits into ovens, melted the tar surfacing and loosened stones which became airborne when kicked up by churning wheels. In practice, Tony Brooks proved that all of the Ferrari bugs had been removed by screaming over the course at 2:19.4 (for a new record). Handling had been greatly improved by modifications to the rear suspension, and Hill was almost able to match his British teammate by posting a time only four-tenths of a second slower. He thus shared the first row, with Brabham's agile Cooper (2:19.7) sandwiched between the fierce red cars. Hill's time had pushed Moss (in a BRM) back into row 2, with Behra, who had insisted on taking over Gendebien's car at the last moment. Gurney and Gendebien were in the fifth row, behind several Coopers and BRMs.

After the final session a candlelight champagne dinner was attended by the driven (held in the famed champagne caves) and much talk centered around the fat first-place money, totaling some $25,000, which would be split between driver and factory. Reims, therefore, was well worth winning.

On Sunday, July 5, the sun lanced down, broiling hot, and the drivers who assembled on the grid were busily sponging themselves; drinking bottles were placed close at hand; buckets of water were used to wet down coveralls, and the general atmosphere was one of great discomfort. This 50-lap race would be a grueling test, and each of the 21 drivers prepared to battle the intense heat as well as his fellow competitors.

At the flag, Brooks got away to a very smooth, fast start in his Dino V-6 Ferrari, and led Brabham and Hill neatly through the first corner. Moss and Gregory moved up rapidly, passing Hill in a shower of loose gravel. A sizable stone slashed Phil's nose, and he felt blood trickling down his face from the cut.

"At first it seemed as though I'd lost my entire nose," Hill says, "because it was numbed from the blow; I couldn't feel it! I thought of stopping at the pits, but decided to go ahead. Actually, the cut wasn't serious, just bothersome."

Hill dropped to fifth as the hail of stones continued. Gregory was struck on the forehead and dizzily pitted, unable to go on. On lap 10 Hill was still fifth, but was pressing the Moss BRM. Soon Gurney was out with a stone through his radiator; and this same malady eliminated Graham Hill's Lotus. Behra had stalled on the grid, getting away in last place; by the 20th lap he had thundered up to third and was attempting to outbrake Brabham into second when he spun, losing two positions. The EZ sign was out at the pits, but Behra ignored it and planted his foot squarely on the floor, equaling the lap record by straining his engine beyond its limits.

Hill joined the parade of drivers who were spinning on the loose cobblestones at Thillois. The road tar had melted on this tricky hairpin, and several competitors came to grief there. Phil whirled about, quickly jammed his foot on the gas to avoid a stall, skidding back to the circuit in a spray of dirt and gravel, his Ferrari howling after the leaders following a loss of only three seconds.

A few laps later, mixing it with Brabham and Behra, he found his groove blocked by the other two machines and took the escape road.

Braking, he geared down, reversed direction and blasted past both drivers within a few hundred feet of the turn, wedging himself firmly in second behind the flying Brooks.

On lap 31 Behra was out with a blown engine. He had broken a piston in his mad scramble up from the rear of the pack and had refused to slow down even when smoke began seeping from the hood of his car. The expression on Tavoni's face indicated that there would be words after the race.

Brooks was pulling away each lap as Hill grew dizzy from the incredible cockpit heat (estimated to be well above 150 degrees!). The American was literally standing up in the Ferrari as he took the long back straight, gasping for air. Moss, in the slower BRM, made his bid and moved up rapidly on Hill, now in no condition to stave off a challenge. Phil was overshooting his brake marks, sliding sideways on several of the curves, half spinning, driving on the ragged edge of control as Moss carved down the gap between them.

Just eight laps from the finish, with Hill well in his sights, Moss made a serious error and spun at Thillois. The clutch had failed on his BRM and this did not help the situation as he slid off the circuit. The engine stalled; Moss pushed. It would not restart. Exhausted, he accepted outside help, disqualifying himself, and motored sadly back to the pits. Brooks, who had never been headed, won the race at the impressive average of almost 128 mph, with the half-conscious Hill finishing 28 seconds behind him ahead of Jack Brabham. Having driven his finest GP race, the Californian had to be lifted out of his cockpit and revived before appearing with Brooks for press photographs and congratulations. (Brabham climbed out of his Cooper without aid, then collapsed to the ground.)

Back in the pits, an angry Tavoni berated Jean Behra for "deliberately destroying" his car, and the hot-blooded Frenchman slapped the team manager's face — resulting in his dismissal. Behra had crashed in the Targa, blown his engine at Monaco and at Le Mans — and had now repeated the process here at Reims. Enzo Ferrari wanted nothing more to do with him.

"Behra had never been happy with us," Hill says. "He resented Brooks as the No. 1, was uncomfortable at the performance of a newcomer like Dan Gurney, complained about always being given the slowest car—which was simply not true—and lost his temper more often than the Italians, which is going some!"

•   •   •   •   •

A strike at the Maranello factory prevented Ferrari from entering the British Grand Prix on July 18, and it was won by Jack Brabham. Moss finished his first GP of the season in trailing the Cooper ace across the line with his BRM.

•   •   •   •   •

"We were all set for the Grand Prix of Germany," says Hill, "and although none of us looked forward to racing at the Avus track we knew that our chances for success were excellent there. About 100,000 spectators, from East and West Berlin, converged on the circuit, and in direct contrast to Reims the weather was dark with heavy clouds building up."

The Avus circuit, chosen in 1959 for "political reasons" over the more suitable and much finer Nürburgring, was basically another Monza, *sans* road course. The five-mile layout in West Berlin consisted of two parallel straights separated by a 50-mph hairpin at one end and a steep, bricked banking at the other. The Ferraris would obviously set the pace in a race such as this, with the smaller cars hoping to tuck in behind and ride their slipstream.

Although no longer connected with a factory team, Jean Behra was at Avus with two Porsches, a single-seater F2 of his own design for the *Grösser Preis von Deutschland* and another sports RSK model for the race preceding the Grand Prix. This event should never have been run, since it began in the rain, and water streamed down the slanted brick banking like a coating of oil. First a Porsche driver spun off the bank, across the double-Autobahn and into a concrete wall. Then another Porsche slid to the top of the bricks, disappearing from sight over the banking. Both drivers escaped with their lives, but as the dangerous contest continued disaster was in the air. On the fourth lap, Behra's furiously driven RSK lost traction on the bricks, spun backward over the lip of the banking, cut itself nearly in half on a concrete blockhouse, pitching its driver into a flagpole. Behra, who had survived over a dozen serious crashes in his hazardous career, died instantly in this one.

The little Frenchman's death cast a dark shadow over the following day's Grand Prix, and the usual light banter and horseplay were missing as the teams assembled on the grid. Hill was puffing nervously on a cigarette, and no one was smiling. The event was to be run in two 30-lap heats, in order to save tires, and the great fear was rain. The sky was still cloudy, but by noon the rain had ceased and the track was dry by race time.

"Dan seemed to take to this banked type of high-speed competition," Hill says, "and his practice time had been faster than mine. Once we got going I tried to stay with him but looked down at my tach and read the needle: 8800. Which was 500 into the red. I figured the engine would blow if I kept up like this, so I dropped back into fourth, letting Tony and Dan go. Masten Gregory was chasing them both in his Cooper, sticking right up there with the Ferraris until his car finally just *exploded* and he was through for the day. Moss had dropped out early. So I was third at the end of the first heat."

Phil discovered that his rev counter was faulty, and that it had been registering some 500 rpm more than he was actually using, thus explaining why the other Ferraris were able to move away without engine strain. Knowing this, he took the lead in the last heat, ceding it to Brooks and coming across the line for second just ahead of Gurney. The opposition fell by the wayside and it was what one journalist termed "a Ferrari walkaway" at flagfall with the Italian cars taking their lap of honor in line abreast, peeling down off the banking like a trio of metal birds as the contest ended.

•   •   •   •   •

Stirling Moss finally overcame his seasonal jinx at the Grand Prix of Portugal in late August by running away with the event in his Cooper-Climax. Brooks hated this twisting tree-and-curb-lined circuit at Lisbon, and finished a poor ninth in his Ferrari. Gurney saved the day for Maranello by taking third behind fellow American Masten Gregory, who drove a fine, spirited race to capture second overall.

"I had nothing but trouble down in Portugal," says Hill. "Our cars were literally jumping out from under us, and none of us made the top rows. I was in the third row with Dan, and Tony was behind both of us. With brand-new tires on my car I couldn't do much with it on the opening laps, taking an escape road on lap 2. Then, four laps later, I came boiling around this blind corner and there was Graham Hill's Lotus broadside across the road. He'd burst his oil cooler and the stuff had sprayed his rear wheels causing him to spin, mount the bank, then slide down directly into my groove. There wasn't a thing I could do but hit him."

Hill was thrown face-first into his steering wheel, getting his second bloody nose of the season, and groggily managed to jam the gear lever into first, applying enough power to move the wrecked Ferrari off the circuit, parking it for the afternoon on a side road. The Lotus had been shunted aside in the crash and was no longer a hazard, and the two Hills counted themselves fortunate to have escaped serious injury.

Brabham was next to crash and he was thrown into the path of Gregory's Cooper. The Kansan braked sharply and missed Brabham, who crawled to the grass verge and safety.

Hill's gloomy prediction after practicing on the twisting circuit ("If one of us doesn't kill himself on this course it will be a miracle") had almost proven to be true, but the race drew to its close without a fatal incident.

．　　　．　　　．　　　．　　　．

The Tourist Trophy at Goodwood during the first week in September was the last event of '59 counting toward the Manufacturers' Championship, and all three competing teams, Ferrari, Aston Martin and Porsche, were out in force. Each factory wanted the title badly, but the Astons were favored since they were on home ground. The Goodwood circuit, with its many fast bends, was laid out on the perimeter of an ex-RAF airdrome in Sussex, and was poorly marked. Hill and Gurney attempted to learn it in a sports Riley; then Brooks, who was quite familiar with the course, took them around in his Testa Rossa, pointing out the fastest line through the corners. Practice found the Ferraris back to their old tricks, handicapped by excessive understeer, and the drivers were discouraged by their performance.

In this six-hour contest, which evolved into a game of musical chairs, Moss was first away in a green Aston, and hummed into a nice lead. Hill lasted less than one lap as his engine dropped a valve. He brought the sick car into the pits, disgusted at the fact that he had been denied a chance to drive, but Tavoni told him to be patient, that he would put Hill in the Gendebien car. This was done but Hill found that the seating was not right for him and he pulled a muscle in his back attempting to adjust. Then Allison took out the car, finally handing it over to Brooks in the closing stages.

Moss also switched cockpits, when his Aston (with Roy Salvadori still aboard) caught fire in the pits, due to sloppy refueling. Salvadori leaped out, coveralls blazing, as the car roared into flame, gutting the entire Aston pit area. He rolled on the ground to douse the flames, suffering minor burns. Meanwhile Jack Fairman was waved in and Moss took off in the second works Aston previously driven by Shelby, which was then running third.

After his fine race in Portugal, Masten Gregory was pushing hard at Goodwood and his brakes failed as he sailed into a sharp curve. The Tojeiro-Jaguar continued straight on into the bank, demolishing itself and tossing Gregory 60 feet from the wreckage. He was hospitalized with a broken leg and shoulder.

"Moss took the lead," says Hill, "and nobody could touch him. Bonnier and von Trips got second, with Tony chasing them like mad to the flag. So Aston Martin got the title in '59 by two points over us and three points over Porsche. The funny thing was, in that pit fire, a whole briefcase full of money burned up—so it cost Aston a little *extra* to win."

———————————

CHAPTER EIGHTEEN

A Season Ends at Sebring

B ACK AT MONZA, the scene of his first factory ride in Formula 1, Hill proved the speed of his '59 Ferrari by breaking his own lap record of the previous year (1:42.9) with a qualifying time of 1:41.2 — but eight other drivers also succeeded in bettering the old mark, and Phil found himself in row 2 on the grid behind Moss, Brooks and Brabham. Gurney was next to him, with the Gendebien and Allison Ferraris behind them.

Enzo himself was in the pits during these qualifying sessions, and in fielding five cars he was making an all-out effort to overcome the nimble little Coopers of Moss and Brabham.

The Grand Prix pattern had become quite clear: the most powerful machine was the Ferrari, but due to weight and handling problems this top speed was overcome by the ultralight rear-engined Coopers, powered by the Coventry Climax "firepump" engines. It took strength and fortitude to wrestle a Ferrari around a turn, while the little Coopers seemed to skim around on rails. At Monza, for example, tire wear on the Ferraris was something fierce, and the drivers were told that tire stops would be a necessity during the 72-lap race. Brabham's Cooper was using up considerable rubber, since the Australian utilized a "dirt-track" technique on the corners, while Moss had installed knock-offs on the rear to replace the usual Cooper bolt-on wheels, and it was assumed he also expected to pit for fresh tires before the end of the contest.

Tony Brooks cooked his clutch at the flag and was out immediately, but Hill and Gurney forged up to tackle the two Coopers, Phil passing Moss coming out of Lesmo and Dan taking Brabham as they completed lap 2. Moss seemed content to let Hill pace him, while Dan was closely shadowing the Englishman, and this lineup continued with all four cars running in tight formation. Moss was slipstreaming Hill as much as possible, saving his tires, and the Californian could not shake the Cooper despite establishing a new record (1:40.4) on lap 32, which was to stand for the race.

"They called me in for rear tires on the next tour," says Phil, "and I lost 30 seconds in the pits. Moss took off like fury and opened up 22 additional seconds, so that I was nearly a minute behind when I got going again."

Ferrari then called in their other three team cars, one per lap, for new rubber, allowing Brabham to ease off and Moss to gain a substantial lead unpressed by the opposition. Hill closed the gap by 12 seconds as the race wound on, but it was apparent that Stirling had things well in hand, and that his tires would now last the distance.

Moss won the Italian Grand Prix by a comfortable margin over Hill. Brabham was third, his tires badly worn, with the three Ferraris of Gurney, Allison and Gendebien filling out the top six places.

Hill had driven well and last, and might have won his first Grand Prix if the Ferrari pit strategy had been anything less than catastrophic. Denis Jenkinson, the noted British journalist, acidly commented: "At Monza Scuderia Ferrari made one of their biggest tactical errors ever, and they have made some pretty big ones. They had five cars ranged against Moss, yet they *let* him win. Ferrari made the big mistake of withdrawing all their forces at once, leaving Moss to tour at his ease and save rubber. Had they allowed Hill (or Gurney) to go on nonstop it would have meant that Moss would have had to go at the same pace, using up his tires. Had he then made a stop, which was likely, the other Ferrari could have won."

•   •   •   •   •

Phil still had another GP race to be run that season, at Sebring in mid-December (the first Grand Prix of the United States), but his year in Europe was over and he headed for the United States and another speed attempt at Bonneville.

"I was assigned the same MG streamliner Moss and I had driven in August of '57," explains Hill. "The only exterior change was the removal of the stabilizer tail fin. I met Captain George Eyston at the flats on October 5, and although I was somewhat bothered by the lack of shoulder harness and roll bar I had no trouble—and everything went off without a hitch. This time we were after several Class E records, from one kilometer to ten miles. And we got all of them, under official FIA timing."

Hill's top speed in the EX181 was 254.9 mph, boosting the previous mark set by Moss by almost 10 mph.

•   •   •   •   •

Phil drove in California that same month, October, at the Riverside Grand Prix for sports cars, and almost washed out his Ferrari in practice. He was handling a 3-liter model, and in his eagerness to qualify faster than Ginther, Gurney and Moss (the hot three) he throttled too rapidly into the first turn and sideswiped the steel guardrail, flattening one side of his mount and bending two wheels. In the race itself, despite the memory of his rail encounter, he engaged Richie Ginther's 4.1 Ferrari in a duel for the front position, while Moss in a 4.2-liter Aston Martin futilely chased both of them, spinning into the dirt on lap 11. By the 26th round Stirling's oil pressure was gone and the Briton was out.

Ginther was next, blowing his engine on lap 35, while Gurney never got into the fight at all, having been rammed on the starting grid. Hill coasted to a $7500 victory with no other serious challengers, breaking what some papers were terming "his California jinx."

•   •   •   •   •

"Then I went to Nassau for the Speed Week doings," says Phil, "where I won the all-Ferrari race and took second behind Constantine's Aston Martin in the main go. Moss blew up again with the 4.2 Aston after charging up into second, and I just kept plugging along till the checker. After the race I packed up and took off for Sebring."

•   •   •   •   •

The United States Grand Prix for Formula 1, at Sebring, Florida, was to decide the 1959 World Championship. It would also provide Stateside spectators with their first look at genuine Grand Prix racing since the pre-war days of the Vanderbilt Cup. Depending upon their performances in this event, any one of three drivers, Brabham, Moss or Brooks, could win the title—and although Brabham led with 31 points, and was rated favorite, the two British aces were very much in the running. Hill was only three points behind Brooks when the teams came to Sebring but he was beyond any chance of taking the crown, even if he won and set the fastest lap. His main job at this final GP of the season would be as a middleman; if Brooks got the lead Hill would attempt to wedge himself in second and help his teammate by holding off Moss and Brabham. At least this was the general plan. Von Trips (having rejoined the team after a stint with Porsche) and Cliff Allison were also instructed to block the Coopers if possible.

Practice confirmed Ferrari's fears: the Coopers were faster on this airport circuit, and both Moss and Brabham made the front row. Brooks made row 2, while the other three Ferraris were sitting back in row 3, side by side. Hill's car had been painted blue-and-white, since he was on home soil, but he had not been happy with it in qualifying runs.

"I didn't last long in that race," Phil says. "By lap 10 I was out with clutch and brake trouble. Allison also pitted with his clutch gone on lap 26, and Tony got shunted by Trips on the first round—which pretty well took care of our team! Brooks was never able to get near the leaders and wound up in third. Moss retired on lap 6 with a broken transmission and Brabham led going into the final lap, then ran out of gas and had to push his car the last 800 yards, while Bruce McLaren won. Still, when he crossed that line, Brabham became World Champion."

The final point standing for 1959:

> *Jack Brabham* *31*
> *Tony Brooks* *27*
> *Stirling Moss* *25½*
> *Phil Hill* *20*

CHAPTER NINETEEN

From Argentina to Monte Carlo

A NGERED BY ENZO FERRARI'S "pressuring" tactics, and feeling that he was not being properly treated with the Italian team, Dan Gurney left the Scuderia of the Prancing Horse in 1960. Therefore, when Hill journeyed to Buenos Aires for the first sports car championship race of the season, he found that his most formidable competitor was his ex-teammate from California. Gurney had joined the American Camoradi team, being assigned a new Tipo 61 2.8-liter "birdcage" Maserati (so-called due to its involved tubular chassis) with Masten Gregory as co-driver.

"It didn't take us long to discover that Dan was going to be a real threat with that ugly Maser," says Hill. "I managed to set fastest practice time down there with our 3-liter, but Gurney wasn't far behind me."

For the 1000-kilometer event Juan Fangio acted as official starter, and the first car off the line was the Gurney Maserati, with Hill in close pursuit. Dan steadily pulled away despite Phil's best efforts and had built up a solid lead when he gave the car to Gregory. At the same time Hill came in to hand over to Cliff Allison. Suddenly the race picture reversed itself, for Allison soon caught and passed the Kansan (not yet fully recovered from his Goodwood crash and driving well off his usual form). Masten was hastily flagged in and Gurney scrambled off in the car trying to earn back lost ground, spun in the process as the shocks weakened, then abandoned completely when the gearbox packed up at midpoint in the event.

"Nobody else gave us any trouble after that and we won," says Phil. "Trips and Richie Ginther, in the second works car, finished behind us—so Ferrari was off to a good start for the season. Still, we were all worried about that birdcage Maser. If it held together it was going to be very hard to beat."

• • • • •

With three consecutive sports car victories in three meets (Riverside, the all-Ferrari go at Nassau and now here in Argentina), Hill was again ready to tackle the Formula 1 machines—and the first Grande Epreuve of 1960 was also set for Buenos Aires, just a week after the 1000-kilometer race.

A very popular gesture on Ferrari's part was to give one of his four cars to the portly Argentine veteran José Froilan González, once known as "the Bull of the Pampas" due to his thrusting style behind the wheel. José came out of retirement just for this event, planning no others, and drove well enough to finish in the top 10, showing much of his old flair in practice and in the early stages of the Grand Prix—before exhaustion slowed him.

Hill, Trips and Allison filled out the Maranello team, but found that their heavy, front-engined cars were no match for the Coopers and a spanking-new rear-engined Lotus. Even the BRMs were faster at Buenos Aires, and no Ferrari made the front row of the starting grid.

"The gas tanks were moved up from the rear to the sides," explains Hill, "in an effort to improve handling. They resembled the old Squalo models, with great whale bellies. Then the engines were moved back to compensate for the shift in weight. Of course this meant that the drivers sat almost a foot farther back too—and this tended to give you the feeling of being on the end of a string, of being *flung*, as it were. The rear end of a racing car isn't stable like the front and it does things in a more violent fashion. A driver who is subjected to these things tends to lose contact, because any time the tail of the car jumps out the driver goes right with it. I never got near the leaders during the race, running back in fifth or sixth, but the fast boys began dropping out—the Lotus and the Bonnier BRM and Moss in his Cooper—so I began trying to get past Brabham who wasn't doing anything spectacular that afternoon, when I felt water spraying back in my face. I thought at first that it was coming from Jack's car, but when I looked down at my own temp gauge I saw the needle climbing fast. Sure enough, I pulled into the pits just as my engine was about to seize and they found a split in the main pipe leading from the radiator. By the time they'd changed the water pipe and hose I had dropped to eighth, where I ended up at the flag. McLaren won in his Cooper and we were pretty discouraged afterwards because it was all too clear that the day of the front-engined Ferrari had passed. The factory was working on a rear-engined model, but we didn't know how soon we'd have it, or how well developed it would be."

.   .   .   .   .

A fuel dispute kept Ferrari from sending his team to Sebring that year, and the race was won by a Porsche, with a private Ferrari in third, reversing the outcome at Buenos Aires and putting the two factories in a points tie for the sports car title. Hill had acted as Richie Ginther's pitman in Florida after Enzo had forbidden him to drive a car there. Although Moss and Gurney dominated the race for eight hours with their birdcage Maserati, it broke down, along with the other 2.8 Masers. The cars were unbeatable when piloted by a top driver, but thus far they had proven too fragile.

.   .   .   .   .

"The Targa was next," says Phil, "and we got there six days ahead of time in order to practice with an old '55 Monza, which was, oddly enough, quite good for the circuit since it gave you power all the time. We were able to thrash that old thing through those 45 mountainous miles each lap and turn in some respectable times. But on the only day the road was closed for practice, Richie finished off the poor old Monza, crashing into a house near the spot where I hit the Vespa scooter two years before. Then Cliff Allison wrote off our new practice car in a very fast 130-mph S-bend when the left front tire suddenly went flat just as he was into the bend. Shot right off the road like an arrow."

Richie Ginther had replaced Gurney on the Ferrari team for 1960, and was assigned a 3-liter V-12 with Allison. Hill and von Trips had a smaller 2.5 liter V-6 with independent suspension at the rear. (According to Hill, this was very helpful in the bumpy Targa.) The only birdcage Maserati was in the capable hands of 1954's Panamericana winner, Umberto Maglioli, backed up by the fast Sicilian, Nino Vaccarella.

The 44th running of the Targa Florio, the world's oldest existing open road race (dating back to 1906), was a wild and woolly affair marked by numerous crashes. The two Rodríguez brothers from Mexico, Pedro and Ricardo, sent their car off the road no less than four times; Ginther wiped out one of the Ferraris against a tree beyond the pits; Trips locked up his front brakes and banged a marker stone; Lucky Casner drove his Porsche over a six-foot drop. The circuit was littered with wrecked cars as the race progressed.

As it had done at Buenos Aires and at Sebring, the Tipo 61 Maserati took firm command, and seemed a sure victor until two laps from the end when it was eliminated with a split gas tank. This allowed the swift, road-hugging Porsche RSK 60 of Bonnier and Hans Hermann to score the winning points for the German factory.

Hill drove a superb race, taking over the car from Trips in fourth and hurling it into second by the final stage. Then Trips brought it over the line just six minutes behind the Porsche, saving the day for Ferrari. The points for the Manufacturers' Championship now stood at 20 for Porsche, 18 for Ferrari.

.   .   .   .   .

"The next round for the title was set for later that May at Nürburgring," says Phil, "but first we all took off for England and the International Trophy meeting at Silverstone. This was not a Grande Epreuve, but it *was* a Formula event and we needed to try to iron out a few kinks before Monaco, so the factory sent me over with Cliff Allison."

A major tragedy darkened the practice sessions when Harry Schell lost control of his Cooper in the wet going into Abbey Curve, overturned, struck a wall and was instantly killed. The popular French-American, who loved parties and practical jokes, would be sorely missed by his fellow competitors, since his spirited sense of fun helped to enliven every race meet. His was a serious loss to the sport.

Dan Gurney, who had signed with BRM for Formula events, qualified the British car up front next to teammate Bonnier. Moss, in the Cooper, and Hill also shared row 1, with Allison behind them. However, the Ferraris were again outgunned, with the finishing order: Lotus, Cooper, BRM, Lotus. Ferrari's best was a poor fifth, Hill up.

"The cars just weren't handling," recalls Phil. "We looked like fools sliding around that course, sideways half the time and getting nowhere fast."

. . . . .

At the Ring, trailing Porsche by two points for the sports car title, Enzo Ferrari fielded four cars, with his main hopes pinned on the Hill / Trips 3-liter V-12, in which Phil posted fast time for the team. But since practice was conducted in the wet, the best overall time was made by Jo Bonnier in the new RS 60 Porsche, and Moss was next in the Camoradi Tipo 61 birdcage Maser (which he was sharing with Gurney).

"All practice took place in the rain," Hill says. "We did a lot of experimenting with different tires, looking for the correct 'bite'— and also changed the roll bar so that the car would 'point' a little better. On the Ring you need to be able to get the tail out a bit; it's that kind of circuit."

The race was a near disaster for Ferrari. First, Ginther's car retired with a water leak; then Scarlatti's car was destroyed by fire in the pits when a careless mechanic allowed gasoline to ignite via a hot exhaust pipe. (The scene was a repeat of the Aston pit fire at Goodwood, with Scarlatti rolling about to quench the flames on his coveralls this time in place of Salvadori.)

"To make matters even worse, the weather threw everything at us in this one," says Phil. "We had mist, then rain, then a heavy fog which cut vision to about 150 yards. The FIA had ruled that you had to have a large windscreen in '60, and it became necessary to sit on a stack of pillows in order to see over the stupid thing. Otherwise you were completely blind. When I took over from Trips we were in second, then I got the lead from Gurney when he pitted the birdcage with a fractured oil pipe. We all thought: 'Uh huh, there goes the Maser, out again!' But they got the car fixed in less than five minutes and Dan busted loose, really driving at his limit and cutting into our lead each time around. Trips took over and we were second again, until the engine blew. We then had one car left out of four, with the Maser leading and two Porsches in front of us. Tavoni called in Allison and gave me the wheel, and I took off after Trintignant in the third-place RS 60, with just a few laps to catch him."

Hill drove furiously over the uphill-downhill 14-mile circuit, and despite the Frenchman's supreme effort the Californian caught and passed the Porsche, giving Enzo Ferrari the vital third-place points he needed to stay in the running for the title.

Gurney and Moss had won, with the Bonnier/Gendebien Porsche second. Masten Gregory brought in the second birdcage Maser for fifth overall, proving, at last, that the Maseratis were not nearly so fragile as had been supposed.

"We still had a chance to win the sports car title at Le Mans, but it was two months away, and all of my thoughts turned to Grand Prix," says Hill. "I was going back to Monaco and try to vindicate myself for my sloppy performance there in '59. On that twisty little circuit, though, we knew we'd have to work damn hard to place, as our cars were anything but suitable. A hundred laps there is a long, long grind—and no matter what the engineers came up with in the way of improved handling we'd never be able to match those little rear-engined bugs from Lotus and Cooper. But at least the terrible problem of cockpit heat had been licked, as everything was sealed off really well."

•   •   •   •   •

The Grand Prix de Monaco, at Monte Carlo, found 24 cars locked in desperate competition for qualifying slots on the grid. The rules in the "round-the-houses" contest were strict, and no more than 16 cars would be permitted to start-on Sunday, May 29. Moss was out in Rob Walker's new Lotus-Climax, and astonished everyone with a final fast time of 1:36.3, shattering the old record by a wide margin. In fact, before the trials had ended, *all* the qualifying drivers had exceeded the previous year's fastest qualifying time. The last car to make the grid was driven by the popular French veteran Trintignant, who fought his Cooper-Maserati to 1:39.1 in a thrilling, roundly cheered, last-minute fight to qualify among the 16. In the new American Scarabs, making their long-awaited European debut in Formula racing, owner-builder Lance Reventlow and his chief driver Chuck Daigh vainly struggled to elicit speed from the two beautifully prepared machines, but their best lap (1:47, set by Daigh) proved that the Scarabs had simply arrived too late, and were already sadly outdated, even by the "red trucks" of Enzo Ferrari.

BRM had also switched to rear-engined models, while Hill and Trips had to manhandle the front-engined brutes around the very tight course. However, to prove that he was well aware of the trend, Ferrari unveiled his first experimental rear-engined car at Monaco, powered by a small 2.2 liter V-6 unit, and gave it to Formula newcomer Richie Ginther. While the new Ferrari was far from perfected, never having been tried out in competition prior to Monaco, Ginther made the fourth row of the grid next to Hill's brute, with a very respectable lap of 1:38.6, with Trips edging them both out by three-tenths of a second for best Ferrari time, landing him in row 3. (Cliff Allison, pushing too hard in practice, sustained a broken arm, crushed ribs and severe spinal injuries when his Ferrari pitched him out after plowing into the harbor chicane barrier.)

Under a glowering sky which promised rain, the pack was flagged off, with the bearded Bonnier thrusting his new BRM to the fore, hard pressed by Brabham and Moss. By lap 5 Moss was second in the Lotus, with Brabham losing ground as Brooks' Cooper and Hill's Ferrari closed in on the Australian.

Lap 20 found Moss in the lead, followed by Brabham and Bonnier. Brooks, riding an insecure fourth, found the big Ferrari of Hill dogging him around the corners. Within eight laps rain had begun to spatter down, mixing with rubber deposited on the turns and causing several drivers to spin. McLaren whirled end-for-tail through the tunnel; Hill rotated at the Casino; Brooks spun at Sainte Devote and Salvadori stalled at the Gasworks after a turnabout. Finally, Brabham mashed into the retaining wall at the Sainte Devote turn, putting him out of the race.

At half distance (50 laps), Hill was riding fifth, having dented his car's nose in a shunt with Brooks. Plagued with a case of severe understeer, he was working very hard to keep the massive car in contention. However, Phil soon managed to scramble up into third in a superb display of wet-road driving, staying inches ahead of McLaren's Cooper and Graham Hill's BRM.

Positions were changing rapidly: Moss pitted to reconnect a loose plug lead; Bonnier forged into the lead; McLaren got past Hill's Ferrari, but the Californian refused to cede his position. As a result of this pressure, on lap 67, McLaren did a complete 360-degree spin at the Gasworks hairpin. Hill nipped by on the outside, wheels spinning for traction, while Graham Hill passed McLaren on the inside, immediately losing control and spinning wildly into a wooden radio shed. Building and car were demolished.

Ginther was out with transmission failure; Gurney's suspension had failed as had Bonnier's—and now Moss again led what was reduced to a six-car race. McLaren and Hill were waging a furious struggle for second far behind Moss, who almost seemed to be sleeping as he neatly scissored the turns, helmet pushed casually back on his head.

"If I hadn't been so exhausted near the end I might have been able to pass Bruce into second," says Hill, "but I'd used up all my energy herding that Ferrari around the circuit, so I was in no condition to make any last-minute sprint. Bruce got it by 10 seconds, almost a minute behind Moss. I was third, and Tony Brooks—the only other car to last out the entire race—got fourth a lap behind all of us. Trips had gone out with a bad clutch, so mine was the only car in our team to finish."

Hill's gallant battle at Monaco against overwhelming odds established him as Ferrari's Number One, a position which he was to consolidate over the remainder of the '60 season. And Phil's driving on that rainy afternoon effectively silenced the critics who had condemned him as "too wild" in his previous run at Monte Carlo. Indeed, in the Ferrari camp, he was the man to watch.

———————————

CHAPTER TWENTY

Fighting the Odds

JUST SEVEN DAYS after Monaco, the Grand Prix of Holland was run at Zandvoort, and since the two circuits were nearly 1000 miles apart this meant much scrambling about on the part of the various factory teams. Damage caused at Monte Carlo to engines, chassis, wheels, transmissions and body shells had to be repaired, and team mechanics worked in round-the-clock sessions in order to put their cars in proper order for the Dutch race.

With Cliff Allison still in the hospital, Ginther was moved to the cockpit of a front-engined Ferrari, with Trips and Hill. The American Scarabs were out for another try, but not much was expected of them.

"We had the rear-engined prototype on the last day of practice," says Hill, "and we all tried it out, with the conclusion that it was far more comfortable and much easier to drive. You didn't have the problem of extreme understeer as you did with the front-engined cars. Trips spent a lot of time in it, but finally pulled out of practice with the engine pouring oil. So we all piled back into our brutes and did what we could with them."

Hill and Ginther sat glumly side by side in the fifth row after qualifying 12th and 13th, while Trips was relegated to row 6, having displaced the Scarab of Chuck Daigh when Reventlow decided against letting his car run. A dispute over starting money was the basis for this action. (Daigh had been lapping at 1:38, a second and a half behind Trips, which would have put him in the back of the grid.) Reventlow himself had lost a wheel while at speed in his Scarab, and this unsettling experience had dropped him far down in the qualifying times.

As the pack got away, with Brabham and Moss in charge, Hill accelerated around the edge of the field and roared up into fifth— fighting to maintain this position over the ensuing laps. On the 11th tour, as Dan Gurney was throttling down the pit straight at 140, his rear brake failed. With the front wheels locked, Gurney cannoned straight into the sand dunes. His BRM shot over a rise and flipped on its back, pinning Gurney beneath it. He survived with minor cuts and bruises, but one of the spectators, an eighteen-year-old youth who had eluded track police and was in the process of crossing the dunes to a fresh vantage point, had been struck down and killed by the rampaging BRM.

Moss, too, came close to disaster. He had been slipstreaming Brabham when the Australian's wheels bit out a chunk of granite curbing, throwing it skyward. It hit the outer front wheel of Stirling's Lotus and burst the tire. This cost the Englishman two laps—and the race.

"By the 41st lap I was at the pits with a sticking throttle," Phil relates. "We were trying out a new system of throttle rods and it just wasn't any good. When my engine began cutting out and in, in and out, I just called it a day on lap 55. Brabham won. Our team got fifth, with Trips, and sixth, with Richie."

· · · · ·

The scene of his next Grand Prix race ideally suited Hill's fighting personality: the arduous Spa-Francorchamps circuit through the brooding forest of Ardennes in western Belgium, almost nine miles of sweeping bends and full-throttle straights demanding precise judgment and unquestioned bravery. This was the quickest road circuit in Europe, and offered the driver of genuine Grand Prix ability a chance to demonstrate the hazardous art of driving a fast bend at over 130 mph with his car alive and trembling at the exact hair edge of control.

"Fangio was the absolute master of the fast bend," says Hill, "and that's one of the reasons he became World Champion five times. I'd never driven at Spa prior to this 1960 Belgian GP, but I felt at home on the circuit after I once learned it. And our cars seemed a lot better here. Some of their former disadvantages, at places such as Monaco, became advantages at Spa. Such as excess power over roadholding; you've got the old hoof down practically all the time and you can use all the power an engine can give you."

For reasons of politics and to further public relations, the young Belgian Willy Mairesse was given a Formula 1 seat at Spa by Enzo Ferrari, replacing Ginther. Hill and Trips had their usual front-engined, all independently sprung Dino 246 machines, and while Trips could do no better than row 5, and Mairesse row 6, Hill put the bit in his teeth and flashed the red monster around the long circuit in 3 minutes 53.3 seconds, earning a place on the front row with the Coopers of Brabham and Brooks.

Moss was missing from the grid lineup. On the final day of practice, approaching the end of the fast downhill right-hand bend at Burnenville in the Malmédy section, his Lotus skimming over the snaking black road at 130, the Britisher was suddenly in very desperate trouble. The left rear stub axle broke, severing the wheel, and the Lotus whiplashed into a series of slewing skids, bounded along a dirt embankment, ejecting Moss, then flung itself across the road, exploding into a ditch with the impact of an artillery shell. Hill was among the first of the drivers to reach the injured Britisher. "He was lying in a fetal position, coughing blood and begging us not to move him till the doctor arrived. He was afraid his back was broken."

Luckily, it was not. But Stirling Moss had suffered his worst crash, and was rushed to a hospital with cracked ribs, smashed vertebrae, two broken legs and a broken nose. He was not expected to resume his career for several months.

No sooner had word reached the pits of the Moss crash than it was announced that a second Lotus had left the road at speed. Michael Taylor's steering column had abruptly snapped, and the car had plunged into the trees. Taylor survived, though his injuries were almost as severe as those sustained by Moss.

The two accidents were blamed on the ultralight construction of the new Lotus machines, Graham Hill remarking: "It's a bloody sprint car. They won't stand up to hard driving, and this circuit proves it." At 900 pounds, the Lotus had shaved a full 100 pounds off the weight of the exceptionally light Cooper—and the general opinion was that the designers had sacrificed basic strength for a few extra miles per hour.

After their abortive efforts at Monaco and Zandvoort, the two blue-and-white Scarabs finally entered their first GP race, starting at the back of the grid. Reventlow only lasted one lap, as his engine let go in a gout of smoke, and Daigh was slowed by numerous troubles, sidelining him for good on lap 17. For the Scarab team, spirit just wasn't enough.

At the start, Brabham and Scotsman Innes Ireland began to pull away, but Hill was not hanging back, and on the third tour he was slipstreaming Ireland's Lotus. When the Scot tried to shake him by zigzag methods the Californian flicked past, setting out after Brabham.

Knowing full well that Hill was the underdog with his massive Ferrari, the crowd urged on the American driver, and Phil responded by pulling abreast of the flying Cooper on the 1.8-mile Masta Straight, bringing a roar from the massed spectators. Brabham could not lose the Ferrari, although by lap 10 he had put six and a half seconds between himself and Hill, establishing a new lap record while he was about it.

By half distance (18 laps) the Australian led Hill by nine seconds, but Phil was still driving full-bore in pursuit, and Brabham kept checking nervously over his shoulder on the Californian's position. Crowd attention was naturally centered on this intense frontline battle, yet the back runners in the pack were trying equally hard to move up, particularly Chris Bristow, a young twenty-two-year-old Britisher with an unhappy record of smashups in club events to his discredit. Tailing the Ferrari of Willy Mairesse, Bristow was wringing every ounce of power from his Cooper. Diving down into the rapid Burnenville corner, where Moss had crashed the previous day, Bristow got out of line, finding himself on the outside of the bend. Trying to correct, he slammed a hay bale with his left rear wheel, throwing the Cooper into the middle of the road. The car struck an iron guardrail, cartwheeled end for end, bounced back on the course, coming to a final stop upside down. Bristow was beyond aid, dead when his body thumped down onto the road.

Just a few laps later, tragedy again struck the Grand Prix of Belgium when a low-flying bird smashed into the goggles of Alan Stacey as he was doing 140 on the Malmédy curve. At this speed, the impact was stunning, and. Stacey's Lotus followed the destructive course of Bristow's Cooper, also killing its driver.

Unaware of the two deaths, Hill was trying vainly to close on Brabham, and was encouraged in his efforts by a BRAVO! sign from Tavoni in the pits. But, on lap 29, just seven rounds from the finish, Phil began slowing.

As he tells it: "My left leg began feeling very cold, and soon I felt an icy blast down there in the cockpit. This turned out to be gasoline leaking from the tube in the fuel pressure gauge, which was getting into the airstream from the ventilation pipe. I hated to stop at the pits, knowing I'd lose second and maybe a chance for first, but within a mile I suddenly saw flames licking around my leg, and there was a smoky, orange, crepes suzette kind of fire going down in the lower part of the cockpit. I stopped in a panic, got the fire on my coveralls put out—which didn't burn me since they were fireproofed—then attended to the car. I had stopped on a hill, and the minute I was out of the car it started rolling. I tried to use my foot as a block on the rear, but the wheel went right over it. Well, I jumped back in and parked the thing against a concrete abutment by the roadside, then got the hood off and began slapping out the fire in the engine. By the time I returned to the pits, got the broken pipe fixed and was able to resume, Jack had a full lap on me. I stood on it, and wound up in fourth behind Brabham, McLaren and Gendebien, all in Coopers. Trips and Mairesse had both already retired in our other two Ferraris."

Phil's fighting run in Belgium proved that the big Ferraris could not be counted out on the faster circuits, and although his excellent showing was overshadowed by the deaths of two young drivers and the Moss accident, track pundits were already prophesying a strong bid from the Italian cars at Reims, early in July.

.   .   .   .   .

"Before the French GP we all headed for Le Mans and the final round of the Manufacturers' Championship," says Hill. "I was sharing one of our V-12 3-liters with Trips, and he was set to take the first stint there."

One hour and 37 minutes after the contest had begun, when running third overall, the Trips/Hill car coasted to a silent halt near Tertre Rouge, its fuel pump clicking madly. The car had run out of gas, due to a miscalculation on the part of the Ferrari engineers, and an astonished

Trips was forced to abandon. Hill, therefore, never got a chance to drive, later angrily remarking: "The less said about this the better."

Tanks on two of the remaining Ferraris also ran dry out on the circuit, but Gendebien was able to coast into the pits. He eventually won the race (aided by Paul Frère), with another Ferrari second. No Porsches finished in the first nine places. The birdcage Maseratis again demonstrated their blazing speed in the early stages, with Gregory leading handily, but all three cars retired with varying troubles.

Thus, due to luck in this case rather than sound pit planning, Ferrari regained the Manufacturers' Championship. And again, as he had done in previous years, Phil Hill contributed heavily to the Italian victory by his win in Buenos Aires, his second in the Targa and his third at the Nürburgring.

·   ·   ·   ·   ·

Hill remained in France for the following week's Grand Prix at Reims, and planned an all-out assault on Brabham in an effort to overcome the Australian World Champion on this "Ferrari circuit." (Actually, with the 1960 Cooper's superior speed and superb handling qualities no course was now ceded to Ferrari, but the Italian machines had won this race each year for the past four seasons, and this imbued the Maranello factory team with a win-or-bust spirit at Reims.)

The ill-fated Scarabs were making their final try in France, with Richie Ginther replacing Reventlow in one of the two cars. Despite Ginther's proven ability, his best lap time of 2:36.1 was barely fast enough to put him in the last grid position, but the Scarab engines were so severely strained that neither car was able to start the race. Throwing in the towel, Reventlow ordered the cars shipped back to California, realizing that to continue in Europe would be foolish and entirely useless.

Willy Mairesse and Trips settled for the second and third grid rows, but Hill was determined to place his Ferrari on row 1, and experimented with lead weights in an effort to improve his car's handling characteristics, finally posting 2:18.1—which was quick enough to put him between Graham Hill's BRM and Brabham's Cooper on the front line.

In a ragged start, Graham Hill was shunted by Trintignant, putting both drivers out, while Brabham took his usual lead. Directly behind him, however, the two Ferraris of Hill and Trips were post-ing notice of their winning intentions, and the Cooper could not pull away. On lap 4 Hill bulled into the lead, putting Brabham between the pair of bellowing red Ferraris. They roared past the stands in this order, leaving the remainder of the field behind them, smoke plum-ing from their tires as they braked from 175 to a crawling 40 in or-der to negotiate the hairpin. Lap 5 saw Brabham dart his Cooper past Hill, but on lap 6 the fighting Californian had regained the lead. The pace was tremendous, and lap speeds were averaging 133 mph.

"It was incredible the tow I was giving Jack with my big beast," recalls Phil. "But when *he* led, with me attempting the same thing, I just couldn't properly slipstream his Cooper since that little thing cut a much smaller hole through the air. To get any advantage at all, I had to be quite close, and aim directly down the center line of his car. As a result, I hit him!"

Hill's Ferrari was described as "rising up on its back wheels, its mouth twisted from the impact." This shunt cost Phil a few precious feet, but he scrabbled back up, clawing his way into the lead within another lap.

"I couldn't hold it, though," he admits. "I was a bit faster on the long straight into the hairpin, but Jack was braking deeper and get-ting out of the hairpin sooner. Trips was right with us all the way, while Jack and I kept switching the lead, usually passing the main stands nose to nose."

Then, on lap 21, Hill attempted to outbrake the World Champion and failed, shooting up an escape road. Trips closed on Brabham's tailpipe while Phil got sorted out, and at the halfway point in this sav-age race, with 25 laps behind them, the three leaders were still bat-tling for every inch of track, the twin Ferrari V-6s howling at 8400 rpms, drowning out the cry of the smaller Cooper.

"I was beginning to wonder how I was going to take care of those Ferraris if the pace continued like this to the end," confessed Brabham. "But right about then I looked in my driving mirror and saw Hill drop sharply back. I knew he was in serious trouble."

For the overstressed Ferraris, the day was done. An input bevel between the engine and the gearbox had broken on Hill's car, and he freewheeled past the stands, braking to a final stop at the edge of the pit area in a round of applause, his hard-fought battle ended. And just two laps later Trips was coasting sadly down the straight, his transmission also broken. The third team Ferrari of Mairesse had retired earlier with a similar malady — and the race was left to the steady Brabham who flashed over the line at the head of an all-Cooper parade. The small British bombs took the checker 1-2-3-4 for a clean sweep at the end of 50 laps.

. . . . .

"Then it was Silverstone and the British GP," says Phil. "Knowing that we had no chance at all on that circuit, Ferrari only sent two cars for Trips and myself. We bounced around at the back of the field, and wound up sixth and seventh. Trips finished just four seconds ahead of me, but we were both two full laps away from Brabham, who won again. Incidentally, Moss acted as the official starter at Silverstone, so we knew he'd soon be strong enough to re-enter GP competition. Fortunately, Stirling had made a remarkably quick recovery."

Hill accompanied Trips to the picturesque Solitude circuit, near Stuttgart, for a Formula 2 race prior to the upcoming Grand Prix of Portugal, and was never competitive in an old front-engined car against the new Formula 2 machines. Trips drove the new rear-engined Ferrari at Solitude, winning the race for the Maranello factory while Hill took seventh.

"This course was a kind of slower Spa," says Hill, "and I wanted to get some experience on it. Since 1922 they'd been running motorcycles at Solitude, but this was the first full-scale Formula race held there. I just toured around, enjoying the scenery. I knew I had a rough time ahead of me at Portugal — since I *hated* that Oporto circuit. It was bad enough in '56 when I drove a sports car there. In a GP Ferrari I knew it would be murderous. But on a team you go where the team goes — and, like it or not, I was going to Oporto."

CHAPTER TWENTY-ONE

After 39 Years: *Bravissimo!*

I N MID-AUGUST, just two months after his crash at Spa, Stirling Moss was back in action in a Grande Epreuve, having chosen the extremely difficult Portuguese Grand Prix for his comeback in the Rob Walker Lotus. He joined a crack field for this event, which was attended by Cooper, Lotus, BRM and Ferrari. John Surtees, the World Motorcycle Champion, driving for Lotus, found the bumpy, cobblestoned 4.5-mile circuit at Oporto to be much like the courses on which he had won his two-wheeled crown, and proceeded to earn pole position with a time of 2:25.5, a tenth of a second faster than Dan Gurney, who was also going very well in practice with a new BRM. Brabham was next, at the outer edge of row 1, while Moss made the second row. The two Ferraris of Trips and Hill were side by side back in row 4, both having made 2:28.4 — and with eight cars ahead of them on the grid their case seemed hopeless at Oporto.

The snaking circuit was designed to test skill and nerve to the utmost, with the start/finish line on the ocean front in the suburbs of town. Its many hazards, beyond the rough cobblestones which covered large sections of the road, were curbs, tram tracks, narrow streets lined with houses, trees, brick walls and an occasional stray dog. It incorporated fast, sweeping bends and tight hairpins over a variety of surfaces, and it was well understood that a serious error here could prove fatal.

Hill found that his original estimate of the circuit was correct, but after two days of practice the severe challenge presented here stirred his competitive spirit, and he began to have more confidence in himself.

"It was so bumpy it made your eyes blur," says Phil, "and the downhill bit with all the trees on the outside, which I recalled vividly from my first trip there, was even more frightening at GP speeds. The independent suspension was getting an unbelievable workout on these cobblestones, tending to fling the brake pads back into the calipers, which meant that when it came time to apply the brakes they were a fair distance away from the discs, demanding a full stroke of the pedal before you had any stopping power. After you passed a bad section of road, it was necessary to use your left foot to pump the brakes back up in order to get the pads against the discs so they'd be ready when you needed them."

Two practice crashes had served to tame even the most incautious: Henry Taylor had overturned his Cooper on the curve beyond the pit area, and Jimmy Clark left the circuit on the same spot, managing to keep his car from upending. Both drivers were shaken, but not seriously injured.

No one was surprised to see Brabham get away first as the race began, but Gurney had the crowd of 50,000 cheering as he charged past the World Champion and got his BRM firmly in the lead as the field completed lap 1. Hill was riding fifth, but moved up when Brabham spun (barely missing Gurney), putting the Australian in eighth. Trips had rammed the bales on the first tour and was trying to make up ground in his bent Ferrari, far behind his teammate.

Surtees was chasing Gurney, and Hill was pressing Moss for third as the pace quickened, but by the tenth lap Gurney's BRM began to falter with a toughening engine. Surtees took the front position, with Moss harrying, and Hill shadowing both of them. But then Stirling began having trouble and pitted for fresh plugs, putting Hill in second. Brabham had meanwhile knifed his Cooper up from eighth and was riding Phil's tailpipe, looking for a chance to pass.

As one journalist described this duel: "Hill's large red Ferrari bounced and slid in nasty attitudes over trolley tracks and pavement changes, roaring up the straight, stopping violently for the sharp left-hander and, on one occasion, throwing up a mass of stones and dirt into Brabham's face."

"The bronze piston inside the clutch-operating hydraulic cylinder started to pick up aluminum from its housing," says Phil, "and in no time it was making a bad seal between the housing and the rubber cup inside. The clutch began to have a very *strange* feel. At times it felt just like a sponge, then it would operate okay, then go soft again. I began to miss shifts now and then because I was driving very, very hard and being merciless with the gearbox. One thing was paramount in my mind: that was to *keep* Brabham behind me. He got closer and closer—and finally he was right behind me. We went around for a couple of laps this way, then he passed me coming into the ocean front, but immediately I got back by him at the end of the straight—but I couldn't pull away, with the clutch giving me trouble again.

"Now, right from the beginning, I had been leaving my braking until 200 meters before that little square turn that goes between the houses—the slowest on the circuit—and I missed another gear change coming in to this one. I was driving in a way that meant everything had to come off exactly right in order to get stopped. To have a proper front-rear braking ratio our cars were so balanced that you needed 8000 revs' worth of engine helping at the back wheels, *right then,* and the minute that the revs dropped under 7000—unless you could gear down for more revs—you started locking up the front wheels. That's just what happened at Oporto. I missed the gear change from fourth down to third, and thought I'd have to take the escape road. But as I was coming up to the turn I decided to make a stab at getting around. Well, I hit the curb and some bales; the radiator wrapped around the front suspension, tie rods and steering idlers, and I stalled."

Up front, Brabham was after Surtees, and the motorcycle ace seemed capable of withstanding the challenge until his foot slipped on fuel which had leaked on the brake pedal from a ruptured tank, and he slammed the curb, splitting his radiator. Brabham took the lead, and with Moss out of the race (spinning off course with a locking brake) it was again victory for the canny Australian, his *fifth* straight GP win—assuring him of his second World Championship in the nimble Cooper.

The luckless Hill refused to quit; he reached the pits after restarting his battered Ferrari, and when the mechanics attempted to wheel the car away Hill intervened, jumped back into the cockpit and again started up the now-clutchless machine. Phil drove it one lap, parking at the finish line with the intention of pushing it over for a last official place. The clerk of the course denied him this privilege and the tired Californian tried to restart for the third time, but stalled again, finally giving up the battle.

· · · · ·

"I went back to England for a Formula meet at Brands Hatch later that same month," says Hill. "This wasn't a Grande Epreuve, but we were still trying to sort out various handling problems, and took advantage of this race to test certain theories. We tried several different types of front suspension geometry there, and hit pretty close to home. But these improvements were rather embarrassing to us, because we had all but scrapped the idea of a front-engined car, so we didn't want to influence our engineers with a lot of enthusiasm for the new changes in the old cars! A number of people at the factory didn't particularly want our cars to look just like all the other little bugs. They wanted to keep the Ferrari in the same classic proportions the racing car has always had, with the engine in the front— so it was with mixed emotions that we greeted these improvements in roadholding. Still, we weren't all that much better, because my best at Brands was fourth among the Coopers and the Lotuses."

· · · · ·

On September 4, 1960, the Italian Grand Prix was held as scheduled at Monza, although none of the British factory teams sent entries to this event, due to the fact that the high-speed banking had been incorporated into the race along with the usual road circuit. This "double" layout had only been used twice for GP racing (in '55 and '56), and on these occasions the rough banking had taken a severe toll of tires and suspension systems. Cooper, Lotus, and BRM all felt that their cars would prove too dangerous on the banking and therefore decided to boycott the race.

Phil comments: "I'm sure if I had been driving on a team where the cars had so little margin of strength that they had failures even on 'normal' roads—such as the Spa circuit in Belgium—I might have been afraid to drive on the banking myself."

Only a dozen other cars were at Monza in addition to the Ferraris, and none of these were really competitive, being slower, out-

The 1960 Grand Prix season opened on a rainy May 29 at Monaco, where Hill deftly handled the 246 front-engined Dino and scored a third behind the nimble Cooper of Bruce McLaren and the Lotus-Climax Stirling Moss took to first place. The steps of the Hotel de Paris serve as the backdrop to Hill's 2.5-liter Ferrari. (Louis Klemantaski/The Klemantaski Collection)

Phil managed a seventh against the mid-engined contingent at the British GP at Silverstone in 1960. (Geoffrey Goddard/GP Library)

Brands Hatch hosted a Formula 1 race in August. The Ferrari team used this non-points event to experiment with suspension settings on the 256 Dinos. (Geoffrey Goddard/GP Library)

The 1960 Italian Grand Prix at Monza proved to be a historic moment as Phil Hill became the first American to win a Grand Prix race since 1921, when Jimmy Murphy drove a Dusenberg to a win in the French Grand Prix.

This would turn out to be the last Formula 1 win for a front-engined Grand Prix car of any marque. (LAT)

At Riverside in 1960, Hill finished seventh with a slipping clutch in the Times Grand Prix for sports cars. The Ferrari 250TR was the one he and Cliff Allison won with in Argentina. *(Bob Tronolone)*

Phil is seated in a Cooper T51 at the American Grand Prix at Riverside—the last event of the 1960 season. *(Jim Sitz)*

Since the Driver's Championship points race belonged to Jack Brabham, Ferrari sent no cars to Riverside. Phil drove the Yeoman Credit Cooper to a sixth-place finish. *(Dave Friedman)*

In March of 1961, Phil Hill and Olivier Gendebien went to Sebring to co-drive a Ferrari 250TRI 61. Behind Hill's hard-cornering 3-liter Ferrari is an Alfa Romeo Sprint Speciale and some of the airport's usual traffic. *(Flip Schulke)*

Longtime friends, fellow Californians, and Ferrari works drivers, Richie Ginther and Phil Hill talk with the press during the 12-hour Sebring event. *(Flip Schulke)*

The team of Hill and Gendebien after winning the 1961 Sebring event, their second win at the airport circuit. *(Flip Schulke)*

After 15 hours at Le Mans in 1961, only 2.5 seconds separated the Phil Hill and Olivier Gendebien No. 10 Ferrari from the entry of Pedro and Ricardo Rodríguez. The Rodríguez brothers retired after 22 hours. The No. 11 Ferrari of Willie Mairesse and Mike Parkes finished second, three laps down to the record-breaking win for Hill/Gendebien. *(LAT)*

It would appear Dan Gurney may have the upper hand in this poker game played out in a hotel room in the Bahamas, circa '61. *(Flip Schulke)*

For the 1961 Monaco Grand Prix, Phil was assigned a Ferrari 156F1 with a 60-degree V-6, while Richie Ginther had an untried, yet lighter, 120-degree unit. By lap 75, Hill, suffering carburetion and brake troubles, let Richie by to chase down Stirling Moss. Moss finished 3.6 seconds in front of Ginther. Hill finished third. *(Louis Klemantaski / The Klemantaski Collection)*

Hill is pictured leading the sun-baked French Grand Prix at Reims in '61. Later, he spun and was tapped by Stirling Moss' Lotus. Hill's V-6 stalled and would not restart. In blazing heat he push-started the Ferrari and finished two laps down. His only consolation—100 bottles of champagne presented to fastest qualifier. *(Bernard Cahier)*

The rain fell hard at Aintree on July 15, 1961, for the British Grand Prix. Phil Hill in the Ferrari 156 has just lapped Lucien Bianchi's Lotus as they go into Anchor Crossing. Hill scored a second to Wolfgang von Trips, after a nasty moment. (Geoffrey Goddard / GP Library)

Hill was the first to break the magic 9-minute mark at Nürburgring, when he put together a flawless practice run through the 14-mile circuit. Three hundred thousand watched the 1961 Grand Prix of Germany, as teammates Phil Hill and Wolfgang von Trips competed for points toward the Driver's Championship. (Ludvigsen Library Limited)

The smoking Ferrari 156 "60" of Ricardo Rodríguez is seen trailing Phil Hill and Richie Ginther on the banking at Monza, Italy in 1961. Teammate Wolfgang von Trips was locked in a close points race with Phil Hill for the Driver's World Championship. Disaster struck on the opening laps as von Trips touched wheels with Jim Clark's Lotus, and the Ferrari careened into the crowd. Fifteen died, including the German Count. *(Bernard Cahier)*

Hill drove the No. 2 car to the checker to receive the winners' wreath, and also the news of the tragedy. *(LAT)*

Hill's point lead after Monza was unassailable, so Ferrari did not send his cars to the last race at Watkins Glen, NY, denying Hill the chance to drive the 156 and claim his title in the U.S. Grand Prix.

Phil Hill was at last given a champion's welcome, when he was fêted at GM's Styling Department. *(Ludvigsen Library Ltd.)*

dated private entries, or Formula 2 machines, so the affair turned into a Ferrari "benefit" from the outset.

Hill set fast time in his front-engined Dino, a new combined-course record of 139 mph, with a lap at 2:41.4, giving him the pole. Richie Ginther was next (by two seconds), followed by Mairesse on the third Formula 1 Ferrari. The rear-engined Formula 2 car had been assigned to Wolfgang von Trips, and he qualified some ten seconds behind Hill in this machine.

In a practice hassle with the always-aggressive Monza track police, Enzo Ferrari threatened to withdraw his cars from the race. It seems that the overactive policemen had arrested a Ferrari mechanic and barred the Commendatore himself from his own pits, having failed to recognize the shirt-sleeved, cap-wearing Enzo. After an official apology the still-angry Ferrari allowed his cars to run; had he not done so the race would have lost all of its interest as a Grande Epreuve, and Phil Hill would have been denied his chance to finally win a Grand Prix victory.

Win he did, taking the lead from Ginther on lap 26, and pacing the field to the checker for an average speed of 132 mph over road and banking, setting fastest lap at 136.6, for another new record. It was not a complete walkaway for Hill, since Ginther was in excellent form and led his teammate to the first tire stop on lap 16, getting back into the fray with a 25-second lead over Hill, whose own stop was bungled, costing Phil over a minute. He set out after Ginther with a will, cutting away at Richie's lead by some vigorous driving, and passing his teammate within 10 tours. Richie was unable to stay with Hill, receiving the checker over half a lap behind for second overall. Mairesse was third, with Trips winning the Formula 2 race against the Porsches by notching fifth behind Cabianca's Formula 1 Cooper-Ferrari. (On team orders, Willy Mairesse had given Trips a "tow" on the straights to help cement the Ferrari's Formula 2 victory, and the Porsche's of Barth and Herrmann were eventually lapped by Trips, thanks to this assist from Mairesse.)

In capturing the Italian race, Phil Hill became the first American driver in 39 years to annex a championship Formula event. On a Duesenberg, in 1921, Jimmy Murphy had turned the trick, winning the French Grand Prix over the original Le Mans course. Americans had tried many times to follow in the fast Irishman's tire tracks, but none had succeeded prior to Hill at Monza. Early-day greats such as Tommy Milton, Peter de Paolo, Earl Cooper, Leon Duray and Babe Stapp all tried their luck in Europe and failed. John Fitch was next, in the '50s, then came Masten Gregory, Gurney, Ginther, and the Scarabs of Reventlow and Daigh. *"Bravissimo!"* shouted the Italian fans as Phil's red Ferrari thundered off the banking and swept under the checkered flag, 39 years, one month and 10 days after Murphy had taken the checker at Le Mans.

The Long Wait was over.

∙ ∙ ∙ ∙ ∙

Phil returned to his home state in the role of "America's greatest driver," a position which never failed to make him uncomfortable. Despite his polished performances at Monza and his furious wheel-to-wheel battles with Brabham that season in Europe, Phil was basically unchanged in his distaste for certain aspects of the limelight. If he could avoid a formal dinner party, he would do his utmost to bypass the affair; if called upon to make a speech he would suffer the agonies of hell in delivering it; if required to attend official functions he would moan his displeasure in the willing ear of Ginther, who would be sure to sympathize.

At Riverside, in mid-October, this "pressure" prevailed. He was Phil Hill, wasn't he? He'd *better* win! Phil had a factory 3-liter from Ferrari, but the car could not cope with the host of birdcage Masers on hand at the desert circuit, and Hill finished seventh after trying vainly to catch his old rival, Shelby, who was fifth in one of the Maseratis. (Roy Salvadori, in a Cooper Monaco, just nipped in ahead of Phil for sixth shortly before the windup.) Two other birdcage Masers (one carrying winner Billy Krause), a Scarab and a remarkably fast home-built Special ("Ol Yaller II") all beat Hill to the flag. However, Phil's spirits might have been eased a bit by World Champion Jack Brabham's performance at Riverside (he was tenth in a new E-Type Jaguar) and by the fact that neither Moss nor Gurney could even finish the race.

∙ ∙ ∙ ∙ ∙

The season's last World Championship event, the Grand Prix of the United States, was also held at Riverside just a month after the sports car event, and although the championship had already been decided in Brabham's favor, Hill wanted to improve on his fourth-place finish in the 1959 listing with a third-place finish in 1960. The points he had earned at Monza put him behind Brabham and Bruce McLaren in the standings, and if he could do at all well at Riverside his third place would be secured. Unfortunately, Enzo Ferrari saw no sense in shipping his cars all the way to California, and Hill was out of a factory ride. Obtaining permission from the Commendatore, Phil snagged a berth with the Yeoman Credit Cooper team, joining Tony Brooks, Gendebien and Henry Taylor. Hill's rear-engined Cooper-Climax impressed him ("The difference in handling between it and our heavy Ferraris was incredible!") but the car was not up to the latest factory Coopers, and none of the Yeoman team could hope for top grid positions.

"I qualified at 1:58.8 for row 5," says Phil, "and managed to stall at the start. With the help of a push, I was away at the tail end of the pack."

Within just a few laps Hill had roared past nine cars, but his forward rush ended at flagfall with a sixth overall, behind Moss, Ireland, McLaren, Brabham and Bonnier. Stirling's victory and the second place earned by Innes Ireland put both drivers ahead of Phil in the final championship standing, dropping him to fifth, six points ahead of Trips (who had taken ninth at Riverside in a borrowed Cooper-Maserati). Despite this bit of end-of-season bad luck, 1960 had been one of Hill's best years.

However, the Californian still had his *finest* year ahead of him.

CHAPTER TWENTY-TWO

The Tables Are Turned

IN LATE MARCH of 1961, when Phil Hill went to Sebring for the classic 12-Hours, he was beginning a fresh season—and since Phil had won his initial race each year for the past three years (Buenos Aires in '58, Sebring in '59, Buenos Aires in '60) the Californian was out to make it four in a row.

Ferrari had once again teamed him with the cool Belgian, Olivier Gendebien, and their mount was a 3-liter V-12, with a reported horsepower of 310. New wind-tunnel tests recently conducted at the factory were responsible for the high-backed, clipped-off look of the new model Ferraris, with their fresh lines giving them an extra 10 mph down the long Sebring straight. The most exciting car at Sebring was the rear-engined V-6 Ferrari, with its humpback housing a detuned version of the 1960 Grand Prix 2.5-liter powerplant. Given to Ginther and Trips as the "sprinter" (in hopes of breaking up the opposition with a sizzling pace), this odd-looking machine was easily the fastest car in practice. The third works Ferrari (front-engined, like the Hill/Gendebien model) was to be driven by Willy Mairesse and the talented young newcomer from Italy, Giancarlo Baghetti.

Facing the machines from Maranello in this first round for the Manufacturers' Championship were five Maseratis and two works Porsches. For 1961, Maserati also sported a rear-engined version of their fast birdcage, the Tipo63, backing up three of the older Tipo61 models. The Masers had an impressive driver lineup including Moss, Hansgen, McLaren, Gregory, and Graham Hill.

In a private modified Testa Rossa Ferrari V-12, the two lion-hearted Rodríguez youngsters from Mexico City, Pedro (twenty-one) and Ricardo (nineteen), were set to battle the works entries, providing the car held together at their punishing pace.

Under a clear, brass-blue Florida sky, the 65-car field roared and sputtered away, according to engine displacement-but the Maserati of Stirling Moss did neither. It remained silent, victim of a dead battery. When Moss finally got into action he was already far behind and it took him almost two hours to tackle the leading cars.

"I was driving strictly according to plan," says Hill, who was fourth as the initial lap was completed. "We were not going to burn up our car in a duel for the lead in a long race such as this, so I stayed just close enough to the front to know what was going on up there."

Plenty was going on, because by lap 3 Pedro Rodríguez was hounding Masten Gregory's first-place birdcage Maser, and had soon passed the Kansan into the lead. Gregory dropped back, and Hill also got by him, letting Rodríguez set the pace. With 15 laps behind them, Rodríguez and Hill led the remainder of the field, but Ginther was pressing from third to pass and go after the young Mexican. Hill gave way and Richie streaked his rear-engined Italian bomb into the lead within a few more tours of the 5.2-mile airport circuit.

At noon, Ginther handed to Trips, Hill to Gendebien and Moss (who had blasted up into second with a series of record lap times) to Graham Hill. These co-drivers proved unlucky for two of the three leaders. First Graham Hill dropped out with a broken exhaust manifold; then Trips lost the steering on the rear-engined Ferrari on a fast left bend and spun into the grass, mowing down a line of rubber pylons. A bent lower-right wishbone and a broken tie rod ended the car's run for the day. Tavoni was quick to switch Ginther/Trips to the Mairesse/Baghetti car (then fifth) but the two works drivers were never able to challenge for the lead in this slower Ferrari.

Ricardo was now in the Rodríguez car, and going like Hell's Hammers. The fact that the Hill/Gendebien Ferrari had lost time in the pits due to poor organization, combined with their plan not to abuse the car in the first half of the race, allowed the Rodríguez brothers to build up a very fat two-lap lead over the works car.

"Phil and I waited till halfway through, which was 4 P.M., before we really began to push," Gendebien later stated. "And for a while there it seemed as if we'd waited *too* long to make our bid. Those Rodríguez kids were really moving."

At 6:47 it was all over. The Rodríguez car pitted with one light out, needing a new generator and a set of disc-brake pads. The lengthy stop was enough to give Hill a chance to make up the two laps, then stretch out to another lap and a half, setting the second-hottest time in the race in doing it (3:13.8 to Moss's 3:13.2). There was no catching the Belgian-American combination after this, and Hill brought the car under the flag at 10 P.M. for his third Sebring victory. Ginther and Trips were second just ahead of the still-charging Rodríguez brothers.

"Although the cockpit heat was brutal for a while," says Hill, "the car ran beautifully all the way. Luckily, the Masers folded up, and the highest-placed Porsche was fifth. So we'd won the first round of the season."

While the victors sipped champagne from the huge silver trophy, scorekeepers toted up their time. A new course record: 12 hours, 1080.5 miles, at 90.4 mph average.

Phil returned to California after his Sebring victory—and ended up in traffic court. Jim Murray, columnist for the *Los Angeles Times,* related the incident:

> Phil was driving through Westwood on a nice sunny day in his innocent little Volkswagen. He got to the Wilshire/Westwood intersection and, seeing that the oncoming traffic was full of drivers with sluggish reflexes, swung left smartly in front of the pack....
> When a cop flagged him down Hill claimed he was in the right. In court, to plead his case, Phil was very patient with the judge, explaining: "Regardless of what people think of the Volkswagen it has a lot of spontaneous torque which you store up in the flywheel. It's like a pole vault—you can hardly keep climbing but you go up pretty rapidly for the first few feet. It's that way with a VW. It virtually *jumps* the first 40 feet! So, as you can see, those other cars were in no danger. I'd made the proper calculations." The judge, figuring him for a wise guy, threw the book at him and Phil didn't help things with the remark: "Our traffic laws are based on the smug assumption that anyone who thinks he is a good driver is probably a very bad driver. It just so happens there *are* a few good drivers around. I pleaded not guilty and that's how I feel—not guilty." Then Phil paid his fine.

The Murray column illustrates Hill's attitude toward current traffic limitations. He admits: "Before I switched to driving a VW I got all kinds of tickets. But, most of the time, in a VW, nobody notices you. In a sports car, you're always a choice target."

. . . . .

On the last day of April the mountains of Sicily echoed the roar of competition engines as the latest edition of the world's roughest road race, the Targa Florio, got under way, with 54 cars accelerating into action at 30-second intervals.

Olivier Gendebien was scheduled to take the first stint at the wheel of the new No. 164 rear-engined sports Ferrari he was sharing with Phil Hill, but just a few minutes before flag time the usually reliable Belgian refused to start, claiming "he didn't feel up to it." Of course, this was not the case. As *Motor Sport's* Denis Jenkinson wrote:

> Trips and Ginther had the race-proven rear-engined Sebring car, but this Hill/Gendebien model was a brand-new, untested Ferrari. It had been agreed that if anything happened to this new car early in the contest then Hill/Gendebien would be switched to the Ginther/Trips car, and Gendebien suddenly realized that if he started the race he might break down out in the wilds and Hill would then be given the second Ferrari—so he quickly feigned temperament and forced Hill to start.

Phil was understandably furious. He had not had a chance to soak his hands in the toughening solution which saved blisters in the Targa, nor did he have his own goggles with him at the line. Dark-faced with anger, he managed to borrow a pair of goggles and get the car off on schedule at 7:34 A.M., ripping away in a black cloud of rubber dust after the two leading Ferraris of Ricardo Rodríguez and Trips.

Phil was driving in a dangerous fit of temper, working out his extreme irritation with his Belgian teammate in a concentrated attack on the road, sliding the red Ferrari around the narrow "country lane" turns of the circuit which now climbed steeply into the dry Madonie mountains. He slammed past the sleepy village of Cerda, with its polished-stone-block paving, still climbing toward the highest point of the 44.7-mile circuit (the town of Caltavuturo, 1800 feet above sea level). He darted the howling Ferrari into a sharp left, where the road dips into a ravine, then snakes upward once more in a series of chilling hairpins to Bivio Polizzi.

The high humpbacked red tail of Trips' Ferrari came into sight, and Hill moved up rapidly on the German, but found no room to pass on the narrow road. Frustrated by the fact that Trips failed to see him, Phil began "gently shunting" the lead Ferrari, hoping that the German would get the idea and move over. Buried in the low cockpit of his machine, deafened by the sound of his own engine, Trips still did not realize that Hill was behind him. He could not imagine that any other car would be catching him this early in the race, and concluded that the thumps from behind indicated mechanical trouble and slowed even further. Out of patience, Phil shunted a bit too forcefully, and both cars spun off, Trips facing in the proper direction, Hill having reversed himself on the other side of the road. After exchanging excited shouts, both drivers gunned their engines and took off again, Trips leading as Hill got his dented car turned in the proper direction and boiled off in pursuit.

This time Trips got the idea and moved well over, letting the angry Californian storm by and accelerate quickly out of sight. As the road angled down in its descent toward the coast, heading for the mountain village of Collesano, Hill caught sight of the race leader, Ricardo Rodríguez, in an older front-engined Ferrari, and jammed his foot hard down on the gas. A surprised Ricardo found himself eating Hill's dust as the American smoked around him on a curve.

Now Hill was in command of the Targa, with little more than 28 miles of the 448-mile race behind him, but he did not ease off his killing pace. He was driving on his emotions, always extremely dangerous in any race, letting instinct guide him around the tight, twisting corners—and the result was inevitable. On the fast downhill section from Collesano, shortly after he had blasted past Rodríguez, Hill misjudged, the tail of his car swinging wide on a blind hairpin turn. In the blink of an eye he was out of control, the body of his Ferrari snapping off a pair of solid concrete posts in its flight from the road, jumping rocks and ditches as it slammed to earth. Seriously shaken, but otherwise unhurt, Phil crawled from the smashed machine. Now his anger was at last spent—but it had cost him the race and very nearly his life as well.

Ironically, Gendebien and Trips won the Targa, having replaced Ginther, but on the return trip to Palermo after the event, driving a rented Fiat 600, the Belgian rolled his car off the road, requiring three stitches to close the painful scalp wound he received. A case, one might conclude, of poetic justice.

·   ·   ·   ·   ·

Having dominated Grand Prix competition completely in 1959 and '60 with their 2.5-liter Climax-engined cars, both Cooper and Lotus were stubbornly opposed to the new 1.5-liter (1500 cc-maximum) Formula for 1961. They had, in fact, been actively battling the FIA on this changeover for two years. Since 1960's Formula 2 (1.5-liters) had now become Formula 1, in line with the FIA's policy to limit ever-increasing top speeds, the British were in trouble, due to the fact that they had been clinging to the unrealistic hope that the old seven-year Formula would somehow be continued. Neither team had put sufficient time or effort into their 1.5-liter engines, and therefore the tables were neatly and decisively turned in '61 when Enzo Ferrari brought three of his new rear-engined 1.5-liter machines to Monte Carlo for this first Grande Epreuve of the season. The Commendatore's rear-engined prototype, thoroughly tested and modified during the previous year (winning two races in the Formula 2 category in the hands of Trips) had now resulted in a superb Formula 1 contender. The new four-cylinder Coventry-Climax Mk 2 engine, used to power the Coopers and Lotuses, was estimated at no better than 155 hp, while the Ferraris were able to produce approximately 180 hp or better at Monaco.

The underdog was suddenly on top again.

"Actually we brought two types of cars to Monte Carlo," explains Hill. "It was somewhat the same setup as Sebring, with Richie, as test driver, getting the latest factory model, in its untried state. This one had the new V-6 engine angled at 120 degrees, which insured better handling qualities. Also his car was about 100 pounds lighter than our V-6s, which were angled at 60 degrees. The 120-degree car had a lower center of gravity in back, and on a really twisty circuit such as Monaco, where you spend a lot of time winding back and forth, this makes a real difference in roadholding. The factory didn't know how this new car would do in a hundred-lap race, so Trips and

I had been assigned the '60' model, which Baghetti won with down in Syracuse in the car's first outing on April 25, three weeks before Monaco."

World Champion Jack Brabham was frantically alternating between Monaco and Indianapolis (where he was to drive a 2.7 Cooper for his first try on the bricks), with the result that he missed more than one practice session and was started last on the grid, with a 1:44 qualifying time. The fastest man at Monte Carlo was the incredible Moss, who was substituting talent for horsepower, and his best of 1:39.1 gave him the pole. Only two-tenths of a second behind him, however, was Richie Ginther in the "120" Ferrari, with 1:39.3, which put him in row 1 next to Moss and Jimmy Clark (who had pulled out all the stops with a 1:39.6 lap in his Lotus-Climax). Graham Hill was next (also with 1:39.6), and both Hill and Trips tied at 1:39.8 in their "60" Ferraris.

Ginther stabbed the road-hugging red charger into the lead when veteran Louis Chiron dropped the flag on the 16-car field, with Hill getting away more slowly in seventh. Trips was tenth in the starting scramble, but quickly moved up as the pack began stringing out. On lap 22 Moss had surged into second, and Bonnier, in a new works Porsche, dogged the Englishman's Lotus. Within eight tours of the tight little Monte Carlo circuit, Moss was just a second behind Ginther. With Bonnier, Gurney and Hill filling the next three slots, the pace was quickening.

On lap 14 Moss took Ginther coming out of the Gasometer hairpin, and Bonnier promptly followed suit. Hill got around Gurney's Porsche and was now in fourth, while Trips continued his forward climb in the rear, also passing Gurney after a brief struggle to join his two Ferrari teammates.

By quarter distance, Hill had passed Ginther and was hot after Moss, approximately 11 seconds ahead. Bonnier was still leading the other two Ferraris, but the Porsche lost third to Ginther on lap 41, and the little Californian moved in behind Phil Hill. By lap 50, with half the race to go, Hill had cut the gap between himself and Moss to seven seconds, lapping faster than *any* car had gone in practice (at 1:38). Bonnier and Trips had fallen well back, and it was a three-man duel: Moss vs. the two Ferraris.

Lap 55 saw the Briton holding a slim four-and-a-half-second lead over Hill, who was using all of his skill to get within passing range. Moss picked up a half second at the Gasworks, but could stretch his lead no further. At 70 laps, Hill was five seconds behind, with Ginther closely shadowing his teammate.

"I began having carburetion trouble," says Phil, "and my brakes were going also, because I'd really been *using* them—and I could see that Richie had more to work with than I did. It seemed likely that he could catch Moss—and on lap 75 I waved him by, having signaled the pits that *he* should do the chasing, and Rich took off after Stirling, who now led us by almost seven seconds."

In the final quarter of this full-throttle race, with Moss and Ginther lapping *below* 1:37, the duel intensified. By lap 84 the Englishman's Lotus was now less than four seconds ahead of the fast-charging Ferrari, and in the final laps Ginther closed this gap to 3.6 seconds—yet it was not enough to catch the flying Moss. He took the checker to win the Grand Prix of Monaco after a tremendous driving display, leading the exhausted Ginther under the checker—while Hill flashed home in third, some 38 seconds behind the leaders. Trips, two full laps behind, and delayed by a faulty throttle and a dead battery, was awarded fourth, ahead of Dan Gurney's Porsche.

None could deny that Ginther and Hill had driven superbly, and only the fabulous Moss, using his keen knowledge of the Monte Carlo circuit and all of his fighting skill, had been able to hold them at bay.

The prancing horses of Enzo Ferrari were once again ready to gallop over the opposition. The pattern was clear: Ferrari was the car to beat in 1961.

––––––––––––––

CHAPTER TWENTY-THREE

A Dutch Duel and Some Ring Records

O N THE FIRST chill morning of practice at Zandvoort, for the Dutch Grand Prix a week after Monaco, BRM, Cooper, Lotus and Porsche had the winding sand-dune circuit all to themselves. No Ferraris had arrived from Maranello, and this cheered the British and German teams considerably. Perhaps Ferrari would not be able to send entries to Zandvoort so close on the heels of the Monte Carlo race. Perhaps further development of the test car, the 120-degree Ferrari, was necessary after Ginther's savage drive. Perhaps...

But all the idle speculation ended when the big Ferrari transporter rolled in at noon, and *three* gleaming new 120-degree cars were unloaded and made ready for practice. Since BRM now had the Mark 2 Climax engines as well as Lotus and Cooper, only Porsche offered any outside competition, and the German engine was definitely underpowered as compared to both Ferrari and Climax. There was much talk of a powerful Climax V-8, still in the testing stage, but for the moment all the excess horses belonged to Italy.

After a great deal of experimentation with tire pressures, carburetion and wheel camber, the trio of red Ferraris began to warm up the cold Zandvoort circuit with some very rapid lap times. When the sand had settled, all three of Enzo's cars occupied the front grid row, with times of 1:35.7 (Hill and Trips) and 1:35.9 (Ginther). Moss was sitting in row 2 with 1:36.2, and Brabham could do no better than row 3 with 1:36.6 in his Cooper. (The World Champion had finished ninth at Indianapolis, and had pulled out at Monaco with engine trouble; and Brabham realized that 1961 was not going to be his year.)

It was decided that Trips should lead and Hill follow, taking care of any members of the opposition who might become aggressive. Ginther would tag along behind his teammates and try for third at the flag for a 1-2-3 Ferrari victory. But the young Scot, Jimmy Clark, and the veteran Briton, S. Moss, had ideas of their own regarding this planned Ferrari conquest in Holland. Clark had the fastest British car on the course (though he was three-tenths of a second slower than Moss in practice), since his Lotus had been cunningly streamlined by Colin Chapman. The front wishbone pivot points had been enclosed, as well as the shock absorbers, and the smoother front-end contours gave Clark an extra 700 rpm on the straight.

The start of this Dutch Grand Prix proved nerve-racking for Phil Hill. As the race was about to begin he discovered that his clutch had packed up, and frantic Ferrari mechanics immediately scampered about the car, working on the hydraulics, while Hill sweated. Observing Phil's condition, Moss employed the needle, feigning impatience: "Push that thing away," he ordered. "It'll only jam up the rest of us." Hill pretended to ignore the Englishman, but Moss tried a new tack. "Oh, *look,* Phil — they're taking the whole bloody back end out of your car!" Hill swallowed the bait, twisting around with a wild "What? Where?" reaction, and an anguished expression on his face. Phil had pessimistically assumed that he would not be able to start the race, and this seemed to confirm his worst fears. But soon the clutch was repaired, and Hill slid into the cockpit as a grinning Moss climbed behind the wheel of his Lotus.

At the flag it was a determined Hill who squeezed out Moss into the first turn, with Trips edging into the lead. Ginther had made a ragged start and was well back as the field began to stretch out. Within five laps the Ferrari of Trips led comfortably, but Clark was flinging his small Lotus into contention, moving up rapidly on Hill and setting what was officially declared the fastest lap in the race on the seventh tour with an astonishing 1:35.5. Hill and the Scot were soon in a furious duel for second, with the Lotus matching the acceleration of the Ferrari despite its lower horsepower. Ginther's engine was misbehaving and he was barely holding off the Lotus of Stirling Moss.

Attention centered on the furious Hill-Clark battle, since Trips was maintaining his lead by four to five seconds, and Phil found that he could not shake the persistent Lotus. The two men were diving side by side into the turns, switching positions as often as five times in a single lap! Neither driver would back off, and the crowd was being treated to a fabulous two-car duel as the laps wound away. Ginther was fighting just as hard to hold off Moss, and Richie's efforts were further complicated by the fact that his seat had come adrift, and he was sliding about in the cockpit on the corners. Only the cool Trips, driving expertly at the front of the pack, could afford to relax somewhat, though it was obvious he would have preferred a larger gap between himself and young Clark.

As the race drew into its final stage, and his gas load lightened, Clark found the Lotus harder to handle; also, his throttle was sticking occasionally, and he was no longer able to match the pace of Hill's Ferrari. The Californian drew away, closing right up on the tail of Trips, and rode home directly behind him, as per the pit signal TRIPS-HILL "freezing" the first two positions. The final lap was a thriller for Moss fans, because Ginther's throttle return spring had snapped and he was forced to lift the pedal with his foot whenever he braked for a slow corner. Moss had been slip-streaming the Ferrari, and made a thrusting bid for fourth overall at the final lap. Ginther slid a bit wide coming out of the hairpin, giving Moss a chance to dive inside and lead the American up the hill into the fast bends on the back of the circuit. As they hit the finishing straight Ginther used the slipstream of the Lotus to gain a final burst of speed and moved out to pass. Ahead of them, the checker was unfurled, and the two cars ripped under the flag for a heart-stopping finish, Moss just inches ahead of Ginther's Ferrari in his dark blue British Lotus.

Thus the final order: Trips, Hill, Clark, Moss and Ginther. Surely this race had been one of the most exciting ever run at Zandvoort, and Enzo Ferrari was given something to ponder by the performances of Clark and Moss. The Lotus was nimble and fast. In mid-June, at the Grand Prix of Belgium, at Spa, the British might prove more troublesome than had been anticipated. But the red cars would be carefully prepared—and Spa was the fastest circuit in Europe.

●   ●   ●   ●   ●

"We had two sports car races before going to Belgium," says Hill. "The first was the 1000-kilometers at Nürburgring, then came Le Mans. On the Ring I teamed with Trips, and Richie with Gendebien on a pair of rear-engined Tipo 246s, the same cars we had at Sicily. The weather was very cold and threatening on race morning—and we'd had rain during practice. The Rodríguez brothers had a front-engined V-12 3-liter, but they weren't on the works team. Maserati was well represented, and two of these Masers were the new rear-engined models. In all, 63 cars in various classes started the race."

As the field got under way after the usual Le Mans sprint start, Jim Clark ripped off in his Aston Martin, hardily pursued by Moss in the RS Porsche. Hill got away in the middle of the pack (though in registering third-fastest practice time his car had been parked next to Moss in the lineup), but by the end of lap 1 he had bulled up into second, screaming by the pits just six seconds behind the Englishman.

Hill had one purpose in mind: pass Moss and build a substantial lead in his nine laps at the wheel, so that when he handed the car over to Trips they would have a "cushion" to offset the predicted rain which was likely to fall as the 44-lap race continued. (The Moss-Porsche combination in the wet on the Nürburgring was a potent one, and *now* was the time to go.)

Foot hard down on the gas, Hill began to go. He whistled past Moss, setting a new lap record on the second tour at 9:31.9, and led the Porsche by 16 seconds as they passed the pit area for the second time. With a dry track in front of him, his car handling beautifully, engine razor-sharp and singing, Phil calmly set his mind to fast motoring. By the fifth lap he had cut his time to 9:25.9—then to 9:22.2 —then, on lap 7, to a fabulous 9:18.4! Nothing had been seen on the Ring like this since Juan Fangio's legendary run in the 1957 German Grand Prix. In his fabled pursuit of Collins and Hawthorn on the Ring in '57 the Argentine World Champion, driving his greatest race, at the peak of his matchless form, had produced the then-staggering time of 9:17.4 in a Formula 1 GP Maserati. Here was Phil Hill, on a "clumsy" 1300-pound sports two-seater, lapping within a second of that mark!

Yet Hill was not done. He was on the toughest circuit in the world, 14 miles of wicked curves, blind brows and roller-coaster tree-lined straights, where few drivers have the courage or capability to extract the full potential from a racing machine—and after proving his car and his talent in a series of successively faster laps, each establishing a new sports record, Phil set out on the eighth tour for one more all-out effort. With the immense crowd of 250,000 roaring approval, he squeezed the last drop of power from his engine and registered the magnificent time of 9:15.8—decisively shattering Fangio's Grand Prix mark and raising the absolute sports car record of Stirling Moss by *more than 16 seconds.*

"After nine laps I pulled in for a tire change and let Trips take it," says Hill. "After our stop we still had a 44-second lead, but then it began to rain like crazy, and I knew we were in for plenty of grief with our open air-cooling vents in the back allowing water to pour right into the engine."

Moss, with rain tires and the nimble Porsche beneath his throttle foot, began moving up as expected. He was then running third behind the Ginther/Gendebien Ferrari, and with the wet track to aid him Moss was slicing away the gap at the rate of 15 seconds per lap. Gendebien spun under this pressure, letting Moss by on lap 20, and the Hill/Trips lead was in question, though the German driver was still well ahead. The freezing rain was soon followed by sleet, then snow began to fall, and the larger cars eased off to keep from leaving the iced road. Hill had taken over once more from Trips, with rain tires fitted on their Ferrari, and was maintaining his lead over the Porsche by some hard and consistent driving in the wet.

On lap 24 the rain stopped, and Hill's Ferrari sounded a bit healthier. He began to extend the car once again, and was running at an estimated 125 mph on lap 25 when his worn rain tires encountered a puddle on the straight coming into Kallenhard. The red car was thrown into a violent spin, whirling end-for-tail several times as it clouted the dirt bankings, sending up clouds of mud and gravel. Phil ducked as the machine headed for a roadside ditch, survived the impact, and leaped from the cockpit when flames began to envelop the car. The blaze was quickly extinguished by track firemen, and a shaken Hill thumbed a ride back to the pits, leaving the battered carcass of his Ferrari smoking in the ditch behind him.

Gregory and Casner won the 1000-kilometer race for Maserati, but Enzo Ferrari scored points for second when the Rodríguez brothers brought their front-engined V-12 over the line a lap behind the birdcage Maser. The Ginther/Gendebien Ferrari was third, with the highest Porsche placement being sixth overall. A rain puddle, worn tires, and perhaps a split second of inattention had deprived Phil Hill of a fine victory, and he was doubly determined that no mistakes would be made at Le Mans.

•   •   •   •   •

"Actually, there were *two* more championship sports car races left for '61," says Phil, "but we were already 11 points ahead of Maserati and if we could win Le Mans then it would be all over as far as the title was concerned. Then there would be no need to concern ourselves over the Pescara race in August. The issue would be settled— so we planned on exerting full effort at Le Mans."

Again, as in many past long-distance events, Hill was teamed with Gendebien, after their altercation in Sicily had been smoothed over. They shared a front-engined 3-liter V-12 Ferrari, of the Sebring-winning type, and another of these cars was in the hands of Mairesse and Mike Parkes (a vigorous young driver, newly risen from club racing in Britain). The V-6 rear-engined car, figured to be less reliable over the long haul, was given to Ginther and Trips. A dark horse in the '61 race was provided by the V-12 Ferrari of the brothers Rodríguez, but the main opposition was expected from Maserati, with four cars ranged against the prancing horse. Two of these, from Briggs Cunningham, were the latest rear-engined 12-cylinder models, producing an honest 320 hp, making them the most powerful cars at Le Mans. An older Tipo 61 completed the Cunningham lineup. Another Tipo 63 Maser, two Aston Martins and four works Porsches were also in the lists against Ferrari (with Porsche running third in points behind the two Italian firms). With 55 brightly painted machines along the pit area facing the track, and a full day and night of speed ahead, it could be anybody's race.

Hill and Gendebien were determined to make it theirs. And although two Aston Martins were first away, snarling under the Dunlop Bridge, the savage red cars of Enzo Ferrari took over on the long Mulsanne straight. Ginther led; Gendebien was in second. Pedro Rodríguez was streaking up from behind, passing Walt Hansgen's briskly driven Maserati by lap 4 and closing on the leaders. On lap 9 the Rodríguez Ferrari, No. 17, had passed both works cars, and the pattern was set. The boys from Mexico City were obviously out to make up for their Sebring defeat.

Shortly beyond the third hour a hard rain drenched the circuit, with the Rodríguez car still pacing the field. Walt Hansgen lost the Maserati at Tertre Rouge, slamming into the bank and putting the fourth-place Maser out of contention. The American escaped with a broken elbow. Then Bruce Halford's Cooper Monaco spun in the wet under the Dunlop Bridge at 120 mph, bounced viciously into the retaining wall and threw Halford into the path of Mike Parkes. The Britisher darted between the dazed driver and the smashed Cooper, narrowly averting a disaster.

From this point on, all through the night into the dawn, the race became a two-way battle: Ferrari vs. Ferrari. The Hill/Gendebien No. 10 against the Rodríguez brothers' No. 17, both 12-cylinder machines, matched on power and acceleration, locked in a fierce duel for the overall lead in this exhausting 24-hour contest.

"The pit kept telling Gendebien to slow down," says Hill, "and, of course, this was the *proper* way to win at Le Mans, but we simply couldn't afford to let the Rodríguez boys build up any kind of sizable lead. I would get out of the pit area, a little farther down the track, and wave Olivier on, so that we kept applying the pressure, hoping to blow up their car. This was a calculated risk but one which I felt was justified."

The duel was unrelenting. In the fifth hour the Rodríguez car led; in the sixth hour it was the No. 10 Ferrari; then the No. 17 again in the seventh hour, Hill in the eighth, Rodríguez in the ninth. After nine full hours of racing the Rodríguez brothers were a bare *eight seconds* ahead of Hill/Gendebien. This was soon reduced to no more than a car length as the twin Ferraris thundered down the pit straight side by side, headlights slicing through the darkness.

The remainder of the field had been all but forgotten in this incredibly extended battle, but Stirling Moss was forced out when riding in fourth overall in his GT Ferrari, resulting from a blown head gasket, and the well-driven Ginther/Trips rear-engined Ferrari eventually stopped with a split fuel tank.

The frontline dogfight continued without letup, although faces in the factory Ferrari pit were dark with worry. If these two machines blew up one another the Pabst/Thompson Maserati, running steadily behind the Italian cars, might move in to claim the victory (as the Shelby/Salvadori Aston Martin had done in '59).

Dawn tinted the sky over Le Mans, and still the red Ferraris dueled, cutting laps of 4 minutes, 3 seconds, impossibly fast after a night-long run. At 7 A.M. the official gap between the Ferraris, after 15 hours of speed, was exactly 2.5 seconds! The crowd groaned, however, when the mud-spattered Rodríguez machine rolled into the pits at 7:30—remaining there for 24 minutes, as a faulty condenser and coil were replaced.

"That stop decided the race," says Hill. "We were able to ease off then, and ride home, despite the fact that the Rodríguez boys made a strong effort to overtake, blowing their engine entirely just two hours short of the finish. Mairesse and Parkes brought in the other works car for second—and the Pabst/Thompson Maser was fourth. None of the Astons finished."

In winning brilliantly for the second time at Le Mans, Hill had broken all records with his Belgian teammate. They had set a new long-distance mark of 2781.7 miles, at an average speed of almost 116 mph. And in addition to this (and $10,000) they were awarded second on Index of Performance, ahead of the Fiats and Porsches, a category which heavily favors the smaller-engined machines.

"This gave the Manufacturers' Championship to Ferrari," says Phil, "so we could all quit worrying about winning Pescara."

As he had done in 1956, '57, '58 and '60, Phil Hill had again made a sizable contribution to Enzo Ferrari's seasonal victory.

CHAPTER TWENTY-FOUR

Hill vs. Trips

A S THE THIRD Grande Epreuve of the 1961 season approached, Stirling Moss and Wolfgang von Trips led in the battle for the World Championship with 12 points each. Hill was next, two points behind them. The Grand Prix of Belgium at Spa, on June 18, was almost certainly going to be a sweep for Ferrari, and Moss had resigned himself to a drop in the standings. In practice for this event, using the Rob Walker Lotus, Stirling had been unable to qualify any higher than row 3, with four Ferraris ahead of him on the grid, as well as Surtees, Graham Hill and Tony Brooks.

Hill made fast time, and had pole position, with Trips and Gendebien next to him in the first row. Ginther was directly behind in another Ferrari. (The Gendebien car, painted Belgian racing yellow, in honor of his participation on his home circuit, was an older "60" while the other three factory Ferraris all sported the faster "120" engines.)

Unlucky Cliff Allison had sustained two broken legs in a spectacular practice crash, wiping out his Lotus, and this incident, combined with the tragic accidents in '60, served to remind the incautious that Spa was a most unforgiving circuit.

In describing it, Denis Jenkinson commented: "Spa-Francorchamps, with its lap speed of approximately 130 mph, and plenty of 150-mph corners, presents the Grand Prix driver with the opportunity to show his true mettle, to demonstrate just how much ahead in ability he is over the ordinary driver."

With a winning car under him at last, Phil Hill demonstrated his skill at Spa in practice by besting all his teammates in a most convincing manner, setting a time of 3:59.3, becoming the only driver at Spa in '61 to get below the 4-minute mark.

None of the British could begin to approach this kind of performance in Belgium. Clark was most unhappy with his car, and a discouraged Brabham was out of the running, consigned to the fifth row with his Cooper.

Based on this practice speed, it seemed logical to assume that Hill would win this Grand Prix, but since Enzo Ferrari had refused to name a team leader ("I believe in letting all my drivers have an equal chance at becoming World Champion") the ambitious and always-fast Count Wolfgang von Trips was a solid threat. Since Phil had been of great help to Trips in the German's victory at Zandvoort the plum here at Spa would fall to Hill, providing he made no mistakes and established himself as fast or faster than Trips. This he had done in practice; now he had to prove himself in the race.

"There had always been great tension with Ferrari," says Phil. "Italians are proud and short-tempered. Ever since I joined the team back in '56 I'd been involved in many flare-ups, and witnessed even more. You could never really relax with Ferrari, because there was always someone who wanted to see you goof, who was ready to take your place if you didn't keep your wits about you. The drivers argued with the engineers and the team manager argued with the drivers and the mechanics argued with everybody—and it was even more unsettling in '61, with the World Championship in the balance. Trips wanted it very much, and so did I. And despite the fact that we were members of the same team we each knew that we'd have to fight with everything we had to win the title. Therefore, the tension continued to build from race to race."

The opening laps of the Belgian GP were a treat for the 70,000 Belgian spectators ringing the long, fast circuit. Their idol, Olivier Gendebien, had taken the lead on lap 1, but had been outbraked into La Source hairpin by Hill, relegating the Belgian to second. By lap 2, however, he had passed Hill for the lead, to be in turn passed by the Californian again. On the ninth tour Gendebien dropped back somewhat, allowing Trips and Hill to move into a secure lead, since his less-powerful engine had been overstrained in the opening stage, and now the Belgian wished only to hold Ginther at bay for third.

Hill and Trips began seesawing the lead back and forth between them, but rain slowed them both and Ginther whipped past Gendebien to move up directly behind his fellow Ferrari drivers, receiving a pit signal from Tavoni: GINT 3RD, meaning that he was not to attempt passing.

In proving his speed and ability to regain the lead, Hill was finally given the official nod from the pits and final positions were "frozen"—with the American eventually leading Trips under the checker by seven-tenths of a second. Ginther and Gendebien made it a 1-2-3-4 conquest for Ferrari. (Moss could do no better than eighth, with Brabham failing to finish.)

"I was virtually blind in one eye for the last third of that race," says Phil. "On lap 20 a pebble was thrown up, lodging in my left eye, but this was nothing compared to the feeling of joy I experienced in winning my second Grand Prix."

Hill was now in the lead for the coveted title, with 19 points. Trips was just a single point behind him, with 18 — with Moss and Ginther tied at 12 points each.

The French Grand Prix, at Reims early in July, would be a very important race, since if Hill could win in France his lead would be consolidated, and much of the pressure would be removed.

.   .   .   .   .

As it had in '59, a searing yellow sun burned over Reims, blasting the track with furnace temperatures, and not a cloud appeared in the French sky on race day to relieve the summer heat. Several of the drivers cut sizable holes in the bonnets of their cars, or removed body paneling in an effort to insure a flow of air into the oven-hot cockpits. Hill (who had won 100 bottles of champagne by setting the fastest practice lap at 2:24.9, a second and a half ahead of Trips) had evolved an unusual method of cooling himself during the race, recalling that severe heat exhaustion in '59 had caused him to nearly black out. He put a large rubberized bag of ice water on the floor of his car, with a hose leading to the upper cockpit. The bag could be squeezed by the driver's legs to send a stream of water through the hose onto his back and shoulders. A strange but practical gimmick.

Since Reims was also a fast circuit, the Ferraris were easily the quickest cars in practice, with Trips and Ginther lined up next to Hill in the front of the starting grid. The young Italian Giancarlo Baghetti was getting his first ride in a Grande Epreuve, driving the slower "60" Ferrari which Gendebien had in Belgium, and although his best time was only good enough to put him in row 5 (as seven British cars and Gurney's Porsche had been faster) it was nonetheless expected that he would finish in fourth overall behind the factory "120" models. Another all-Ferrari sweep was in prospect.

Supporting pre-race predictions, Hill and Trips blistered by the pits at the end of the first lap well in command of things, with Ginther harried by Moss, riding the American's slipstream. Stirling managed to get by Richie when the Ferrari pilot spun in the fifth lap, but Ginther immediately repassed as Moss fell back, his bid over and done. The inexperienced Baghetti was battling a gaggle of British and German cars in the center of the pack, while Hill continued to stretch his lead, followed by Trips who seemed a bit worried by the pace Phil was setting.

No one really knew which Ferrari had been pegged to win the French GP, but Denis Jenkinson witnessed a scene in the pits prior to this race, later summing up the Ferrari strategy in *Motor Sport:*

> When pre-race orders indicated that—despite his fast practice time—Hill was *not* to win this event, there was some umbrage, and in the opening laps the American was obviously pressing on, to show that when he relinquished the lead it was only to obey pit orders. On lap 8 he began to slow down to wait for Trips, and on lap 13 Hill lifted off, letting Trips go by into the lead.

On lap 17 both Trips and Hill were given the SLO sign from Tavoni, and Ginther began catching them both as per the Ferrari plan. The race was duplicating the pattern set in Belgium when suddenly the crowd gasped. The front-running car was in the pits, engine smoking, water leaking from the exhaust pipe. A stone had pierced the radiator and the Ferrari had blown up in the fierce heat. Trips was out of the race.

Smiling broadly at this piece of good fortune ("Lady Luck seemed to be with me right then!"), Hill took over the lead he had so reluctantly ceded to Trips, with Ginther a safe 14 seconds behind. Baghetti was well back, still hassling with several GP veterans, and it looked as if Hill had the victory in his pocket.

But Reims, in 1961, was a race of many surprises. On lap 28 Ginther slid on the floating gravel which covered the melted tar at the Thillois hairpin and looped in a most spectacular fashion. However, he was soon away, still a secure second ahead of a still-struggling Baghetti.

Riding far ahead of the field under the hot sun, his engine sounding crisp and healthy, Hill allowed himself to relax, sure of the victory which seemed solidly within his grasp. He was taking it easy, running 10 seconds under his best practice time, when he entered lap 38 (with only 14 more laps remaining). As he sailed serenely down the straightaway into Thillois, Phil was counting up the extra championship points in his mind, points which would give him a comfortable edge on his German teammate.

But trouble waited at Thillois. The Lotus-Climax of Stirling Moss had closed on the Hill Ferrari down the long straight, and although several laps in arrears (due to wheel problems) the Englishman seemed intent on going by into the hairpin. Phil, suddenly aware that he was being pressed, attempted to outbrake the Lotus into Thillois, instantly spinning on the hot gravel-and-tar surface.

"This spin was horrible," says Phil. "It should have been a simple 360-degree turn, costing me no more than a few seconds at most before I was back on the course. Richie had just spun at Thillois with no serious results, and there was no real problem involved. Even if you stall, each GP car has a self-starter, so you can get going again right away. Well, Stirling gave me a gentle clout as he came around wide, and this jarred my foot off the throttle. The engine went dead. I punched the starter. Nothing. Now, usually the thing would restart easily on the battery, but I had a leak across the alternator and in such terrific heat—the track temperature was 122 degrees—the water had just cooked right out of the battery. So the starter was useless."

In a panic, Hill jumped from the cockpit and began to push the Ferrari down the road under the blazing sun. He would get the car rolling, leap back into it, try to fire the engine by putting it in gear, fail, jump out and start pushing again. This strength-sapping procedure was repeated a dozen times and, as one reporter observed: "It was heartbreaking to see this man, already nearly exhausted, pushing and repushing to get a start and hold onto that lead."

Finally the engine burst to life, but Hill had clapped the car in gear with one hand while pushing with the other. As a result, the Ferrari almost got away on its own, and Phil was forced to summon the final reserve of his strength to run and catch it, pulling himself back into the cockpit and resuming the race in a state of near collapse.

But he had no chance of victory. Eight other cars had passed while he fought the stubborn Ferrari, and he resumed over a lap behind Ginther.

Richie was now tasting the sweet fruits of victory as he led the French Grand Prix, but his hopes ended as abruptly as they began when the oil pressure gauge needle dropped alarmingly. The radiator had become completely blocked by gravel, seriously overheating the engine, and on lap 41 Ginther was out, stopping just short of the moment when he knew his engine would seize.

Now, with only a few laps to the checker, Baghetti became the hero of the hour by engaging Bonnier and Gurney in a fabulous battle for the lead, blowing up the Swedish driver's Porsche and leading the American under the flag by less than a car length. The "rookie" had saved the day for Enzo Ferrari, and the Commendatore had achieved his third consecutive GP victory.

A dispirited Hill, trailing by two laps, came over the line for ninth, thoroughly demoralized by his error at Thillois.

"That stupid spinout robbed me of the psychological lift and substantial points lead that winning at Reims would have provided," says Phil. "I was still ahead of Trips by one point, but this was little consolation to me, since I knew that from here on to the end of the season the pressure would be intensified tenfold. And all because of my own mistake."

· · · · ·

On July 15, at Aintree, the British Grand Prix was scheduled as the fifth Grande Epreuve of the season. Hill drove up to the circuit almost a week before the race, hoping for some advance practice time in his own car over this unfamiliar English course. Aintree, home once each year for the world famous Grand National, is exactly three miles in length, laid out on the grassy steeplechase grounds, and it roughly parallels the horse track. Almost entirely flat, it is nonetheless dodgy, with huts, hedges, gates, wooden barriers and the like to keep the drivers fully occupied. Near the end of the back straight is Melling Crossing, where the road snakes right, then left in two fast bends, passing through heavy wooden gates, built of 18 x 18 beams backed by spiked fences and padded by hay bales. Since Melling is approached at a near-flat-out rate of speed it can prove hair-raising to a driver who loses control there, as three members of the Ferrari team were to discover in this upcoming Grand Prix.

Located in the bleak North of England, the site is just five miles outside Liverpool, that grim gray industrial port city with its many factories belching black smoke into the sky, and despite the grass surrounding the circuit and its huge grandstands, Aintree is anything but a cheerful spot.

Phil was not allowed to drive his own car on the course, so he methodically began to walk its three miles, detouring over fences and water jumps, in an effort to familiarize himself with road characteristics. Subsequently, in practice, he was the first driver to set a time of 1:58.8, which was later matched by the Ferrari of Trips and Ginther and by Bonnier's Porsche. (Apparently the timekeeping watches only read to the nearest fifth of a second, which explained the fact that these *four* drivers all qualified at 1:58.8, while several of the slower times were also identical.)

The fourth Ferrari driver, Giancarlo Baghetti, seemed out of his depth at Aintree, and he spun twice at Melling, cutting a series of deep furrows in the soft grass, while his fastest qualifying lap landed him far back on the grid, on row 8, next to Jack Fairman in the new four-wheel-drive Ferguson.

After having been subjected to the killing heat of Reims, the GP drivers were now harassed by cutting wind and rain, and since Aintree did not drain properly, deep puddles caused no end of concern for the unhappy chauffeurs. Race morning promised more rain, as the sky over Aintree was soot-dark, a combination of factory smoke blown downwind from Liverpool and fat-bellied storm clouds. Therefore, rain tires became the order of the day, and by starting time, 2:30 P.M., rain was falling hard and steadily on the 30-car field.

Hill had the pole, with Ginther and Bonnier next to him, Trips just back of them in row 2 with Moss. As the Union Jack was lowered, Hill jumped ahead of the pack into Waterway Corner (aptly named!), his red Ferrari lost in a blur of spray. Behind him, in a veritable curtain of blinding water, Trips and Ginther held off Moss and Bonnier. The Swedish pilot dropped back quickly, but Moss, who had won more than once here at Aintree on a GP car, and whose uncanny skill in the wet was well known, decided to give the Ferraris a run for their money, and hung on, grimly riding Ginther's tailpipe.

For five laps Hill led Trips in the torrential downpour, but on lap 6, speedboating his Ferrari down the back straightaway at high revs, he got slightly out of line braking into Melling, his front wheels losing adhesion on the glare-ice road. Phil got off the brakes, but was forced to use them again to diminish his speed for the bend. Immediately he was skidding sideways, still at a rapid rate, and found himself heading straight for one of the stout wooden gateposts.

"I could see that big post coming right at me," recalls Hill, "and I thought of my two crashes in the Targa and at Nürburgring—but then, I just barely managed to get pointed in the proper direction again and, using all my power and what traction I still had, shot through the gate and on down the road. I remember thinking: 'They can have the damn Championship!'—and I slowed down, figuring my life was worth more than a world title. The thing was, I had changed the braking ratio during practice when the course had been dry, putting more on the front. It was my fault; I'd requested it, and on the wet road it was bad, since you don't get so much weight transfer forward. When I hit the brakes the front wheels skated out from under me. That was a frightening moment, and it affected my entire performance during the remainder of the race."

Trips had passed Hill as the Californian eased off, and it was then Ginther's turn to get sideways at Melling, which allowed Moss to nip by into third. Henry Taylor, in a Lotus, had also fallen victim to the treacherous crossing, but had been unable to avoid a crash. His car spun into the grass, demolished a sign, then scraped along a wooden wall. A splintered section of this wall punctured Taylor's fuel tank, trapping him in the cockpit as the car blazed, but he escaped with minor burns and some cracked ribs.

By lap 9 Moss was pressing Hill, who had definitely slackened his pace, and the Englishman passed to a round of frantic applause from the stands on lap 10, setting out after Trips. Moss kept charging, and on lap 24 was very close to the leading Ferrari when he joined the parade of Melling spinners, skidding sideways at 100 mph in the slippery bend and exchanging nose for tail before resuming the chase.

Just four laps later, at Waterway, the back-running Baghetti was forced to swerve when the car ahead braked early, and got into a roadside puddle, losing all traction and crashing backward through the railing to put him out of the race. The young Italian sat out the remaining laps as a spectator.

Ginther now passed Hill into third, then got by Moss, whose Lotus was obviously in trouble and falling back. The rain had stopped and conditions had improved accordingly. Hill applied fresh speed, passing Moss, as the Briton's race was run. A fractured brake line sent him into the pits.

The Moss retirement removed the only threat to Trips, and as the track dried under a late sun, he led smoothly to the checker, Hill having moved ahead of Ginther on team orders into second. (Richie had backed off to let Hill go by just as Phil had done for Mike Hawthorn in '58, giving his California teammate precious extra points in the championship struggle.) Ginther's official third place gave the Maranello cars a 1-2-3 finish, with the highest-placed British car taking fourth overall in the hands of Jack Brabham (for the World Champion's best race of the season). In winning at Aintree, Wolfgang von Trips now headed the points listings with 27 to Hill's 25. (Ginther had 16, Moss 12.) Trips had driven a superb race, making no mistakes in the wet, and had strengthened his avowed intention to bring the world title to Germany in 1961. On home ground, at the forthcoming German Grand Prix in August, Trips would be hard to beat. For Phil Hill, the pressure was still building.

———————————

CHAPTER TWENTY-FIVE

A New World Champion

THE HOME OF Count Wolfgang Berghe von Trips was located just 60 miles from the Nürburgring, and for this sixth Grande Epreuve of 1961, to be fought on German soil around the wicked, twisting 174 curves of the Ring, a huge crowd of spectators swelled into the circuit, pitching tents in the dark Eifel forest and in the rolling meadows and deep-grassed fields, hoping to see their current idol, the dashing Trips, emerge victorious in this difficult Grand Prix. By race day, August 6, they were 300,000 strong, estimated to be the largest crowd at the Ring since the glorious days of Mercedes and Auto Union. Practice, over this exacting circuit, had already taken a toll of the competitors: Michael May had climbed one of the bankings, upending his British mount—and Jimmy Clark, diving into the fast Schwedenkreuz curve, had his steering fail completely at speed, resulting in a serious crackup. Fortunately, only the *cars* were badly injured.

Phil Hill came to the Ring in a state of high tension, afraid that even if he managed to outdrive Trips in the German's own backyard he would not be given the official nod which would allow him to stay ahead. It would be smarter team politics to let Trips score in Germany, and Phil was keenly aware of his discouraging position. Perhaps because he was once more the underdog and had always been able to come from behind with amazing performances, he swung into the rhythm of the circuit (after a day of camber adjustments, suspension changes involving higher or lower roll centers, etc.) and began taking each curve progressively faster. The red Ferrari's rising scream echoed through the Black Forest as Hill slammed around the 14-mile strip of road, unwinding like a great dark ribbon behind him.

The timing watches clicked out the figures: 8:55.2—for a stagger-ing new course record. Phil Hill had become the first driver in history to officially break the 9-minute barrier at Nürburgring. The Californian now held both the sports car and GP records at the Ring, having knocked a full 14 seconds off the Vanwall mark set by Moss in '58.

Hill, therefore, won the pole, with Brabham, Moss and Bonnier next to him in row 1. The Australian World Champion, whose season to date had been quite unsuccessful due to his underpowered Cooper, now had the latest engine from Coventry, a V-8 Climax rated at 175 hp, representing a 20-hp gain over the Mark 2. Only one of these new V-8s, so long-awaited by the British, was available for the German GP, having just been installed in Brabham's Cooper chassis for its race debut. Even in an untested state, the V-8 was definitely a dark horse, and as Brabham had qualified at 9:01.4, the new powerplant looked capable of giving the Ferraris some real competition.

Plagued by sticking valves and a mishandling car, Trips had not made the first row of the grid. He had been over 10 seconds slower than Hill, but he had a new engine in his Ferrari for the race (having upped his time considerably with it on the final practice day) and was expected to lead the American once the event got properly under way. (The other two Ferraris, in the hands of Ginther and Mairesse, were far back on the grid, surrounded by British and German cars.)

Juan Fangio, who was to drop the flag, made a warmly applauded "tour of honor" in a 300SL Mercedes, then coolly stepped forward to start the race. As the field thundered toward Sudcurve, Jack Brabham surged ahead in his V-8 Cooper, holding a slender lead over Moss and Bonnier. On the North Curve the Australian fought dog-gedly to maintain his advantage, but an error in judgment was soon to put him out of contention. He had installed soft rain tires on the front wheels, leaving hard tires on the rear. His road-holding, under such an arrangement, was severely affected.

"I was behind the leaders at this early stage," says Phil, "and I had my eye on Brabham when he lost control. He got onto a wet patch of road, under one of the overhanging trees, and slid violently sideways, tried to correct, couldn't, and disappeared through the hedges, stuffing his car into the forest. He wasn't hurt, but he sure was out of things for the day."

On the same initial lap Gurney's Porsche and Graham Hill's BRM made contact, with the Britisher plunging down a grass slope to stop well off the road, while Gurney continued with one side of his Porsche flattened from the impact.

Moss had passed Bonnier into the lead, but Hill now came charging up, overwhelming both drivers into the Adenau crossing. However, by the Karussell, Moss was ahead of the red Ferrari, driving masterfully. With the first lap completed, Moss led Hill by two seconds, and was widening the gap.

On the second fast tour, Innes Ireland's Lotus caught fire at 100 mph, and by the time the driver had leaped out the car was blazing fiercely. Sadly, Ireland saw it devoured by the flames.

By the fifth lap of this 15-lap race, with Trips closing fast behind him and Moss pulling away in front, Hill was having his troubles: his gearbox had momentarily jammed, forcing him to cover half a lap at 10,000 rpm. Also, his car was bottoming on the uphill sections, slowing him further. In two more tours of the circuit, Trips was only a second behind him, and snapped past on lap 8 to a thunderous roar of delight from the German spectators. On the ninth lap Trips set a new mark at 8:59.9 — but Hill was fighting back with all the skill and stamina he possessed, registering a fantastic 8:57.8 on lap 10, which was to stand as the race record.

Yet Moss led them both, still pulling away. No one was going to catch the English Ringmaster on this day, and much of the crowd's attention centered on the bitterly fought duel for second. On lap 11, at the South Curve, Hill gunned around his German rival, holding the inside position on the North Curve as Trips attempted to repass. At Adenau it was Trips leading Hill, and down the pit straight both cars were tied together, engines howling at high revs into the Sudcurve.

On lap 13, with less than 30 miles to go, a light rain began to fall, enabling Moss to stretch away from the two Ferraris to a 15-second lead. (He had installed rain tires on his Lotus at the outset and Ferrari had not; this was the final edge Moss needed to defeat the Italian cars.) So, first place was already secured.

Behind the flying Briton, the wheel-to-wheel battle for second continued, with the crowd solidly behind Trips. A groan went up from the packed mass of spectators on lap 14 when Hill stabbed past the German in his final desperate bid. The question in Phil's mind: *Can I hold him to the flag?*

On the final lap Hill led Trips out of the Karussell, but when the two Ferraris ripped onto the back straight they were side by side; then Trips tucked in behind Hill to ride his slipstream, with the intention of using his slightly lower axle ratio to gain the few hundred extra revs he needed to whip out and pass the American before the checker fell.

Whether this plan would have been successful will never be known, for the skies opened at this moment, and as the two cars topped the crest of the hill at the Antonius bridge, they ran into a sudden, solid wall of water. Lacking rain tires, both drivers scrabbled for traction, sliding sideways together. Trips recovered control just a split second ahead of Hill, and aimed the red snout of his Ferrari at the waiting checker. As the flag whipped down, and the crowd rose en masse in the stands, Wolfgang von Trips led Hill across the line by the snap of a finger.

The German Grand Prix had ended. Finishing with a 21-second lead in his underpowered Lotus, Stirling Moss had defeated his Ferrari competitors in a dazzling display of driving mastery, and Trips had scored valuable points for second overall. In losing to the German, Hill trailed 29 to 33 in the season-long fight for the title. Moss now had 21 points and Ginther, who finished eighth at the Ring after Mairesse crashed the third Ferrari, still had 16.

The upcoming Grand Prix of Italy, on September 10, 1961, was fated to decide the issue. The world would have a new champion after Monza.

•   •   •   •   •

As they had done in 1960, the Italian race organizers at Monza specified that the entire road-course-plus-banking must be used in this GP event, and the boycott imposed by the British factory teams the previous year was reluctantly dropped in 1961, although team spokesmen made it known that they would have been much happier without the banking. Thus, full entries from Lotus, Cooper, BRM, Porsche and Ferrari were received, backed up by many private entries including three Cooper-Maseratis. Of the 37 entrants, all but five made the starting grid.

Hill is pictured with one of the Rodríguez brothers from Mexico City. Phil was paired with Ricardo Rodríguez for the 1962 Daytona Continental 3-Hour Race. At nineteen, Ricardo was the younger of the lionhearted brothers. *(Flip Schulke)*

Phil is shown in the No. 1 Ferrari 246SP that he and Ricardo drove to a second after posting the fastest lap at the 1962 Daytona Continental on February 11.
(Flip Schulke)

On May 27, Hill and Gendebien drove a 246SP to a win in front of the spectators at Germany's Nürburgring circuit.
(Flip Schulke)

Phil and the new 250 GTO in the extensive Ferrari garage area at Sebring. (Flip Schulke)

And at speed in the 12-hour race held in March of 1962. Phil Hill and Olivier Gendebien earned a second overall, and first in the GT class. (Flip Schulke)

Two feet on the brakes were not enough to keep Phil Hill's 268SP from leaving the road when the throttle stuck wide open during the 46th running of Sicily's Targa Florio. *(Peter Coltrin)*

With eight laps remaining in the 1962 Grand Prix of Monaco, Hill was in second, 17 seconds behind Bruce McLaren's Cooper, when he started to reel McLaren in, finishing just 1.3 seconds behind the Cooper. "Another lap and Hill would have won," said team owner John Cooper. *(Flip Schulke)*

Entertaining Dan Gurney and others with stories at the post-race dinner party, after a remarkable drive at the Grand Prix of Monaco in 1962. *(Flip Schulke)*

Phil Hill is leading teammate Ricardo Rodríguez through a practice lap on the circuit of Zandvoort, prior to the 1962 Dutch Grand Prix. *(Geoffrey Goddard / GP Library)*

At Le Mans in June of '62, Ferrari entered Phil Hill and Olivier Gendebien in an experimental 4-liter Testa Rossa. They brought it home first—for the pair's third win for Ferrari in the 24-hour French classic. (Flip Schulke; Top right—LAT)

Phil Hill spent a frustrating 1963 Grand Prix season driving the underdeveloped ATS. A broken suspension joint ended Phil's wet drive at Mexico City. *(Dave Friedman)*

At the Grand Prix of Italy at Monza, Hill finished eleventh in the V-8 powered ATS. This was the best showing in a dismal season with the ill-fated, Carlo Chiti designed Formula I car. *(Geoffrey Goddard / Road & Track)*

At Le Mans in 1963, Phil Hill drove the very fast Aston Martin Project 215. On lap five, he narrowly missed an overturned French coupé spinning like a top in the middle of the track. The Aston Project 215 was retired in the third hour when the transaxle failed. Co-drivers Lucien Bianchi and Phil Hill converse while team manager John Wyer (to Hill's left) passes the bad news. *(Nigel Snowdon/The Klemantaski Collection)*

For the Sebring 12-Hour Grand Prix of Endurance in March 1964, Phil was paired with Jo Schlesser in one of Carroll Shelby's Cobras. They finished sixth overall, ahead of the Ferrari GTOs. *(Flip Schulke)*

In April 1964 the Shelby American team went to Sicily for the 48th
Targa Florio. After four-and-a-half hours of competition, the No. 142
Cobra of Phil Hill and Bob Bondurant was slowed as a rear suspension
mount tore loose. Each lap consisted of over 1000 corners and 44.7 miles
of rough road. They retired after eight laps. (Geoffrey Goddard / GP Library)

Hill drove one of two Cobra Daytonas entered on August 29, '64, at Goodwood for the
Tourist Trophy. On the 17th lap he brought in the smoking Coupé with a hole in the oil
cooler. They were sent back out to finish at a reduced rate. (Dave Friedman Collection)

An inferno resulted when Hill went off course into the hay bales at the Zeltweg airfield circuit, site of the 1964 Austrian Grand Prix. (Geoffrey Goddard / GP Library)

Dan Gurney is visible behind Bruce McLaren, Jim Clark, Jo Siffert, and others considering the remains of Hill's charred Cooper. (Geoffrey Goddard / GP Library)

Team owner John Cooper, obviously upset over the loss of equipment at Zeltweg.
(Geoffrey Goddard / GP Library)

Things had not gone at all well for Phil at the Grand Prix of Austria. First, his Cooper T73 was badly damaged in a crash during practice. Then, on the 59th lap of the race itself, Hill crashed the ill-handling backup car through the straw bales, where it burned to the hulk seen below. Luckily, Phil safely escaped before the blaze erupted.
(Geoffrey Goddard / GP Library)

At the Belgian Grand Prix on June 14, 1964 at the Spa-Francorchamps circuit, engine trouble forced Hill to retire the V-8 Cooper T73. *(Flip Schulke)*

On October 4, at Watkins Glen for the USGP, Phil's uncompetitive Cooper No.10 qualified last for the grid, then expired on the fourth race lap with ignition failure. *(Dave Friedman)*

Mexico City was the last race of '64, the last race with Cooper, and the last Grand Prix Phil Hill would start. A six-year career as Grand Prix driver would end, yet Hill would remain competitive in GT racing, the Can-Am and Tasman series. *(Flip Schulke)*

Hill joined the Ford GT40 program in 1964 and, for the Le Mans 24-hour race, he was paired with Bruce McLaren. Hill set a new lap record, and was running third when the Collotti transaxle failed after 13½ hours of racing. *(Geoffrey Goddard/GP Library)*

Late in '64, Phil drove a GT40 for the Nassau Tourist Trophy, but did not finish. The non-point Bahamas Speed Week events were to serve as a shakedown. The GT40s suffered mechanical woes, including suspensions that came adrift. *(Dave Friedman)*

For the 1965 endurance race at Le Mans, Hill was paired with Chris Amon in one of Ford's two experimental 7-liter MKII's. After seven hours and a new lap record, mechanical failure forced the retirement of the No. 2 car. *(Geoffrey Goddard / GP Library)*

At the Northwest Grand Prix at Kent, Washington in October 1965, Phil drove Bruce McLaren's M1B team car to a new lap record and a second-place finish in the first heat. He was leading the second heat until trouble with the throttle linkage ended his only appearance in one of the McLaren Group 7 sports racing cars. *(Cam Warren)*

Chaparral's only Can-Am victory came with the one-two finish of Jim Hall and Phil Hill in heat one of the 1966 season finale at Laguna Seca Raceway. (Cam Warren)

Hill on his way to an important win in '66 at Nürburgring. (Kurt Worner/Road & Track)

Le Mans '66, No.9 Chaparral 2D of Phil Hill/Jo Bonnier retired with a dead battery, while the promising '67 bid with the No.7 Chaparral 2F of Phil Hill/Mike Spence was retired due to failure of the automatic transmission. (Geoffrey Goddard/GP Library)

The BOAC 500 6-hour race at Brands Hatch in July 1967 turned out to be Phil Hill's last professional race. Teamed with Mike Spence in the 7-liter Chevrolet powered Chaparral 2F, they beat the Ferrari P4s, Ford GTs, Lolas, and Porsches. "How many drivers win their last race?" *(Geoffrey Goddard/GP Library)*

Jim Hall and Phil Hill enjoyed two good seasons together. *(Dave Friedman)*

A 1976 family portrait shows Jennifer seated, a young Vanessa standing, and Phil's wife Alma holding their infant son, Derek John Hill. *(Stephen Green-Armytage)*

Now in his twenties, Derek John Hill is driving in competition. He dominated the final race of the 1996 Barber Dodge Pro Series, leading from wire to wire. In '95 Derek went to Italy for the Ferrari Challenge at Mugello. He won all three events entered—shades of Philip Toll Hill in an MGTC at Carrell Speedway in 1949. *(Richard Dole)*

Hill drove up to Monza with Dan Gurney (who was set to handle a works Porsche), via the Autostrada del Sole turnpike. Before they arrived at the circuit they spent the night at the Hotel Auriga in Milano, rolling into the Monza Autodrome in time for Friday's first afternoon practice session.

Hill was given a new Ferrari for this important Grande Epreuve, with a slightly hotter "120" engine, giving a few more horsepower at higher revs, but he was not satisfied with the car, and his best practice lap on Friday was 2:48.9, which Richie Ginther bettered by two full seconds in another "120." In his most ambitious effort of the season, Enzo Ferrari had brought six cars to Monza, four of the "120" models for Hill, Trips, Ginther and Baghetti, an older "60" for Ricardo Rodríguez (who was entering his first Formula 1 Grand Prix) as well as a "Muletta," or practice car. Rodríguez managed to break the Muletta's chassis on the uneven banking, scraping back to the pits — but on Saturday, the second and last day of practice, the fiery young Mexican hammered around the 6.2 miles of Monza in the "60" Ferrari at tremendous speed, clocking a lap of 2:46.4, which was just one-tenth of a second slower than Trips (who had earned the pole with 2:46.3).

Hill was grim-faced, sweating to match his teammates with an engine he didn't trust. And although he knocked more than a second and a half from his Friday time he was still not able to reach the times of Trips, Rodríguez, or Ginther. Only Baghetti, among the red cars, qualified slower.

Enzo Ferrari, who was in the pits during these practice sessions, chided Phil for letting the "new boy," Rodríguez, beat his time, and the angry Californian insisted that another engine be installed in his car. Shrugging at this display of "temperament" on the part of the nervous American, Ferrari ordered his mechanics to do as Hill wished. On race morning, though they would have to work on his car all through the night, Phil would have a new engine.

Three of the more-powerful British V-8s were in evidence at Monza, and drivers Moss (Lotus), Brabham (Cooper), and Graham Hill (BRM) all qualified their cars with the new powerplants installed. The BRM got down to 2:48.7, but the machine was withdrawn, along with the Moss Lotus, since both V-8s were plagued with water loss through the relief valve. Brabham's engine was also losing water, but he elected to try it out anyway in the race, just to see if he could give the Ferraris any competition in the opening stage. It was obvious that the Climax V-8 still needed work, but the potential was certainly there, as Jack had proved for those few sizzling miles at the Nürburgring.

On Sunday, September 10, as a hot sun began to climb the cloudless sky, the roar of racing engines began at 7 A.M. with the first of two Gran Turismo races under way. For six hours the GT cars occupied the circuit, and when the Grand Prix machines were finally rolled into position the turns were already coated with oil and rubber.

A vindicated Phil Hill slid into the tight cockpit of his No. 2 Ferrari. His insistence on a new engine had been fully justified, since a broken inner valve spring on one cylinder had been discovered during the overnight teardown. Enzo Ferrari was not at the track (as he never attended the actual races) but the Italian mechanics who had scoffed at Hill's "hunch" now wore sheepish expressions. (If Phil had started the Grand Prix with his practice engine, he obviously would never have finished at Monza.)

A confident, smiling Trips was answering questions fired at him by a host of energetic reporters. Yes, he was a real Count, heir to his family's Rhineland castle and estate near Cologne, and he possessed a university degree in agriculture. Yes, he had started his racing career on motorcycles in 1948 when he was twenty, graduating to a Porsche and winning the 1300-cc Class in the 1954 Mille Miglia. Yes, he had been nicknamed "von Crash" due to his many smashups. Two of them had occurred here at Monza (when he was trying out for Ferrari in '56 and again on the first lap of the '58 Italian GP). In both cases his cars had been completely demolished. Was he now a much better driver? "No, only luckier," he replied. Did he have a wife? "I am married to one of these," he said, gesturing toward his waiting Ferrari. Was he looking forward to the event this afternoon? "I love motor racing—where one has to fight to win. To do this you must drive close to the limit, which I am always prepared to do. There is a very thin line between winning and crashing; you have to walk it like a tightrope."

Hill said nothing. He was a coiled spring, wound tight. When reporters approached him he brushed them aside. No smiles. No waving for the camera. He unbuttoned the collar of his light blue Dunlop coveralls, buttoned it again, wiped his already-spotless goggles. His feet, encased in soft black-leather cycling shoes, tested the pedals. Fine. He inserted a pair of rubber earplugs, donned his white helmet, adjusting it for maximum comfort, then pulled on his perforated driving gloves, carefully fitting each finger. He was ready.

At the one-minute signal, Lord Howe, the starter, edged forward with the flag of Italy, slowly raising it as the final seconds ticked away. In staggered lines of two, the gleaming GP cars stretched far back along the grid. Hill was in the second row, next to Ginther, with Trips and Rodríguez ahead. Now all the drivers were revving their engines in a rhythmic rising and falling cadence. Since the Ferraris were pulling very high axle ratios at Monza, they would lose time in the initial getaway, and Hill was prepared to sort his way through some traffic in his bid for the lead.

The flag dropped. With a deafening explosion of sound all 32 cars surged forward, the red Ferraris menaced by a sea of British green and German silver. Trips was tardy in his move off the line, and as the pack streamed away toward Curva Grande the German tucked in behind Brabham. Jimmy Clark had knifed up from the fourth row to tackle the Ferraris, but Hill and Ginther both passed him, one to either side, along the banking. Behind the two Americans and Clark rode Rodríguez, Graham Hill and Baghetti.

Seven cars, all closely bunched, whipped down off the South Banking to end the first lap, with Hill pacing the field. Behind him, waging a six-car war, Ginther, Rodríguez, Clark, Brabham, Trips and Baghetti were only inches apart, switching positions on each curve.

With his American rival beginning to open a lead, Trips made his bid, taking Brabham and then Clark with two full-throttle bursts of power. As the pack swept through the Ascari Curve and down the fast straight to the "Parabolico," or South Curve, at the start of Veldano, Trips had his sights firmly set on Rodríguez in the older "60" Ferrari. Passing him should be no problem—and then he could try to deal with Ginther and Hill. He would yet bring home the World Championship to Germany....

Suddenly: disaster! In cutting ahead of Clark's Lotus, Trips had shaved his margin too fine, and both cars made contact at well over

100 mph. Trips' rear wheel grazed the Scot's front wheel; neither driver could maintain control—and the Lotus spun wildly, slamming the dirt bank, coming to a dusty halt at the edge of the road. The Ferrari whiplashed into a steel guardrail, ricocheted across the track with the force of an exploding shell, and sideswiped the chain-link fence, behind which the packed spectators were struck down in a nightmare moment of horror, then continued its thrashing end-for-end flight back onto the road, where it finally came to rest, a tangled mass of smoking wreckage. Wolfgang von Trips was sprawled facedown on the grass verge, some 30 yards from his car, his body broken by the impact. He did not survive—and 14 others died with him. Clark was stunned, but otherwise unhurt.

Beyond the scene of tragedy, the race continued with Hill and Ginther exchanging the lead, unaware of their teammate's fatal crash.

"As we came around on the next lap I saw the two cars by the edge of the road," says Hill. "But I really didn't worry too much, because people had been crashing all season and there had been no fatal accidents. This looked bad, but no worse than many others. I turned my thoughts to the job at hand: winning the Italian Grand Prix."

On lap 9 Brabham was out, his V-8 overheating seriously. Then, with almost two-thirds of the race to go, Rodríguez smoked into the pits, oil smearing his windscreen. His furious pace in the slower car had finished the engine, and the Ferrari was wheeled away. Next, directly behind him, Baghetti retired with valve spring trouble, leaving the race to Ginther and Hill.

Phil was driving fast and skillfully, pacing Ginther along the bankings and around the boomerang-shaped road circuit, with Moss and Gurney battling for third behind the two red cars.

Then Hill checked his mirror. Richie was slowing, falling back. As his fellow Californian pulled into the pits to retire, Hill was all alone in front. Richie's engine had also failed due to a broken valve spring—and now only Hill's Ferrari: remained in the race.

Moss and Gurney were closing behind him, but he increased his speed just enough to maintain his solid lead. The final laps ticked away as Moss dropped from the battle with a collapsed wheel bearing—and now the checker was in sight.

Philip Toll Hill threw up a hand to acknowledge his victory as the checkered flag descended, making him the official winner of the Grand Prix of Italy, and new Champion of the World. He had covered the 43 laps at an average speed of over 130 mph, and Dan Gurney's second-place Porsche was a full 31 seconds behind him.

. . . . .

"When they told me the news, that Trips was dead and more than a dozen spectators with him, I was stunned, deeply shocked," says Hill. "The papers reported that I broke down and sobbed, but that was not true. There were no tears. When you've lived as close to death and danger as long as I have then your emotional defenses are equal to almost anything. Trips died doing something he loved, and he was willing to accept the risks. Just as I am willing. When I love motor racing less my own life will become worth more to me, and perhaps I will be less willing to risk it."

. . . . .

The last act in the tragic drama that was Monza, 1961, took place in Germany, as Wolfgang Graf Berghe von Trips was buried with honor. Three separate services marked the passing of the great German driver, the first being conducted in the family castle, near Cologne, Burg Hemmersbach, a massive structure of stone surrounded by a moat, seemingly unchanged since the Crusades.

"Richie and I came up from Modena to serve as pallbearers," relates Hill. "After the Funeral Mass at the castle, our procession formed outside. It was raining, but none of us wore raincoats. We walked, bareheaded, beside Trips' casket, carried on his open Ferrari sports car. The dark Ferrari was driven very slowly behind a band, dressed in black, playing Chopin's Funeral March. The pace was set by an ancient woman, also dressed entirely in black and carrying a symbolic brass lantern—and we trudged along the cobbled road in the rain for a mile, to the church, where another interminable Mass was sung."

The procession again formed outside the church for the final mile to the cemetery, with the rain beating down steadily, drumming on the flower-decked casket in the open car. The family chapel was on a high knoll, and Hill describes their difficult passage up the rain-soaked hill.

"We clambered up, eight of us, slipping and sliding on the mud, bearing the heavy casket. There, at the chapel, the last service was held and poor Trips was finally entombed. I have never experienced anything so profoundly mournful as that day. Afterwards, I went to the house of a friend and took a boiling-hot bath."

That same evening Hill was asked to visit the castle and talk to Trips' mother.

"Now, ever since leaving Italy I'd had a pain, a kind of stitch in my side. I knew it was purely psychosomatic; it told me that I was tense, that I must relax. Well, that pain began to ease when I talked to Frau Trips. She was composed. She even scolded me gently for not accompanying her to the Salzburg Music Festival as I had promised to do earlier in the season. I sensed, as we spoke, that she did not condemn racing. I knew that of course she was terribly hurt at the loss of her only son, but he had freely chosen a dangerous career and now that he was gone she accepted the fact like a Spartan mother. I left the castle without pain, strangely relaxed for the first time in days."

For Hill, the battle to win the most honored title in motor sport was finally over. It had ended tragically for one man, triumphantly for the other—and a bitter price had been paid. But each man had taken the same risk in reaching for the same glittering goal.

From the long years of struggle, from the many races in the United States, Sicily, Mexico, Argentina, France, Venezuela, Germany, Portugal, Sweden, Cuba, Morocco, Holland, Monte Carlo, England, Belgium, the Bahamas and Italy, from the smoke of motorized battle across many continents just four words tell the story:

PHIL HILL: WORLD CHAMPION

CHAPTER TWENTY-SIX

The Post-Championship Years

A T THE END OF THE 1961 SEASON Hill pondered the question: "Should I retire?" He had serious doubts about continuing to race. In taking the Grand Prix Championship home to America, Phil had captured the richest prize in motor racing; there seemed no higher goal to pursue. Additionally, the element of physical risk loomed larger than ever in his mind. Although he'd never suffered more than minor scratches in a decade and a half of all-out racing, he wondered how long he could defy the odds. Drivers were constantly dying around him, race to race. (When Fangio retired in 1958 he was quoted in *Time:* "Twenty of my friends have died behind the wheel. All of the greats are gone.") And beyond his doubts, there were substantial changes in the Ferrari camp.

Enzo Ferrari's successful '61 team disintegrated at the season's close when chief engineer Carlo Chiti, team manager Romolo Tavoni, and engineer Giotto Bizzarrini all parted company with the Maranello firm. This major shake-up took place as a result of certain demands, financial and otherwise. The Commendatore, always a stubbornly proud man, refused to meet these demands; no compromise could be reached. Richie Ginther left Ferrari to sign with BRM, and rumors that Hill would also join the British team were widespread when Phil visited the BRM organization in England.

But the Santa Monican once again signed with Enzo Ferrari for his seventh season of European competition, ending all speculation as to his possible retirement or his plans for a team change.

The alarming statistics involved in the upper echelon of motor racing were finally put aside by Hill, but he did comment on this frightening aspect of the sport: "The obvious truth is, we are all likely to kill ourselves if we drive over our heads. Personally, my driving has always contained a high caution factor."

As the team's number one driver, Hill had been promised a newly-designed, faster GP Ferrari for the 1962 season, but this promise was not kept. "Our cars simply got a facelift," he declared. "We were totally outclassed in power and speed."

With the introduction of the Coventry-Climax V-8 engine, Phil's V-6 Ferrari 156 was no longer competitive against the BRM 48, the Lotus 25, and the Cooper T60. Hill realized that his chance at a second GP crown had been lost, but he was committed and would give Enzo Ferrari his best.

In sports competition the Ferrari was still a potent contender. That February, teamed with Ricardo Rodríguez, Hill racked up a strong second in the Daytona 3-Hours and, with Gendebien, took home a first in the Grand Touring class (and a second overall) at Sebring in a Ferrari GTO after twelve long hours of speed.

In Formula 1, despite his car's handicap, Phil got off to a solid start for the season by notching a pair of thirds at Aintree and in Holland. Switching to a sports Ferrari for the '62 running of the Targa Florio in Sicily, he set fastest practice time around the formidable 45 miles of open roads at 41 minutes, 58 seconds. But suddenly he was in trouble. A journalist from *Motoring News* described the situation:

> About five miles from Cerda, on a short uphill stretch ending in a right-hand turn, Hill's throttle jammed wide open at 85 mph. Braking as hard as possible, he rammed down the brake pedal with *both* feet, switching off his engine at the same time. Hill laid black skid marks for some 70 feet. They ended abruptly where the Ferrari, leaving red paint on a boundary stone, dived over the edge of the road, plunging down a rough bank (which formed a most fortunate ramp) into a field, ending up near a farmhouse approximately 40-50 yards from the course.

Once again, as had been the case at the Nürburgring and in the '61 Targa, Phil escaped injury, although his Ferrari was considerably mashed in its erratic flight down the mountainside.

Stirling Moss was far less fortunate, having crashed at Goodwood just two weeks earlier in England. Moss also failed to make a turn, but his speed (120) was far higher than Phil's as his Lotus whipped across 150 yards of grass and exploded directly into an embankment, totally demolishing the Grand Prix machine and trapping Moss inside. It took 30 minutes to free the Englishman. His condition was critical: in addition to a gashed face, two broken ribs, cracked knee and a torn shoulder, Moss also sustained what doctors termed a "severe bruising of the right side of the brain."

In reporting the crash, *Time* included an earlier quote from the Britisher: "I wouldn't drive a racing car unless there was an element of danger involved. Does a bullfighter want to fight a bull without horns?"

With Moss absent from the professional racing scene, Hill felt more confident of his abilities. Again teamed with Gendebien, he next tackled the difficult, always dangerous Nürburgring and scored a very impressive Ferrari victory there. This winning run may have inspired his truly astounding performance a week later in Monte Carlo.

Hill's competition for the Monaco Grand Prix included Clark in a Lotus-Climax, Gurney in a Porsche, Surtees in a Lola-Climax, Brabham in a Lotus, Graham Hill in a BRM, and Bruce McLaren in a Cooper-Climax. As the race progressed, Hill picked off his rivals one by one—as other cars crashed or failed on the difficult, round-the-houses circuit. With just eight laps remaining, Phil was running a solid second, but was a full 17 seconds behind Bruce McLaren. Surely, this late in the race, there was no way to close such a gap. But Hill set out to do just that, expertly powering the red Ferrari over the twisting, oil-slick course with a precision worthy of Moss at his best. Taking the Gasworks Hairpin in full opposite-lock slides, he was relentlessly moving up on the Cooper, cutting down McLaren's lead by two seconds per lap. In the final run for the checker, as the crowd cheered him on, Hill was directly at McLaren's back—losing by only 1.3 seconds after nearly three hours of furious racing.

John Cooper, whose marque notched the victory, commented with awe: "Another lap and Hill would have won. Bruce was going every bit as fast as he dared, yet Hill kept catching him."

Never again, in Formula 1, would Phil Hill surpass this inspired run over the streets of Monte Carlo.

He went on to earn a hard-fought third at the Grand Prix of Belgium and to win, with Gendebien, at Le Mans that summer in a 4-liter Testa Rossa, last of the fabled front-engined Ferraris. It was Phil's third victory in this French classic, making Hill/Gendebien the most successful duo in the history of long-distance sports car racing. One journalist dubbed them "The Roadmasters."

But Hill's success at Le Mans was not repeated in Formula 1. Over the final six months of 1962 he failed to complete the GPs of Britain and Germany, and in the Italian Grand Prix, at Monza, he finished a distant eleventh.

This marked the end of his extended tenure with Ferrari.

"I wasn't sorry to leave," says Hill. "Enzo Ferrari never understood me. I wasn't his type, not super gung-ho enough to suit him. A lot of fine drivers died racing for him and he always favored the man who would take that extra risk in a live-or-die situation. I won a lot of races for him—which is why he kept me around—but I was never his kind of driver. I wasn't willing to die for Enzo Ferrari. I wasn't willing to become one of his sacrifices."

Hill was satisfied that he'd done his best in '62 with an inferior car: "It handled better that year, but it was much slower on the straights. Over the tighter circuits I was able to hold my own and, in fact, I was running a close second for the championship with Graham Hill as late as Belgium in June. Of course, Graham went on to win as things got worse and worse for us. But there was nothing I could have done to change the results."

For the 1963 season, Hill signed on to drive for ATS (*Automobili Turismo e Sport*), which he later admitted was "one of the poorest career decisions I ever made, because these cars were far from ready."

Carlo Chiti, Ferrari's former engineer, had designed the new V-8 rear-engine ATS machines, but proper financial backing was not available and the GP cars were never fully developed or perfected.

"Things just kept breaking," Hill recalls bitterly. "In the GP of Belgium it was the gearbox. In Holland I lost a rear wheel, and in Mexico I was out when a wishbone joint snapped. In Germany it was a split fuel tank. And at Watkins Glen the oil pump failed. My best for the season was an eleventh in the Grand Prix of Italy. The ATS was a total disaster."

In sports cars that year, driving a variety of marques, Phil's only success came at Sebring where he beat the Corvettes to win his class in a Cobra. At the Ring, in an 8-cylinder factory Porsche, he was leading when a wet patch of roadway sent him into the banking. At Le

Mans, as he was winding up the big GT Aston Martin to 160 mph beyond Dunlop Bridge, a competing car suddenly went to pieces in front of him. Phil managed to miss the tumbling machine, but ran over its hood. A pit stop was made to check for damage. Three hours later he pited for good with a broken transmission.

Gregor Grant, in ranking the top competitors for *Autosport,* wrote of Hill: "He is still a first-rate driver in spite of a dreadful season. When his car was going properly the former World Champion showed all of his old skill."

And Anthony Pritchard, in *World Champions From Farina to Stewart,* dubbed the '63 season "a waste of Phil Hill's very considerable talents."

Phil drove a Centro-Sud BRM into a fourth at Snetterton that March while awaiting a GP contract for the upcoming season. He hoped to reverse his downward spiral by signing with John Cooper for 1964. As the team's number two driver (behind Bruce McLaren), Hill would take the place of Tim Mayer who had been killed in a practice crash in the Tasman series.

In 1959 and 1960 Jack Brabham had won back-to-back World Championships driving Cooper's GP machines—but by 1964 the cars were badly outclassed and Hill was facing another "impossible" season.

At Monaco the Cooper's seat didn't fit, and Phil was forced to hunch over the wheel. Also, the interior cockpit heat was scalding and he suffered blisters on several parts of his body. A broken rear suspension ended his bid.

Hill finished eighth in the Dutch GP at Zandvoort, two laps behind McLaren (who was seventh). In Belgium his car caught fire in practice, and on lap 14 of the race his engine blew. ("It just let go," he declared. "Absolutely not my fault.")

He did a little better in the French GP, finishing seventh. His only championship point for the season was earned with a sixth in the British GP at Brands Hatch.

At the Ring, for the GP of Germany in August, while engaged in a fierce duel with Jack Brabham, Hill made a rare and costly mistake: he missed a shift. The result was another blown engine. This time he freely admitted that the fault was his. As bad as this seemed, things soon got worse.

In Austria that same month, on his first practice lap over the rough and bumpy Zeltweg airfield circuit, Phil misread a slow bend for a fast one, went in "too hot," slid wildly and slammed into the bales, severing a front wheel.

Back in the pit area, John Cooper began a fierce verbal assault, shouting at the Californian in front of a startled crowd. ("I was feeling bad, really guilty, so I took it," says Hill.)

Badly shaken, driving a spare practice car in the race itself, Phil entered the *same* slow corner and crashed again. This time the machine was consumed in flames.

In a cold rage, Cooper fired him from the team.

"That second crash wasn't my fault," declares Hill. "The rear suspension broke going into the bend, but since the car was totally gutted by fire, I could never prove it."

Only because he needed the starting money, Cooper allowed Phil to drive in the season's final two GP races. At Watkins Glen for the U.S. Grand Prix, Hill qualified last on the grid with a snail-slow machine. It expired on the fourth lap when the ignition failed. In Mexico City, for the Mexican GP in late October, Hill noticed that his oil pressure was dropping to a dangerous low. He signaled this information to the pits and they ignored it. Instead, he received an order: "GO FASTER!"

He did as instructed, and took a perverse pleasure in blowing the Cooper's engine sky-high.

There was one final consolation. Driving formula cars for Bruce McLaren in the 1965 Tasman Trophy series of races in Australia and New Zealand, Phil took home two solid third places—in the Sundown event and in the Australian GP.

In sports cars the 1964 season had started well. Partnered with Pedro Rodríguez in a 250 GT Ferrari, Hill scored an impressive victory in the Daytona 2000 and went on to distinguish himself at Le Mans (paired with Bruce McLaren) in a new GT40 Ford. He'd signed on with the Ford factory under the management of John Wyer to help develop and race their cars.

Starting trouble on the grid and a stuttering engine early in the event dropped Phil to forty-fourth position at the end of the first hour. But with his mechanical problems solved, Hill was soon chopping his way past other cars, flashing his lights to warn slower machines, going like the furies and setting a new lap record in the process. After McLaren spelled him at the wheel, Hill again took over the GT40, working his way up through the long French night to an amazing third overall. "Then," says Phil, "the gearbox packed up and we were out."

Despite his frustrating non-finish, Hill had clearly demonstrated the class and talent of a true champion, yet ill fortune plagued him that season.

Phil set another lap record at Spa in a Shelby Cobra—until fuel trouble defeated him. Driving the Ring, the GT40's suspension came adrift. At the Tourist Trophy, the Cobra coupé's oil cooler failed. In the Targa, a wishbone mount tore loose.

Disheartened by these setbacks, Hill once again considered retirement at the end of the season, but decided against it. "I just couldn't go out on such a low note," he said. "I had to prove myself to the people who still believed in me."

Avoiding the pressure of Grand Prix competition, he concentrated his full efforts on sports car events.

Phil turned in another outstanding performance at Le Mans, teamed with Chris Amon in a 7-liter GT Ford. He set fastest qualifying time (a full five seconds ahead of the factory Ferrari) and had worked his way up to second overall in the 24-hour contest, establishing a new lap record, when the Ford's clutch began to slip. By the seventh hour the car was out.

At the Ring, Hill was running a strong second to the leading Ferrari when the gearbox seized. He switched to another car and snared eighth overall. When his GT40 failed at Sebring in the third hour, he once again switched cars (this time to a Cobra) for a shared 21st-place finish.

Phil's best run that season was at Kent, in Washington state, where he took over Bruce McLaren's M1B and cinched the lap record, taking a strong second in the first of two heats. The fans grinned. Ole Phil would eat up the competition. And he almost did. Grabbing the lead in the second heat, he had the crowd roaring. But a sticking throttle ended his bid. Despite a series of superior performances and newly-established lap records, he has won no races in 1965.

"Phil is still a tremendous driver," declared Bruce McLaren at the close of that season. "He's as good as they come when things are going right."

Again, Phil refused to quit; he would not allow a sequence of mechanical failures to force his retirement, Maybe in '66 things *would* go right.

Hill functioned in a double capacity this season: as a racing adviser and driver in the spectacular film production, *Grand Prix*, which was "fictionally" based on his own career, and as a legitimate competitor in various sports car events.

Rumor had it that Phil was due to join the Honda team for GP rides, but this did not materialize. He remained with sports cars. Partnered with Jo Bonnier, he signed with Jim Hall to drive the Texas-built Chaparral. Phil praised the car as "really wild and innovative with lots of potential."

At Daytona, however, after a promising start, he dropped from second to fifty-fourth after three hours, due to minor problems. Eight hours later he had slammed back up to seventeenth and was still gaining on the leaders when the rear hub carrier shattered. Out.

An oil leak knocked him from the race at Sebring, and a dead battery ended his run at Le Mans.

At the Nürburgring, however, the car's potential paid off. Paired with Bonnier, Hill whipped the big Chaparral around the twisting German circuit to score an impressive win over the Ferraris and Fords. This well-deserved victory restored his confidence.

He almost got back in Grand Prix competition that season as he was called in to practice for the GP of Italy in a Gurney Eagle, but the car was not properly prepared and he was not able to drive it in the race. Phil was scheduled to handle an Eagle at Watkins Glen, but ill health kept him out and Bob Bondurant took the wheel. Hill's GP career was finally over—but he was still a talent to reckon with in sports cars.

The final months of the 1966 season saw him battling fiercely for the Canadian-American crown. He won at Laguna Seca after scoring a solid second in Canada. Vapor lock in a fuel line knocked him out of Riverside. Yet by the end of the series Hill entered the Stardust GP at Las Vegas tied for the championship with John Surtees. He outgunned Surtees to qualify in row one next to boss Jim Hall. If his luck held, he could take home the championship.

But it didn't. A first-lap shunt cost him race time. The Chaparral's flipper went haywire and had to be cut away. Phil finished seventh in a bent, wingless machine. His fourth position in the final Can-Am standings and a purse of $17,750 failed to cheer him for the title loss.

He talked yet again of quitting. "If I could get out of this sport with any real ego left, I would. Racing brings out the worst in me, and I'm not sure I like the person I am now."

Yet his talent was undiminished.

At Daytona, paired with Mike Spence for the 1967 event, Hill was back in top form at the wheel of Jim Hall's 2F Chaparral, dominating the race in the first four hours and setting a new lap record. He was leading forcefully when he entered a banked turn at speed, hit a section of broken asphalt, slid sideways, and banged the retaining wall. The resulting suspension damage ended a superb effort.

At Le Mans, where he always drove at his best, Phil was running a strong third in the Chaparral at halftime, with twelve hours to go and two Fords to catch, when an oil seal let go in the gearbox. Again, he was unable to finish.

A shredded tire eliminated him in the Targa, and at Sebring he suffered a sudden attack of appendicitis on the eve of the race. Into the hospital. An irony; Hill had never been hospitalized in twenty years of racing.

In practice at Spa, piloting the big white Chaparral 2F, he set the all-time fastest lap over the Francorchamps circuit at 146 mph, earning pole position and totally eclipsing the speed of the vaunted factory works P4 Ferrari. The Chaparral's high, rear-mounted "wing" (controlled by a foot pedal) kept the rear wheels glued to the track, allowing Phil to go flat out around Spa's sweeping, high-speed curves. But misfortune struck again as the car "packed up" during the race. Another non-finish.

At the always-difficult and treacherous Nürburgring Phil set another race lap record and was leading the field on the ninth lap when the drive shaft failed. A bitter dropout.

July, 1967. Brands Hatch, England. The 6-hour BOAC 500. Hill was there to co-drive the V-8 Chevy-powered Chaparral 2F with

Mike Spence. No one really expected much of the Chaparral by this time; after all, old chap, the bloody thing just never finished a bloody race! Besides, the P4 Ferraris and GT Fords were out in force, the Lola-Chevys were very hot, and the 8-cylinder Porsches were extremely quick on this tight, twisty little Kentish circuit.

Jackie Stewart and Chris Amon were paired in one of the swift P4 Ferraris and proved to be the team to beat. But Hill and Spence were determined to demonstrate the speed and endurance of their American machine.

By the fifth hour, Hill was leading the thundering P4 Ferrari by 18 seconds, and when Stewart took over after Amon's pit stop the Chaparral's lead continued to increase. Both cars finished on the same lap, but the Hill/Spence/Chaparral combination had won decisively over the Ferrari by 58.6 seconds after their fierce six-hour battle.

Denis Jenkinson, reporting for *Motor Sport,* declared it "as fine a long-distance race as we have seen this season and certainly the best in England for many a year. The Chaparral victory was loudly applauded... a joy to Phil Hill and Mike Spence."

Although he didn't know it at the time, this hard-won event turned out to be Phil's last professional motor race.

"I never officially quit," he later explained. "I sort of retired by degrees. Jim Hall didn't have the new Chaparral ready for me to drive in the upcoming Can-Am series and my other racing plans just fizzled out. Then one day I woke up and said to myself, 'It's over. It's finally over.' At least I'd gone out a winner, and that was very satisfying."

Reflecting on his retirement, Phil later admitted: "I no longer had the drive I did when I was younger, that hunger to win, and I felt that I wasn't really evolving, just repeating year after year—and you need to do more than that to stay on top."

He talked about the tensions of high-speed competition: "I never totally relaxed when I was driving a race car. I was afraid of the damn things, afraid that if I *did* relax they'd turn around and bite me."

From time to time during his career Phil was asked if he ever intended to get married. No, absolutely not. He was emphatic on the subject: "A wife would never understand my risking my life week after week in a racing car. She'd worry and fret, and this would harm both of us."

However, by 1971, at age 44, with his last race four years behind him, Phil finally did give up his long-standing bachelorhood. He married Alma Varanowski, a 33-year-old divorcee who had a pre-teenage daughter, Jennifer. In taking a wife, Phil surprised himself. "Frankly, by then, I never thought I'd get married. I was pretty set in my ways and marriage seemed very unrealistic. I was mainly a 'thing' person. I lived inside a world of cars and antiques. Cars made sense to me in a way people never did. But Alma was different... open. She taught me how to be a 'people' person."

Their daughter, Vanessa, was born in November of the following year, and they soon had a baby son, Derek John Hill. Fatherhood was a whole new experience to Phil; it gave him "a broader perspective." He was no longer alone, isolated, self-absorbed. Life had greatly expanded.

Alma says: "Philip has undergone a psychic change. He's remade himself. I look at all those old racing photos of him and I see another person. That's not Philip. Not now."

Another change: Hill became an official business owner in 1972 when he and a partner, Ken Vaughn, opened a restoration garage as Hill & Vaughn in downtown Santa Monica. They quickly gained a reputation as one of the most respected restorers of concours-winning classic cars in the U. S. Customers happily paid up to $75,000 for a Hill/Vaughn restoration job, despite a two year wait for delivery.

"Phil was incredibly meticulous," declared one of Hill's garage employees. "Every screw and bolt from the frame up had to be totally authentic and if a matching part couldn't be found, it would be machine-tooled here at the garage. The car's original color was carefully duplicated. Seat and floor fabrics had to match the originals precisely. This is why each job took two years or more. You can't do this kind of work over a weekend."

Hill would religiously attend vintage car shows, "wandering among the nuts and bolts," checking out parts that could eventually be used in these painstaking restorations.

He found an almost mystical pleasure in the work: "By taking a rusted, broken machine and bringing it back to its original state of perfection, it's as if the car becomes a time machine, taking me to another, earlier era."

Phil didn't simply restore old classics, he also collected them. By the early 1970s he had more than a dozen "beloved" automobiles, several of which he had personally restored. They filled his home garage and six other garages scattered throughout the Santa Monica area.

Beyond his 1931 Pierce Arrow LeBaron town car, Phil also owned a 1905 double-chain rear-wheel drive Panhard touring car, a sister to the machine that won the Vanderbilt Cup; a 1911 Packard 18 touring car; a 1912 Packard Model 30, with gas-operated headlamps; a 1906 Fiat Landaulet, once the personal car of Mexican President Díaz; a 1918 Packard Twin Six Fleetwood town car, the world's first production V-12; a 1925 Packard straight-eight sports roadster; a 1929 Pierce Arrow touring car; a 1931 custom-body Packard that once belonged to silent film comedian Harold Lloyd; a 1931 Alfa Romeo supercharged Grand Sport Zagato 1750; a 1931 Marmon convertible 491 V-16; and a 1931 Le Mans 4.5-liter supercharged Blower Bentley in racing green. Phil's personal favorite was the classic he'd spent ten months in restoring — a 1938 V-12 Packard with a Brunn all-weather Cabriolet body, the car that he'd used to ferry Alma home after their church wedding.

Another favorite was his 1913 Mercer Type 35-J Raceabout. Only a rare few exist today. "She was the lightest car of her time," Hill declares. "A mile in 51 seconds, guaranteed. Four-cylinder 306-cubic-inch T-head engine. She'll still do 85, but I'd never push her that hard. In '13 you could have bought her for two and a half thousand! Imagine that!"

In August of 1975, at Laguna Seca for the Second Annual Monterey Historic Automobile Races, Hill was reintroduced to the '38 Alfa Mille Miglia Spyder he had driven to victory in the 1951 Del Monte Handicap at Pebble Beach. Participating in a five-lap exhibition race on the circuit that weekend, he crossed the line first in the Alfa, handling the classic machine with extreme care. It was "a real joy" to him.

A month later Phil was at the Long Beach F5000 street race, tooling the course between heats in a Toyota identical to those also being driven by Dan Gurney and Graham Hill. In a prearranged gesture of camaraderie, all three drivers crossed the finish line together.

Hill's love of cars has never diminished; for decades now, as a contributing editor for *Road & Track,* he's been conducting road tests of exotic (mostly vintage) automobiles for the magazine. In the spring of

1976 he was called to the Riverside Raceway to try out a Formula 1 B3 Ferrari. Phil had not driven a GP Ferrari for 14 years and was amazed (but not surprised) at the improvements made by the factory.

He reported that the new Ferrari had "marvelous control and was extremely honest so far as integrity in a racing machine is concerned," adding that, at 490 horsepower, he had "never driven anything this powerful. My old '61 Ferrari GP car generated only 190 horsepower. This one does zero to a hundred in just over four seconds, with a top speed very close to 200 mph. Driving it at Riverside was a terrific experience, one of the high points of my life in an automotive sense."

Phil's record as the only American Grand Prix champion remained unbroken for 17 years. Then, in 1978, Mario Andretti became the second American in GP history to win the world title. There was an ironic and bitter parallel to Andretti's victory. The race which cinched the championship for him was the same one in which Phil had earned *his* title: the Grand Prix of Monza in Italy, and a major death darkened each of these events. In 1961 Hill's teammate, Wolfgang von Trips, had met his death at Monza; in 1978 it was Andretti's teammate, Ronnie Peterson, who crashed in the race and died.

Phil spoke often about "the risk factor" in professional racing, about how grateful he was to have survived his years of speed. Since 1948, when he began running his MG on the West Coast, over 100 drivers had been killed in high-speed competition in the United States and abroad. Some 20 of these deaths have occurred during races in which Phil had been involved. The colorful stars of yesterday—Ascari, Wimille, Sommer, Marimon, Collins, Hawthorn, Portago, Schell, Musy, Musso, Castellotti, Bonetto, Behra, Lewis-Evans, Rosier, Levegh, Wharton, Scott-Brown, Fraser, Cole, Whitehead, Bueb, Vukovich, Bryan—were all dead. Mike Spence was also gone, smashed against a wall at Indy, and Bruce McLaren had crashed fatally while testing a car at Goodwood.

"Motor racing has always been extremely dangerous," Phil admits. "But for all the lives it has taken, the sport has saved millions more. Every day, all over the world, people are riding in cars, buses, trucks, and even landing in jet liners using accident-preventing equipment that has been developed directly from auto racing. Risk is part of the business. And it's valid. Without the risk, without a driver at the wheel who is willing to push a competition machine to its limits, to find out what parts fail under pressure, racing would have contributed nothing to our store of useful, lifesaving knowledge." Hill nods. "A great many racing drivers have died for a purpose." Then he grins. "I'm just glad I wasn't one of them."

Celebrating the 30th Anniversary of his Formula 1 championship in 1991, Hill was fêted at several racing events. He was grand marshal for the Eleventh Annual Vintage Grand Prix at Road Atlanta in October, and spoke at a special dinner given in his honor that weekend in which he was introduced as "one of the most accomplished and talented racing drivers in the history of American motorsport."

He was also guest of honor at Palm Springs in November for "A Weekend Tribute to Phil Hill."

Phil talked about his retirement: "In looking back, I see clearly now that I had this desperate need to prove that I could race successfully and stay alive. I kept telling myself, for many years, that I couldn't be killed in a racing car, that sure, it happens to other drivers, but it can't happen to me. Part of it was that I had this extra sense of perception that always warned me that something was going wrong before the 'something' reached a critical stage. That was my 'edge of safety.' But, in 1967, I had a premonition that if I kept racing, I was ultimately going to kill myself. So leaving the sport was obviously the right thing to do."

*   *   *   *   *

Today, in the 1990s, as a revered racing veteran, Hill continues to attend vintage car events; he particularly enjoys Laguna Seca on the Monterey Peninsula. Inevitably, he is asked to drive a classic machine during these weekends. The owners know that he will treat their cars with genuine respect and restraint; they never worry about bent metal with Hill at the wheel.

In 1995 Phil drove a classic Bugatti to first place in an exhibition race over the Monterey circuit, making sure not to stress the vintage machine. "I've always been very sensitive to a car's limits," he says. "I never do anything excessive. Just being able to drive these wonderful old automobiles is reward enough. I'm not out to prove anything."

Phil's acute sensitivity to every element of an automobile is legendary. Bill Devin has observed: "During his racing days, after a practice run on the circuit, while other drivers were adjusting tire pressures by five to ten pounds, Phil could tell which tire needed just a quarter of a pound of air."

Indeed, Hill's knowledge of cars is uncanny; he can recall the make, model, color, year, and gearshift pattern of every automobile he's ever driven.

With Alma, he still lives in the expansive, richly-furnished Spanish-Moorish home his aunt willed to him in 1959, with its dark-beamed ceilings, polished wood floors, and inlaid tile stairways. Inside the house, Phil surrounds himself with beauty: a carefully-preserved 17th-century Dutch Bible; a shining array of antique music boxes; shelves of leather-bound, gilt-edged volumes; tastefully framed Renaissance prints; a rare, restored and playable violano under glass; old, trumpet-speaker phonographs; and several gleaming player pianos, restored to perfection by Hill himself and programmed to reproduce "with exact nuances and phrasing" some of the finest piano virtuosi in the world.

"When I put in a piano roll," Hill declares, "I have the pianist right here in the room, performing just for me."

He selects a favorite, slots it into his Steinway grand, and suddenly a Rachmaninoff concerto is being played, ghostlike, by the famous composer himself.

And while Phil glories in symphonies and chamber music, and has (inside his head) the scores of countless operas and concertos, his tastes are broad and all-encompassing—from rock to blues to country.

Jazz virtuoso Allen Eager claims that "Phil has the finest ear of any non-musician I've ever known."

From the music of a Ferrari engine at full revs to the trembling piano chords of a Bach concerto, Phil Hill savors the full range of classic sound.

Perhaps most remarkable, decades after his retirement, Phil is once again fully active in the arena of professional motor racing. His son, Derek John Hill, has become a skilled competitive driver, carrying his father's legendary name into modern motorized combat.

"Derek straps himself into a race car every chance he gets," says Hill. "Alma and I did nothing to encourage him to compete, but racing has proven to be his great passion. At first I was a bit apprehensive about it—the dangers and all—but his driving has literally swept me away. He's *very* talented."

Derek, who started with go-karts, subsequently enrolled in the Skip Barber Driving School, which provided him with the ideal training required for open-wheel competition. He began in a 140 horsepower Dodge-engined machine, then drove a 2-liter open-wheel car at Indianapolis Raceway Park, where he finished third.

At Thunderhill, the SCCA track in northern California, Derek set a new track record. Then, in the weekend's main, he spun into the grass while leading, pitted to make sure everything was okay, then roared off in sixth, 20 full seconds behind the leader. Closing fast, he broke his own lap record, passing the leader on the final lap to win. A most impressive performance.

For the 1995 Ferrari Challenge series, driving the same marque that had made his father a legend, Derek notched an overall second place in this series behind the wheel of a Ferrari 348.

This showing led to an invitation to compete in the European Ferrari Challenge at Mugello, Italy, on a special factory circuit some 30 kilometers north of Florence. Derek's mount was an F355 Ferrari — and young Hill went on to win all three of his events in grand style, besting many skilled Ferrari veterans in the process.

In what proved to be a double triumph for the Hills, Phil drove a classic 1958 Ferrari Testa Rossa to a vintage-car victory that same weekend at Mugello. They were photographed together, arm in arm in the trophy ceremony, sharing a golden moment of motor racing history.

"I'm extremely proud of him," Phil declares, with the emotion shining from his eyes. "I never expected Derek to become a professional racing driver, but it's happened — and I love it!"

Thus, the cycle continues — from Philip Toll Hill to Derek John Hill — from the first American Grand Prix champion to a potential champion in the making.

A new legend is building in the roaring world of international motor sport.

INTERNATIONAL SUCCESSES

Reflecting first, second, and third-place showings in Formula and sports car events, 1954–1967, and including International records established in 1957 and 1959.

NOTE: *All racing successes attained in sports and GP Ferraris except where noted. Speed records attained in MGs.*

1954

November 19-23		*Carrera Panamericana (Mexico)*	2nd

1955

March	13	*Sebring 12-Hours (U.S.)*	2nd w/Shelby (1st in Index)
December	9	Nassau Governor's Cup (Bahamas)	2nd
December	11	Nassau Trophy (Bahamas)	1st

1956

January	29	*Buenos Aires (Argentina)*	2nd w/Gendebien
May	27	*Nürburgring (Germany)*	3rd w/Gendebien and Portago
June	17	Grand Prix of Portugal (Oporto)	2nd
August	12	*Grand Prix of Sweden (Kristianstad)*	1st w/Trintignant
August	25	Messina 5-Hours (Sicily)	1st

1957

July	13-14	Reims 12-Hours (France)	2nd w/Seidel
August	11	*Grand Prix of Sweden (Kristianstad)*	2nd w/Collins
November	3	*Grand Prix of Venezuela (Caracas)*	1st w/Collins
December	6	Nassau Governor's Cup (Bahamas)	1st
December	8	Nassau Trophy (Bahamas)	3rd

International Speed Records established at Bonneville, Utah, in 1957:
In Class G, 750–1100 cc, supercharged model MG EX179 w/Ash and Wisdom

200 Miles	131.89 mph
500 Kilometers	132.39
500 Miles	131.38
1000 Kilometers	131.34
3 Hours	132.62
6 Hours	132.13
12 Hours	118.13 (The same car, unsupercharged.)

NOTE: *Italic entrees indicate that event counts toward sports car Manufacturers' Championship. Bold italic entrees indicate that event counts toward Grand Prix World Championship.*

1958

January	26	*Buenos Aires (Argentina)*	1st w/Collins
March	22	*Sebring 12-Hours (U.S.)*	1st w/Collins
June	21-22	*Le Mans 24-Hours (France)*	1st w/Gendebien
June	29	Monza 500 (Italy)	3rd w/Musso and Hawthorn (result of 3 heats)

Formula 1

| September | 7 | *Grand Prix of Italy (Monza)* | 3rd |
| October | 19 | *Grand Prix of Morocco (Casablanca)* | 3rd |

1959

March	21	*Sebring 12-Hours (U.S.)*	1st w/Gendebien, Gurney, and Daigh
June	7	*Nürburgring (Germany)*	2nd w/Gendebien
September	5	*Tourist Trophy (Goodwood, England)*	3rd w/Gendebien, Brooks, and Allison
October	11	Riverside (U.S.)	1st
December	1	Nassau Trophy (Bahamas)	2nd

Formula 1

July	5	*Grand Prix of Europe (Reims, France)*	2nd
August	2	*Grand Prix of Germany (Avus-Berlin)*	3rd (result of 2 heats)
September	13	*Grand Prix of Italy (Monza)*	2nd

International Speed Records established at Bonneville, Utah, in 1959:
In Class E, 1501–2000 cc, model MG EX181:

```
 1 Kilometers ............. 254.91 mph
      1 Mile ............. 254.53
 5 Kilometers ............. 232.97
      5 Miles ............. 238.36
10 Kilometers ............. 234.49
     10 Miles ............. 191.03
```

1960

January	31	*Buenos Aires (Argentina)*	1st w/Allison
May	8	*Targa Florio (Sicily)*	2nd w/Trips
May	22	*Nürburgring (Germany)*	3rd w/Allison and Mairesse

Formula 1

| May | 29 | *Grand Prix of Monaco (Monte Carlo)* | 3rd |
| September | 4 | *Grand Prix of Europe (Monza, Italy)* | 1st |

1961

March	25	*Sebring 12-Hours (U.S.)*	1st w/Gendebien
June	10-11	*Le Mans 24-Hours (France)*	1st w/Gendebien

Formula 1

May	14	*Grand Prix of Monaco (Monte Carlo)*	3rd
May	22	*Grand Prix of Holland (Zandvoort)*	2nd
June	18	*Grand Prix of Belgium (Spa-Francorchamps)*	1st
July	15	*Grand Prix of England (Aintree)*	2nd
August	6	*Grand Prix of Europe (Nürburgring, Germany)*	3rd
September	10	*Grand Prix of Italy (Monza)*	1st

1962

February	11	*Daytona 3-Hours (U.S.)*	2nd w/Ricardo Rodríguez
March	23	*Sebring 12-Hours (U.S.)*	1st in GT Class w/Gendebien
May	27	*Nürburgring (Germany)*	1st w/Gendebien
June	23-24	*Le Mans 24-Hours (France)*	1st w/Gendebien

Formula 1

April	29	Aintree (England)	3rd
May	20	*Grand Prix of Holland (Zandvoort)*	3rd
June	3	*Grand Prix of Monaco (Monte Carlo)*	2nd
June	17	*Grand Prix of Belgium (Spa-Francorchamps)*	3rd

1963

March	23	*Sebring 12-Hours (U.S.)*	1st in Class w/Gurney (Cobra)

1964

February	15	*Daytona (U.S.)*	1st w/Pedro Rodríguez

1966

June	5	*Nürburgring (Germany)*	1st w/Bonnier (Chaparral)
September	24	Canadian Grand Prix (Canada) (Can-Am series)	2nd (Chaparral)
October	16	Lagua Seca (U.S.) (Can-Am series)	1st (Chaparral)

1967

July	30	BOAC 6-Hours (England) (Hill's last professional race)	1st w/Spence (Chaparral)

INDEX

A

Aintree Circuit 193–196, 208, 225
Alfa Romeo 25, 74
Alfa Romeo 2900B Mille Miglia 36, 37, 218
Allard 13–15, 33, 34, 37, 38, 40, 44, 51, 61, 68
Allison, Cliff 128–131, 133, 134, 144– 146, 148–153, 155, 157, 188, 224
Amon, Chris 213, 216
Andretti, Mario 219
Argentine GP 99, 150
Ascari, Alberto 45, 46, 61, 64, 65, 71, 75, 219
Ash, David 89, 91, 223
Aston Martin 78, 79, 97, 103, 104, 107, 109, 110, 123, 130, 133, 136, 137, 138, 143, 144, 147, 183, 185–187
Aston Martin DB-2 37
          DBR1 102, 105, 106, 134
          DBR2 97, 123
          Project 215 211
ATS (*Automobili Turisimo e Sport*) 210
Austin Healey 61, 65
Auto Union 197
Autosport (magazine) 211
Avus Circuit 141, 224

B

Baghetti, Giancarlo 172, 173, 178, 191–193, 196, 201, 203, 204
Bahamas Speed Week 97, 223, 224
Baracca, Francesco 74
Bari Circuit 78
Barlow, Roger 28, 29
Barth, Edgar 119, 169
Beebe, Lucius 65

Behra, Jean 72, 76, 80, 94, 95, 96, 103, 118, 124, 125, 128–131, 133–141, 219
Belgian GP 158–160, 161, 188, 189, 209, 210, 211, 225
Beverly Circuit 66
Bira, Prince Birabongse 131
Birkin, Sir Henry "Tim" 17
Bizzarrini, Giotto 207
BOAC 500 215
Bondurant, Bob 214
Bonetto, Felice 45, 46, 53, 57, 219
Bonneville Salt Flats 88, 89, 91, 146, 223, 224
Bonnier, Joakim 80, 87, 96, 97, 106, 111, 115–117, 123, 124, 129, 144, 150, 152–156, 171, 178, 193–195, 198, 199, 214, 225
Brabham, Jack 105, 116–118, 132, 133, 138–141, 143, 145, 146, 148, 150, 155, 158–167, 170, 171, 178, 181, 189, 190, 198, 201, 203, 209, 211
Bracco, Giovanni 45, 46, 48, 53, 61
Brands Hatch 168, 211, 215
Breeze, Bill 14
British GP 211
BRM 116, 125, 128, 133, 138–141, 150, 152, 155, 158, 162, 165, 166, 168, 180, 199, 207–209, 211
Brooks, Tony 102, 105–107, 128–133, 135, 138–140, 142–144, 146, 148, 155, 156, 159, 171, 224
Bryan, Jimmy 31, 113, 114, 219
Bueb, Ivor 66, 105, 108, 219
Buenos Aires Sports Car Races 58, 71, 94, 110, 149, 162, 172, 223, 224
Bugatti 25, 220

C

Cahier, Bernard 88, 115
Can-Am Series 215, 216, 225
Carrell Speedway (Gardena) 30, 31, 32, 34, 37
Carrera Panamericana 44, 53, 61, 66, 223
Casablanca/Ain-Diab Circuit 122, 123, 125, 224
Castellotti, Eugenio 39, 53, 72, 73, 76, 80, 81, 84, 85, 219
Centro-Sud 211
Chaparral 2D 214
  2E 225
  2F 215, 216
Chapman, Colin 181
Chesebrough, Jerry 44
Chevrolet Corvette 73, 95, 210
Chinetti, Luigi 39, 45, 49, 51–53, 61, 65, 69, 71
Chiron, Louis 61, 131, 178
Chiti, Carlo 207, 210
Clark, Jim 166, 178, 181, 182, 183, 189, 197, 203, 209
Cobra (Shelby American) 210, 213, 225
Cole, Tom 52, 219
Collins, Peter 72, 76, 77, 79–81, 84, 86, 87, 88, 94–96, 99, 102–105, 117–120, 183, 219, 223, 224
Cooper, John 209, 211, 212
Cooper 118, 119, 131, 133, 138, 140, 142, 150–152, 154, 155, 159–163, 165–169, 171, 177, 180, 181, 189, 211, 212
Cooper-Climax 77, 128, 131, 142, 171, 209
  -Maserati 154, 171, 200
  Monaco 170, 186
  T60 208
Coventry-Climax 177, 208
Cramer, Bill 38
Crawford, Ed 93, 114
Cunningham, Briggs 39, 43, 50, 68, 70, 92, 129, 185

D

Daigh, Chuck 54, 124, 129, 154, 157, 160, 170, 224
Daytona Races 208, 212, 214, 215, 225
Devin, Bill 220
Duesenberg Automobiles 10, 169
Dundrod Circuit 71
Dutch GP 133, 157, 180, 181, 208, 210, 211, 225

E

Eager, Allen 221
Ecurie Ecosse 79, 87, 105, 107, 113
Edgar, John 97
Edwards, Marvin 27, 28, 29, 31
Edwards, Sterling 41, 53
Elkhart Lake Circuit 38, 43, 45, 66, 123
Eyston, Captain George 147

F

Fairman, Jack 134, 135, 137, 144, 194
Fangio, Juan Manuel 34, 37, 53, 56, 57, 63, 64, 68, 72, 73, 75, 76, 80, 81, 84, 85, 87, 94, 95, 98–101, 103, 113, 114, 116, 117, 119, 121–126, 131, 149, 158, 170, 183, 198, 207, 209, 211, 212, 214, 215, 216, 218, 219
Farina, Dr Giuseppi 131
Faulkner, Walt 29, 31
Ferrari, Enzo 37–39, 41, 42, 64, 71, 74, 75, 77, 80, 81, 84–86, 97, 103, 105, 110–112, 120, 123, 128, 138, 140, 145, 149, 151, 153, 154, 159, 169, 177, 179, 180, 182, 185, 187, 189, 193, 201, 202, 207, 208, 210
Ferrari 121 Le Mans 65, 74, 85
  212 Barchetta 39–41, 51
  212 Berlinetta 39, 43, 45–48
  246 S Dino 151
  246 SP Dino 172, 208
  250 GTO 208

Ferrari 250 GTO64 212
   250 Mille Miglia 53
   250 Testa Rossa 99, 105, 133,
                    134, 143, 172,
                    222
   250 TR59 147, 149
   250 TR60 151, 153, 161, 170
   250 TRI61 172, 183, 185
   268 SP Dino 208
   290 Mille Miglia 80
   296 "Monza Special" 112
   330 TRI62 209
   335 S 86, 88, 94
   340 America 41, 45, 46, 48
   340 Mexico 50–54, 56
   348 222
   375 Mille Miglia 55, 58, 61,
                     62, 66
   375 Plus 61, 62, 63, 86, 97
   410 Special 66
   410 Sport 72, 82
   412 MI 123, 124
   412 "Monza Special" 112, 114
   500 Mondial 71
   500 Testa Rossa 81
   625 Le Mans 78
   750 Monza 64, 74, 77
   860 Monza 73, 74, 76, 82, 85
Ferrari F1 156 208
   F1 246 159
   F1 256 120
   F1 B3 219
FIA *(Federation Internationale de
   L'Automobile)* 120, 124, 147, 153,
                177
Fitch, John 38, 43–46, 48, 50, 52, 60,
   73, 170
Ford GT40 212, 213
   MKII 213
Francis, Alf 77, 78
Fraser, Mac 87, 219
French GP 111, 161, 191, 211
Frère, Paul 76, 79, 87, 138, 162

G

Gendebien, Olivier 71, 72, 76, 78, 84,
   87, 94, 99, 103–109, 118, 120,
   126, 128, 129, 132–138, 143, 145,
   146, 154, 161, 172, 173, 175, 177,
   183–191, 208, 209, 223–225
German GP 196–200, 224, 225
Gilmore Stadium (San Bernardino) 31,
   32
Ginther, Richie 14, 35, 41, 53, 61, 93,
   97, 98, 147, 150, 151, 153, 155,
   157, 159, 162, 169, 170, 172–175,
   177–182, 184, 185, 187–196, 198,
   200, 201, 203, 204, 207
Golden Gate Park Circuit 40, 51
Goldie-Gardner, Major A.T. 88
González, José Froilan 72, 150
Goodwood Circuit 143, 144, 149, 153,
   208, 219, 224
Graffenried, Baron Emanuel de 131
Graham, Mike 14, 15, 40
Grand Prix (book) 25
Grand Prix (movie) 214
Greenspun, Gene 92
Gregory, Masten 51, 58, 70, 71, 73, 86,
   87, 94, 95, 97, 98, 101, 113, 115,
   121, 122, 124, 130, 139, 142–144,
   149, 154, 162, 170, 172, 173, 185
Grove, Doug 31
Guiberson, Allen 43, 45, 61, 64
Gurney, Dan 115, 123, 124, 128, 129,
   133, 134, 136, 138–140, 142, 143,
   145–147, 149, 151, 153, 154, 156,
   158, 165, 166, 170, 178, 179, 191,
   193, 199, 201, 204, 205, 209, 218,
   224, 225
Gurney Eagle 71, 84, 207, 210,
   211–218

H

Halford, Bruce 130, 131, 186
Hall, Jim 214–216
Hamilton, Duncan 78, 105–109
Hansgen, Walt 73, 92, 172, 186

Hawthorn, Mike 64, 66, 76, 77, 79, 80, 84, 87, 88, 94–97, 102–105, 106, 110, 112–117, 119, 120–122, 126, 127, 183, 196, 219, 224

Hearst, George 23, 27, 28

Hermann, Hans 152

Hill, Alma 9, 217, 218, 221

Hill, Derek 217, 221, 222

Hill, Graham 139, 142, 155, 159, 162, 172, 173, 178, 188, 199, 201, 203, 209, 210, 218

Hornburg, Charles 38, 39, 44

HWM 60

I

Indianapolis (Motor Speedway) 45, 61, 65, 112, 113, 178

International Motors 28, 29, 32, 34

Ireland, Innes 160, 171, 199

Italian GP 39, 40, 168, 169, 200, 202, 204, 210

J

Jaguar C-Type 43, 44, 49, 51, 52
 D-Type 64, 66–68, 71, 79, 80, 87, 92, 94, 102–108, 110, 113
 E-Type 170
 SS-100 30
 XK120 13, 15, 32, 34, 36, 38, 40, 43

Jenkinson, Denis 175, 188, 191, 216

Johnston, Sherwood 68–70, 92

K

Kent, Washington Circuit 213

Kessler, Bruce 108, 123

Kimberly, Jim 66, 68

Kling, Karl 44, 46, 48–51, 53, 54–56, 58, 68–70, 121, 152, 200

Kurtis Kraft 53, 61, 64

L

Laguna Seca Raceway 220

Lancia 45, 46, 48, 49, 53, 57, 65, 86, 112

Lang, Herman 44, 46, 48, 49

Las Vegas Circuit 214

Le Mans 10, 39, 43, 49, 51, 65, 66, 71, 72, 78, 79, 86, 93–95, 102, 104–106, 110, 136, 137, 161, 169, 170, 185–187, 209–215, 224, 225

Levegh, Pierre 65, 219

Lewis-Evans, Stewart 121, 125, 126, 219

Lilly, Gib 27, 28, 31

Lisbon Circuit 86, 142

Lister-Jaguar 102, 113, 129, 130

Lola-Chevy 216

Lola-Climax 209

Lotus 25 208
 Mark XI 87
 -Climax 77, 154, 178, 192, 209

Lotus 130, 133, 139, 142, 143, 150, 152, 154, 155, 158–160, 165, 168, 177, 179–183, 188, 195, 199, 200, 203, 208, 209

M

MacDill AFB Circuit 50

Macklin, Lance 61, 65

Madera Airport Cicuit 44, 53

Maglioli, Umberto 45, 49, 53, 55, 61–63, 65, 80, 93, 134, 135, 151

Mairesse, Willy 159, 161, 164, 169, 172, 173, 185, 187, 198, 224

Malbrand, George 38

Manzon, Robert 44, 46, 80, 81

Maranello 75, 133, 138, 141, 142, 150, 162, 164, 172, 180, 207

Marimon, Onofre 219

Marmon 18, 218

Maserati 60, 67, 70, 72, 76, 77, 80,
81, 84–88, 92, 94, 96, 97, 99, 103,
113, 121, 123, 128, 149, 151, 152,
154, 162, 170, 172, 183–187
    250F 111, 115, 116
    Tipo61 "Birdcage" 149, 152,
        153, 172, 185
    Tipo63 "Birdcage" 172, 185
Mayer, Tim 211
McAfee, Ernie 45, 66, 74
McAfee, Jack 34, 38, 45–49
McCluggage, Denise 111
McLaren, Bruce 119, 132, 148, 151,
155, 156, 161, 171, 172, 209,
211–213, 219
McLaren M1B 213
Mercedes-Benz 45, 47–49, 64, 94, 197
    300SL 45, 71, 82, 93,
        198
    300SLR 65
    540K 102
Mexican GP 210
MG 14, 25, 28, 35, 37, 219
    EX179 89–91, 147, 223
    EX181 88–91, 223, 224
    Magnette 30, 88
    TC 28, 29, 30, 31, 32
    "2Jr" (V8 60 Special) 38
Mille Miglia 36, 60, 75, 86, 94, 202
Milton, Tommy 170
Modena 17, 74, 75, 85, 92, 205
Moffett AFB Circuit 52
Moll, Guy 39
Monaco GP 130, 131, 154–156, 178,
179, 209, 211, 224, 225
Monterey Historic Automobile Races
218
Montlhéry Circuit 16, 93, 94, 210,
216
Monza 500 "Race of Two Worlds"
111–114, 121, 224
Monza Circuit 10, 77, 111–113, 120,
121, 125, 132, 145, 146, 151,
168–171, 200–202, 205, 210, 219,
224, 225
Moroccan GP 125, 224

Moss, Stirling 11, 72, 76, 77, 79, 80,
83, 84, 87–89, 99, 101, 102, 104–
106, 113–115, 119–122, 125, 126,
128, 131, 132, 134–137, 139–148,
150, 152, 154–156, 158, 159, 161,
165, 167, 170, 172, 173, 174, 178,
179, 181–184, 188, 190–192, 195,
196, 198–201, 204, 208, 209
Motor Sport (magazine) 175
Motoring News (magazine) 208
Mugello Circuit 222
Murphy, Jimmy 169, 170
Musso, Luigi 59, 72, 76, 84, 87, 88,
94, 96, 97, 103, 104, 112–116,
126, 219, 224
Musy, Benoît 77, 80, 219

N

Nassau 10, 69, 70, 82, 83, 97, 98, 123,
147, 150, 223, 224
Neumann, John von 66, 84
Nürburgring Circuit 16, 60, 61, 73,
74, 76, 79, 87, 104, 118, 133, 134,
141, 152, 153, 162, 183, 195, 197,
198–200, 202, 209, 210, 214, 215,
223–225

O

Oakes Field Circuit 97
Offenhauser 27, 68, 112
Oporto Circuit 76
OSCA 51, 52, 70

P

Pabst, Augie 187
Packard 18, 20, 29, 101–103, 218
Palm Springs Road Races 10, 33, 35,
37, 38, 73, 82, 85
Palm Springs Vintage Races 220
Parkes, Mike 185–187
Parkinson, Don 15, 25, 31, 40
Parravano, Tony 41, 45, 85
Pebble Beach Concours d'Elegance 65,
218

Pebble Beach Road Races 10, 13, 35–37, 39, 51, 55, 64, 73

Peterson, Ronnie 219

Pierce Arrow 19, 58, 59, 65, 82, 218

Pikes Peak Hill Climb 34

Pollack, Bill 37, 38, 40, 41, 44, 51, 64

Pomona Fairgrounds Circuit 84

Porsche Cars 70, 96, 99, 104, 105, 118, 119, 129, 133–136, 138, 141, 143, 144, 148, 151–154, 162, 172, 174, 178, 180, 184, 185, 187, 191, 193, 199, 200, 202, 209

Porsche 550 73

    RS 93, 183

    RS60 153

    RSK 141

    RSK60 152

Portago, Alfonso "Fon" de 39, 61, 69, 70, 76, 78, 79, 80, 82, 84, 85, 86, 87, 93, 219, 223

Portuguese Sports Car Races 76, 86, 223

Portuguese GP 142, 144, 164

R

Rathmann, Jim 113, 114, 124

Reale Hotel 17

Reims Circuit 52, 60, 77, 86, 87, 93, 99, 111, 115, 116, 118, 138–140, 161, 162, 190–194, 223

Reventlow, Lance 124, 154, 157, 160, 162, 170

Riverside Circuit 10, 61, 124, 147, 150, 170, 171, 214, 219, 224

Road & Track (magazine) 38, 218

Road America Circuit 66–69, 82, 92, 93

Road Atlanta Circuit 220

Rodríguez, Pedro 152, 172, 173, 186, 212, 225

Rodríguez, Ricardo 152, 172, 173, 175, 176, 201, 208, 225

Rose Bowl Circuit 27

Rouen Circuit 77, 78, 94

Ruesch, Hans 60

Ruttman, Troy 31, 114–117, 124

S

Said, Bob 58

Salvadori, Roy 78, 102, 103, 105, 124, 132, 137, 144, 153, 155, 170, 187

Santa Barbara/Goleta Airport Circuit 29, 52, 66, 86

Scarab 124, 125, 154, 157, 160, 162, 170

Scarlatti, Giorgio 87, 116, 136, 153

Schell, Harry 39, 80, 88, 96, 113, 115, 116, 121, 131, 132, 152, 219

Seafair Circuit 66

Sebring Airport Circuit 10, 16, 85, 88, 94, 101–103, 106, 110, 128, 129, 146–148, 151, 152, 172, 174, 175, 177, 186, 208, 210, 213–215, 223–225

Seidel, Wolfgang 87, 93, 97, 105, 106, 107, 108, 109, 119, 223

Shelby, Carroll 58, 61–64, 66, 74, 82, 84, 85, 92, 97, 98, 101, 105, 116, 122, 124, 130, 137, 138, 144, 170, 187, 223

Silverstone Circuit 32, 129, 152, 164

Skip Barber Driving School 222

Snetterton 211

Solitude Circuit 164

Sommer, Raymond 39, 219

Spa-Francorchamps Circuit 158, 165, 168, 183, 188, 189, 213, 225

Spear, Bill 50, 51, 58, 61, 68

Spence, Mike 216, 219, 225

Sports Car Club of America (SCCA) 13, 51, 58, 66, 71, 222

Stead AFB Circuit 53

Stewart, Jackie 216

Stubbs, Arnold 14, 27, 29–31, 40, 45

Summers, Art 59

Sumpter, Rudy 27–29, 31

Surtees, John 165–167, 188, 209, 214

Swedish Grand Prix of Sports Cars 81, 89

Sykes, David 60

Syracuse Circuit 178

T

Targa Florio 74, 103, 104, 133, 140, 151, 162, 175, 176, 195, 208, 213, 215, 224

Taruffi, Piero 53, 61, 76, 80, 131

Tasman Series 211, 212

Tavoni, Romolo 115, 126, 129, 132, 134, 136, 137, 140, 153, 161, 173, 190, 207

The Racers (movie) 60, 61

Thompson, Dick 187

Tilp, George 66, 67, 77, 82, 85, 94

Time (magazine) 174, 207

Tojeiro-Jaguar 144

Torrey Pines Road Races 10, 41, 42, 49, 59, 66, 71

Tour de France 39, 93

Tourist Trophy 213, 224

Trintignant, Maurice 76, 80, 81, 84, 87, 101, 105, 107, 131, 132, 138, 153, 154, 162, 223

Trips, Count Wolfgang von 80, 81, 84, 85, 97, 100, 104–106, 108, 117, 120, 121, 126, 129, 130, 144, 148, 150, 152, 153, 155–157, 159, 161–166, 169, 171–179, 181–185, 188–191, 193, 195–203, 205, 206, 219, 224

Triumph TR-2 59, 74

U

U.S. Grand Prix 147, 212

V

Vaccarella, Nino 151

Van Dyke, Louis 28, 29

Vanwall 116, 118–120, 121, 125, 126, 128, 198

Villoresi, Luigi 44, 80

Volkswagon 78, 97

Vukovich, Bill 31, 65, 219

W

Walker, Rob 154, 165, 188

Wallace, Chuck 94

Walters, Phil 43, 45, 52, 64

Watkins Glen Races 33, 44, 123, 210

Wharton, Ken 76, 219

Whitehead, Peter 110, 219

Wimille, Jean Pierre 219

Windsor Field 82

Wisdom, Tommy 89, 91, 223

World Champions From Farina to Stewart (book) 211

Wyer, John 212

Y

Yeoman Credit 171

Z

Zandvoort Circuit 133, 157, 160, 180, 189, 211, 225

Zeltweg Circuit 212